T0330192

Welfare Measurement in Imperfect Markets

NEW HORIZONS IN ENVIRONMENTAL ECONOMICS

Series Editors: Wallace E. Oates, *Professor of Economics, University of Maryland, USA* and Henk Folmer, *Professor of General Economics, Wageningen University and Professor of Environmental Economics, Tilburg University, The Netherlands*

This important series is designed to make a significant contribution to the development of the principles and practices of environmental economics. It includes both theoretical and empirical work. International in scope, it addresses issues of current and future concern in both East and West and in developed and developing countries.

The main purpose of the series is to create a forum for the publication of high-quality work and to show how economic analysis can make a contribution to understanding and resolving the environmental problems confronting the world in the twenty-first century.

Recent titles in the series include:

Sustainability and Endogenous Growth
Karen Pittel

The Economic Valuation of the Environment and Public Policy
A Hedonic Approach
Noboru Hidano

Global Climate Change
The Science, Economics and Politics
James M. Griffin

Global Environmental Change in Alpine Regions
Recognition, Impact, Adaptation and Mitigation
Edited by Karl W. Steininger and Hannelore Weck-Hannemann

Environmental Management and the Competitiveness of Nature-Based
Tourism Destinations
Twan Huybers and Jeff Bennett

The International Yearbook of Environmental and Resource Economics 2003/2004
A Survey of Current Issues
Edited by Henk Folmer and Tom Tietenberg

The Economics of Hydroelectric Power
Brian K. Edwards

Does Environmental Policy Work?
The Theory and Practice of Outcomes Assessment
Edited by David E. Ervin, James R. Kahn and Marie Leigh Livingston

The International Yearbook of Environmental and Resource Economics 2004/2005
A Survey of Current Issues
Edited by Tom Tietenberg and Henk Folmer

Voluntary Approaches in Climate Policy
Edited by Andrea Baranzini and Philippe Thalmann

Welfare Measurement in Imperfect Markets
A Growth Theoretical Approach
Thomas Aronsson, Karl-Gustaf Löfgren and Kenneth Backlund

Welfare Measurement in Imperfect Markets

A Growth Theoretical Approach

Thomas Aronsson

Professor of Economics, Umeå University, Sweden

Karl-Gustaf Löfgren

Professor of Economics, Umeå University, Sweden

Kenneth Backlund

Assistant Professor of Economics, Umeå University, Sweden

NEW HORIZONS IN ENVIRONMENTAL ECONOMICS

Edward Elgar

Cheltenham, UK • Northampton, MA, USA

Published by
Edward Elgar Publishing Limited
Glensanda House
Montpellier Parade
Cheltenham
Glos GL50 1UA
UK

Edward Elgar Publishing, Inc.
136 West Street
Suite 202
Northampton
Massachusetts 01060
USA

A catalogue record for this book
is available from the British Library

Library of Congress Cataloguing in Publication Data
Aronsson, Thomas, 1963–
    Welfare measurement in imperfect markets : a growth theoretical approach /
Thomas Aronsson, Karl-Gustaf Löfgren, Kenneth Backlund.
        p. cm — (New horizons in environmental economics)
    A completely rewritten update of: Welfare measurement, sustainability, and
green national accounting / Thomas Aronsson, Per-Olov Johansson, Karl-Gustaf
Löfgren. c1997.
    Includes bibliographical references and index.
    1. Economic development—Environmental aspects—Econometric models.
2. Welfare economics—Econometric models. 3. Environmental auditing. 4. Social
accounting. I. Löfgren, Karl-Gustaf. II. Backlund, Kenneth. III. Aronsson, Thomas,
1963– Welfare measurement, sustainability, and green national accounting. IV.
Title. V. Series.

HD75.6.A764 2004
363.7—dc22

2004047065

ISBN   1 84064 779 5

Printed and bound in Great Britain by MPG Books Ltd, Bodmin Cornwall

Contents

Figures and tables

FIGURES

TABLES

Preface

When we started to work on what finally became this book, we were in the process of deciding whether to rewrite our earlier textbook on social accounting or to write a new one. We chose the latter option. Our first textbook, *Welfare Measurement, Sustainability and Green National Accounting*, co-authored with Per-Olov Johansson, appeared in 1997. In that book, we focused the analysis on social accounting in economies with technological change and external effects of environmental damage. To a large extent, we disregarded other issues associated with resource allocation in decentralized (and possibly imperfect) market economies – human capital and uncertainty were two exceptions. We also neglected the possibility that environmental damage created by production and/or consumption in any country might spill over to other countries. Since 1997, our research on social accounting has concentrated on questions that were not addressed in the previous book, such as transboundary environmental problems, issues related to the public sector, as well as the choice of metrics for the welfare measures. It therefore seemed increasingly self-evident that we should try to write a new book instead of rewriting the old one.

Clearly, writing a book is not merely a three-man job. Many people have been involved at various stages of the process. First of all, we would like to thank Geir Asheim, Henk Folmer and Wallace E. Oates. Henk and Wallace gave their general reactions on an early version of the manuscript, which encouraged us to proceed and write the final version, while Geir provided more detailed comments on part of the book at a later stage. Several colleagues at the Department of Economics here in Umeå have also contributed: in particular, Tomas Sjögren and Magnus Wikström read and commented on different parts of the manuscript. Marie Hammarstedt helped us with the editing process and some of the typing. Throughout, our colleagues have never complained, despite the fact that by now we have given (too) many seminars on social accounting. Special thanks are also in order to Chuan-Zhong Li and Kaj Nyström. Li co-authored two papers that comprise part of the material in Chapter 3, while Kaj co-authored a paper that serves as part of the basis for Chapter 9. Kaj also helped us make the mathematical analysis in Chapter 9 understandable (perhaps even to a mathematician). We are very grateful to Julie Sundqvist for thoroughly checking our use of the English language; her work improved the text considerably.

Someone else has also been involved in the process, albeit in an indirect way. Martin Weitzman, whose early work laid the foundations for what later became green accounting, not only produces an almost continuous flow of new ideas; he is also interested in exchanging ideas. Part of his recent work is the most important source of inspiration for Chapter 3. He also visited the annual Ulvö Conference in 1997, where he acted as discussant for what later became Chapter 6.

Finally, we gratefully acknowledge a research grant from The Swedish Research Council for Environment, Agricultural Sciences and Spatial Planning.

Thomas Aronsson
Karl-Gustaf Löfgren
Kenneth Backlund
Umeå, October 2003

1. Introduction

1.1 BACKGROUND

For several decades, a considerable amount of research has been devoted to issues surrounding the use and design of the national accounts. One of the basic ideas behind this research has been to provide a coherent framework for measuring national well-being. This idea is closely related to the concept of social accounting. According to *The New Palgrave Dictionary of Economics*, 'social accounting' refers to 'the body of data that portrays a nation's economic activity in terms of output produced and incomes created, the stocks of capital goods and other inputs required, and the financial pathways and instruments used'. In accordance with this definition, as well as with a broader perspective that includes many nations in a global economy, a welfare economic theory of social accounting has been developed. This book addresses the theory of social accounting, with particular emphasis on valuation problems facing imperfectly competitive market economies.

One of the basic issues in the theory of social accounting is the idea of associating a comprehensive measure of net national product (NNP) with the welfare of a dynamic economy. It is easy to argue that this idea has practical appeal. If it were possible to measure welfare solely by means of a static and (in principle) observable indicator, welfare comparisons would become manageable in practice. Meanwhile, it is quite clear that the conventional NNP does not constitute such an indicator. The only type of consumption included in the conventional NNP refers to goods and services, whereas the concept of net investment is limited to physical capital. A comprehensive concept of consumption should reflect consumer preferences, and not be restricted to conventional goods and services; it would also be likely to include other 'utilities' such as leisure and environmental quality. Similarly, a comprehensive measure of net investments should include all capital formation undertaken by society and not merely changes in the stock of physical capital. Other stocks of importance for production and/or utility are natural resource stocks, stocks which represent or have an impact on environmental quality and the stock of human capital. The net changes in these stocks, measured over a period of time, should also qualify as capital formation, since they are an integrated part of the 'investment policy' undertaken by society. Such extensions of NNP, which are motivated by the objective of measuring welfare, are commonly referred to as 'national product related welfare measures', 'comprehensive NNP' or 'green NNP'. In what follows, we use these concepts synonymously.

The preliminaries give rise to an important question: is there a rigorous welfare economic foundation for welfare measures based on a comprehensive concept of NNP, or does it simply serve as an approximation to more complicated exact welfare measures? Indeed, one of the most important contributions to the theory of social accounting involves providing an *exact* welfare measure based on an extension of the conventional NNP. However, there are also arguments against the idea of trying to measure welfare by comprehensive, or green, NNP. First, additional complications are associated with measuring the welfare contributions of technological change and market imperfections. It is well known that the welfare contribution of technological change is not always recoverable from market data. Similarly, in a 'distorted' market economy, prices might not reflect social opportunity costs and, in certain situations, markets might even be missing. Here, the concept of distorted market economies should be interpreted in a broad sense, so as to include both 'traditional' market imperfections and distortions associated with policy implementation. Second, measures related to NNP do not in general reveal how consumption possibilities are distributed across individuals, households or generations. The argument is that the information that is relevant for measuring welfare is not captured by an aggregate such as green NNP. Third, many environmental (and possibly other) aspects of economic behavior are not measurable in a complete way on a *national basis*. An example is transboundary environmental problems, where environmental damage caused by a particular country affects the welfare of individuals in other countries. If all welfare effects of economic behavior are not appropriately measured on a national basis, the resulting national green NNP is likely to be a biased welfare indicator. We return to these arguments below.

Welfare measurement can also refer to the welfare changes associated with policy projects and/or other parametric changes in the economic system. This is closely related to the principles of cost–benefit analysis in dynamic economies. It should be emphasized that although projects may be small or temporary, they are likely to have intertemporal consequences. Therefore, the study of cost–benefit analysis in dynamic economies might generate insights that are not easily gained in static models. Part of this book concerns cost–benefit analysis of environmental policy with particular focus on environmentally motivated taxes.

The above perspective gives rise to several pertinent questions:

1. What are the conditions under which green NNP, as we have come to know it from the literature, constitutes a welfare measure?
2. How does technological change contribute to welfare measures?

3. What does an appropriate welfare measure actually look like in an imperfect market economy with, for example, uninternalized external effects or imperfect competition?
4. Are market imperfections empirically relevant in the context of social accounting, or is it possible to neglect them in empirical applications without too much loss of information?
5. How are welfare measures affected by policy objectives, such as distributional concern, and/or restrictions on the set of available policy instruments due to, for example, the necessity of raising revenues through distortionary taxes?
6. To what extent are global environmental problems important in the context of social accounting?
7. How should cost–benefit rules be derived in dynamic general equilibrium models?
8. How can deterministic results regarding social accounting and cost–benefit analysis be transformed into a stochastic environment?

The purpose of this book is to answer, or at least discuss, these issues.

1.2 IMPORTANT ISSUES AND BASIC RESULTS IN PREVIOUS RESEARCH

Welfare measurement has been a vital area of economics for a long time. References to previous studies will be given throughout the book. Here, we only briefly outline some of the fundamental results. Most of the early welfare measures were wealth-like concepts such as the present value of future utility or consumption; see, for example, Samuelson (1961). However, although such measures are accurate, they are not very useful from a practical point of view. This explains the quest to measure the present value of future utility by a more easily observed static indicator: green NNP serves this purpose. The welfare interpretation of green NNP comes originally from Martin Weitzman (1976), where green NNP is shown to be an exact indicator of welfare under certain conditions. More precisely, in a dynamic economy with a stationary technology and perfect competition, where the social objective is to maximize the present value of future utility,[1] Weitzman was able to show that green NNP measured in utility terms is proportional to the optimal value function, defined as the maximized objective function. One important aspect of Weitzman's result is, therefore, the interpretation of green NNP as a *static equivalent to future utility*. In technical terms, the result derived by Weitzman indicates that the *current value Hamiltonian* of the underlying optimal growth problem is proportional to the present value of future utility facing the representative consumer. The current value Hamiltonian is, in turn, interpretable as green NNP in utility terms, since it measures the utility value of current consumption plus the utility value of the current net investments.

Although Weitzman himself did not mention the term 'green NNP', the concept of NNP in Weitzman's paper may (and should) be interpreted in a broader sense than has become the convention in actual systems of national accounts. Weitzman discussed the concept of capital explicitly and argued that in addition to physical, man-made capital, 'pools of exhaustible natural resources ought to qualify as capital, and so should stocks of knowledge resulting from learning or research activities'. This view of NNP has inspired much of the subsequent research on social accounting and welfare measurement, where different aspects of capital formation have been addressed.[2]

It should be emphasized that the welfare interpretation of the current value Hamiltonian of the underlying optimal growth problem is based on a set of assumptions which may be somewhat restrictive. Weitzman's fundamental result was based on the assumptions of a stationary technology and perfect competition. The first assumption rules out disembodied technological change, whereas the second implies that green NNP welfare measures, as they are commonly defined in the literature, are fundamentally related to a first best resource allocation. If either of these two assumptions is relaxed, the welfare measure will contain unobservable forward looking terms (in addition to the current value Hamiltonian underlying the optimization problems facing consumers and firms), which cannot be estimated by using the observable set of shadow prices that supports the resource allocation. For obvious reasons, this makes it difficult to apply the theory of social accounting in practice.

We have analyzed welfare measurement problems under technological change and market imperfections in a series of papers, which will be discussed throughout the book. At a theoretical level, the main complication for welfare measurement associated with technological change and market imperfections is that the economic system becomes non-autonomously time dependent. In other words, time itself has a *direct* effect on utility and/or production in addition to its influence via the equilibrium variables and via the utility discount factor. If utility and/or production exhibit explicit time dependence, so does welfare, thereby implying that there is no simple relationship between the current value Hamiltonian and the optimal value function. Therefore, the exact welfare measure depends on the functioning of the economic system, suggesting that a distinction between perfect and imperfect market economies is imperative in the context of social accounting.

The step from theory to practical applications involves several noteworthy and challenging issues. One such problem that has to be considered is whether market imperfections are empirically relevant in the context of social accounting, or if they can be neglected in practical applications without too much loss of information. This can be analyzed using numerical methods aimed at assessing the relationship between welfare contributions associated with various sources of market imperfections and the welfare contribution of the current value Hamiltonian. In the numerical simulations carried out by Aronsson et al. (1997), Aronsson et al. (2001) and Backlund (2000, 2003), the analyses focused on external effects. The results suggest that certain external effects may have only a minor impact on the welfare measures, whereas others may have a considerable influence. These results are useful not only from the point of view of testing the empirical relevance of the theory of social accounting; they are also useful in pointing out the direction in which to look for welfare significant information.

Another issue of relevance in the context of practical applications refers to the unit of measurement. Regardless of whether a first best resource allocation or an imperfect market economy is under consideration, the exact welfare measures are typically expressed in utility terms. The problem, of course, is that utility is not observable, so that practical applications of the theory of social accounting necessitate a transformation of the welfare measures into real terms. The traditional way of carrying out such a transformation is to linearize the current value Hamiltonian. The linearized current value Hamiltonian can typically be transformed into a measure of green NNP in real terms. However, an obvious disadvantage of the linearized current value Hamiltonian is that it only constitutes an approximation of the current value Hamiltonian. A welfare measure based on the linearized current value Hamiltonian is, therefore, only an approximation of the correct welfare measure, and the accuracy of the approximation depends on the functional form of the instantaneous utility function. Weitzman (2000, 2003) suggests a more rigorous welfare foundation for the linearized current value Hamiltonian. Weitzman's idea is to normalize the instantaneous utility function such that the normalized utility function becomes commensurate with the money-metric value of consumption (broadly defined) at the time the measurement is conducted. Another approach to the 'unit-of-measurement' problem in a first best setting is to derive an exact welfare measure in real terms, which can be shown to consist of the sum of green NNP and the consumer surplus. This comes from developing the analysis carried out by Weitzman (2001), and implies that the consumer surplus represents the information lost by linearizing the Hamiltonian.

1.3 THE PLAN OF THE BOOK

The basic idea behind this book is to integrate the research on welfare measurement and social accounting briefly outlined above. In a previous book (Aronsson et al., 1997), we focused on external effects associated with environmental damage and analyzed their role in the context of social accounting. The present book takes a broader perspective by considering a wider spectrum of resource allocation problems in real world market economies.

In Chapter 2, we introduce a 'benchmark model' to be used and elaborated on in later chapters. The benchmark model is a dynamic general equilibrium model with stock pollution, originally developed by Brock (1977). It is an extension of the traditional Ramsey growth model in that energy is added to the other production factors (labor and capital). The use of energy releases emissions, which give rise to a stock of pollution. Such a model is particularly convenient from the point of view of 'greening the national accounts', since it recognizes that the environment may serve as both a consumption good (by being part of the instantaneous utility function) and as a capital good (by being part of the capital concept). We start by considering the welfare measurement problem in a first best resource allocation. We then examine uncontrolled and imperfectly controlled market economies, and show how the welfare measures differ from their counterparts in the first best. Another issue concerns the principles of cost–benefit analysis in dynamic general equilibrium models. The chapter is, to some extent, a recapitulation of some of the results from our earlier book (Aronsson et al., 1997). They are, nevertheless, repeated here, since they serve as a natural point of departure.

The 'unit-of-measurement' problem is dealt with in Chapter 3. By concentrating on the first best resource allocation, we derive a money-metrics analogue to Weitzman's (1976) welfare measure. More specifically, the analysis shows that a generalized measure of the present value of future consumption is proportional to the sum of green NNP in real terms and the real instantaneous consumer surplus. We also derive cost–benefit rules in real terms, which are analogous to the utility based cost–benefit rules in Chapter 2. The final part of the chapter concerns the possibility of measuring changes in welfare by using changes in real green NNP (an alternative view of green NNP discussed in the recent literature) as well as provides an interpretation of the concept of 'genuine saving'.

Pigouvian emission taxes might serve (at least) two purposes in the context of a market economy: they bring the economy to the first best optimum, and they are directly useful in social accounting by exactly measuring the shadow price of additions to the stock of pollution in real terms. At the same time, Pigouvian taxes are very difficult to implement in practice, since their implementation would require information about future preferences. This is the starting point of Chapter 4, where we analyze static approximations of dynamic Pigouvian taxes. The information required to design these taxes is, in principle, recoverable by using the willingness-to-pay method. The basic idea is to arrive at a close approximation of the shadow price of pollution, in which case the Hamiltonian may become a close approximation of the correct welfare measure in an imperfectly controlled market economy. Two questions are important here: (i) is a market economy controlled by the approximation of the Pigouvian tax welfare superior to the uncontrolled market economy, and (ii) is the approximation of the Pigouvian tax useful in social accounting in the same way as a correct Pigouvian tax would be in a perfectly controlled market economy? Both questions are addressed by using the model set out in Chapter 2. Numerical simulations supplement the theoretical analysis.

In Chapters 2–4, the first best resource allocation constitutes a natural reference case. This is so because the external effect associated with environmental damage constitutes the only imperfection in the market economy under consideration. As a consequence, if the government is able to design Pigouvian emission taxes, it is able to implement the first best resource allocation. In Chapter 5, we assume that the government finances a public good by means of distortionary taxes on labor income and capital income. It is well known that if the government is restricted to collecting tax revenues by means of distortionary taxes, the first best resource allocation will in general be unattainable. We show how green NNP in utility terms, derived in Chapters 2 and 4, might become an incorrect welfare measure in an economy with distortionary taxes. We also derive a second best analogue to green NNP in utility terms. Chapter 5 then turns to the welfare effects of policy reform. The motivation is that even if the government wants to combine revenue objectives and environmental goals, it may not be able to implement the second best resource allocation. We consider the welfare effect of a change in the tax mix, which is designed to include an increase in the emission tax. This extends the cost–benefit analyses carried out in Chapters 2 and 4 to an economy with preexisting tax distortions. It also complements some previous studies on environmental tax reform, carried out using static models.

Chapter 6 concerns welfare measurement when countries are confronted with transboundary environmental problems. We extend the benchmark model by introducing two distinct countries as well as allowing the pollution generated by emissions in each country to spill over into the other country. The purpose is to relate the properties of national and global welfare measures to the functioning of the economic system and, in particular, to whether or not there is international cooperation in order to correct for transboundary external effects. We compare a cooperative equilibrium, a non-cooperative Nash equilibrium and the equilibrium in an uncontrolled market economy from the point of view of welfare measurement. In addition, some aspects of the analysis carried out in Chapter 4 are extended here to a global economy by studying approximations of Pigouvian emission taxes.

Chapter 7 also deals with welfare measurement in a global economy by focusing on numerical applications. The first part of the chapter complements Chapter 6 by considering a numerical version of the model set out there. Using real world data as a basis, we also consider welfare measurement problems in a hypothetical 'world economy', where the world is divided into a rich and a poor region. The interaction between regions refers to a transboundary external effect in production from greenhouse gases.

Chapter 8 concerns three emerging issues: welfare measurement in the context of (i) differential games, (ii) unemployment and (iii) distributional objectives. In Section 8.1, we address differential games, thus extending the analyses in Chapters 5 and 6 by considering some additional aspects of the welfare measurement problems implicit in Nash games of open-loop and feedback-loop forms as well as Stackelberg games. Section 8.2 deals with the implications of unemployment from the point of view of welfare measurement. This is topical not only as a technical extension of the analyses conducted in previous chapters; it is also relevant in light of the high (and possibly permanent) unemployment experienced in many countries. The implications of distributional objectives are analyzed in Section 8.3. The basic issue here is whether or not distributional objectives invalidate the welfare interpretation of the current value Hamiltonian.

In Chapter 9, we incorporate uncertainty into the study of social accounting and cost–benefit analysis. Welfare measurement under uncertainty in a dynamic model requires other mathematical tools than those used in preceding chapters, which motivates a brief introduction to stochastic control theory. This is accomplished in the context of a well known growth model introduced in its basic form by Merton (1975), where the growth rate of the labor force is stochastic from the social planner's point of view. We then extend the analysis by introducing uncertainty into the benchmark model of Chapter 2, by assuming that the stock of pollution is also stochastic from the social planner's point of view. This extension is motivated by the fact that the environmental consequences of economic behavior are often uncertain. The results explain the importance of the attitudes towards risk in the context of welfare measures. Moreover, the welfare measures and cost–benefit rules derived under perfect certainty are shown to be nested special cases in this more general model, which takes us back to the basic question of the potential inherent in augmenting NNP in order to obtain an exact welfare measure.

NOTES

1. To be more specific, the social objective commonly applied is 'discounted utilitarianism', which means that the objective is to maximize a discounted sum of instantaneous utilities using a constant discount rate.
2. See, for example, Hartwick (1990), Dasgupta and Mäler (1991) and Mäler (1991) for applications of this welfare analysis to economies where environmental and/or natural resources are important components of the economic system. The term 'green NNP' originates from applications of the theory of social accounting to such economies. See also Aronsson and Löfgren (1996), who consider welfare measurement in an economy with human capital.

2. Our workhorse: the Brock model

Let us now introduce, in an intuitive manner, the mathematical results which underlie the core of the subsequent analysis. We also introduce the particular dynamic growth model that will be our workhorse in the chapters to follow.

Many features of welfare measurement in an imperfect market economy are more general when contrasted with the corresponding analysis in a perfect market economy. Weitzman's classical result, that the Hamiltonian of a typical Ramsey growth model is directly proportional to future welfare, rests on a property of the optimal control problem. This property typically refers to the system as being not 'fundamentally' non-autonomous. This implies that the time dimension enters the problem solely through the state and control variables, and a constant utility discount rate. When externalities, distortionary taxation, unemployment, imperfect competition and distributional considerations are introduced into the economy, the model turns out to be 'fundamentally time dependent' or non-autonomous. As we explain below, in order to convert the market economy into a non-autonomous system, it is sufficient to introduce one of the market imperfections just mentioned. Each imperfection is a special case of a fundamental complication when measuring welfare in a non-autonomous dynamic growth model.

In other words, as soon as first best principles are left behind, Weitzman's fundamental theorem of welfare measurement breaks down, although it does so in a very systematic way. Even if it is not problematical to generalize his result in what then becomes a non-autonomous environment, the new situation introduces a difficult practical measurement problem. We not only have to know entities observable at present, but also in the future.

Valuation of the future components of the new welfare measures is in turn related to the cost–benefit rules that are generated when, say, a perfect dynamic economy is distorted by the introduction of a new project, which can be represented by a parametric change. This is one reason why we introduce a method of carrying out cost–benefit analysis in a generalized Ramsey growth context, but it is not the most important reason. The main reason is that there will be numerous opportunities to address comparative dynamic issues, and we cannot do so without an efficient technique.

We start by deriving a general result, which is very valuable for welfare measurement, and follows directly from the necessary conditions for an optimal control problem.

2.1   A NON-AUTONOMOUS OPTIMAL CONTROL PROBLEM

We think of an economy which evolves over time. The state of the economy at time t can be described by a vector of real numbers

$$\mathbf{x}(t) = [x_1(t),...,x_n(t)] \quad \text{(state variables)} \tag{2.1}$$

The capital stocks in the different sectors of the economy are typical examples of state variables. The state variables can be controlled in the sense that a vector of control functions

$$\mathbf{c}(t) = [c_1(t),...,c_m(t)] \quad \text{(control variables)} \tag{2.2}$$

influences the processes. The control variables are typically the decision variables of households and firms, such as consumption and the input of production factors. The processes or, more precisely, the state variables, are governed by a system of differential equations of the form

$$\frac{dx_1}{dt} = f_1(x_1(t),...,x_n(t),c_1(t),...,c_m(t),t)$$

$$\vdots \tag{2.3}$$

$$\frac{dx_n}{dt} = f_n(x_1(t),...,x_n(t),c_1(t),...,c_m(t),t)$$

$$x_i(0) = x_0^i$$

or in vector notation

$$\dot{\mathbf{x}} = \frac{d\mathbf{x}}{dt} = f[\mathbf{x}(t),\mathbf{c}(t),t] \tag{2.3a}$$

$$\mathbf{x}(0) = \mathbf{x}_0$$

Hence, it is assumed that the time derivatives of all state variables in general depend on all state variables, all control variables, and, in addition, time itself. The latter argument makes both the system and the optimal control problem non-autonomous. This is necessary if we want to allow for exogenous factors such as technological progress not explained by any state variable, population growth, as well as other imperfections in the market economy. Discounting also enters the problem in this manner. An optimal control problem may be created by introducing an objective function

$$V = \int_0^T f_0(x_1(t),...,x_n(t),c_1(t),...,c_m(t),t)dt = \int_0^T f_0(\mathbf{x}(t),\mathbf{c}(t),t)dt \quad (2.4)$$

where explicit time dependence can represent a (time dependent) discount factor as well as an externality in consumption, or both. In economic problems, it is typical to let the time horizon T approach infinity. The reason is that if the optimization is stopped in finite time, the remaining stocks will have to be valued at the time horizon, and the only reasonable way to do this would be to discount what they could produce in the future. For the time being, we will retain a finite time horizon.

In applications of optimal control theory, the control function, $\mathbf{c}(t)$ is usually assumed to have, at most, a finite number of discontinuity points on each finite interval with finite jumps at each point of discontinuity, and to take value in a fixed set U in R^m. According to these properties, $\mathbf{c}(t)$ is referred to as a piecewise continuous function.

Furthermore, an assumption typically imposed on the functions $f_j(\cdot)$, $j = 0,1,...,n$, is that they are continuously differentiable with respect to $\mathbf{x}$, $\mathbf{c}$ and t.

The maximization problem can now be formulated as

$$\underset{c(t)}{Max} \int_0^T f_0(\mathbf{x}(t),\mathbf{c}(t),t)dt \quad (2.5a)$$

subject to

$$\dot{\mathbf{x}} = f\left(\mathbf{x}(t),\mathbf{c}(t),t\right) \quad (2.5b)$$

$$\mathbf{x}(0) = \mathbf{x}_0 \quad (2.5c)$$

$$\mathbf{x}(T) \text{ free} \quad (2.5d)$$

Here, $\mathbf{x}_0$ is the value of the vector of stocks at the starting time, and the last condition in (2.5d) means that there are no restrictions on the stocks at the time horizon.

To derive the main results emanating from this control problem, consider first the necessary conditions of an optimal path. From the maximum principle,[1] we know that if a piecewise continuous control function $\mathbf{c}^*(t)$ solves the optimization problem (2.5) and if $\mathbf{x}^*(t)$ is the associated vector of state variables, then there exists a continuous piecewise differentiable vector function, $\boldsymbol{\lambda}^*(t) = [\lambda_1^*(t),...,\lambda_n^*(t)]$, such that for all $t \in [0,T]$

(i) $c^*(t)$ maximizes $H(x^*(t), c(t), \lambda^*(t), t)$ for $c \in U$, that is, $H^*(x^*(t), c^*(t), \lambda^*(t), t) \geq H(x^*(t), c(t), \lambda^*(t), t)$ for all $c \in U$

where $H(\cdot) = f_0(\cdot) + \lambda f(\cdot)$ is the Hamilton function (Hamiltonian).

(ii) Except at the points of discontinuities of $c^*(t)$

$$\dot{\lambda}^*(t) = -\frac{\partial H^*(\cdot)}{\partial x}$$

(iii) If U is convex and $H(\cdot)$ is strictly concave in $c(t)$, then $c^*(t)$ is continuous.

(iv) $\lambda^*(T) = 0$

Remark: Since the lambda variables are determined by (ii), (iv) and equation (2.3), the top index can be left out, but we have chosen to include it for reasons of clarity. We frequently compare two solutions in which case our 'over-complete' notation comes in handy. Sufficiency follows if the Hamiltonian is concave in x and c.

Next, following, for example, Seierstad and Sydsaeter (1987), we introduce a result which is highly important for the subsequent analysis:

Proposition 2.1 *If $f_i(x(t), c(t), t)$, for $i = 0,...,n$ are C^1 functions of (x, c, t), then*

$$\frac{dH^*}{dt} = \frac{\partial H^*}{\partial t}$$

at all points of continuity of $c^*(t)$.

If $c^*(t)$ is in addition, differentiable, the proposition follows directly from the first order conditions for an optimal path. To see this, we differentiate the Hamiltonian along the optimal path totally with respect to t to obtain:

$$\frac{dH^*}{dt} = \frac{\partial H^*}{\partial x}\dot{x}^* + \frac{\partial H}{\partial c}\dot{c}^* + \frac{\partial H^*}{\partial \lambda}\dot{\lambda}^* + \frac{\partial H^*}{\partial t}$$

Since[2]

$$\frac{\partial H^*}{\partial x} = -\dot{\lambda}^*, \ \frac{\partial H^*}{\partial c} = 0, \text{ and } \frac{\partial H^*}{\partial \lambda} = \dot{x}^*$$

it follows that

$$\frac{dH^*}{dt} = \frac{\partial H^*}{\partial t}$$

At a point of discontinuity of $\mathbf{c}^*(t)$, such as a switch point along a bang–bang control solution,[3] the problem is that $\dot{\mathbf{x}}$ does not necessarily exist, and the solution curve of the state variable has a kink at the switch point.

In intertemporal economies, as soon as the future is discounted, a fundamental time dependence arises through the discount factor. Other forms of time dependence may always enter into such problems. For example, until the mid-1980s, technological progress was typically modeled by adding a time argument in the production function of the economy. Later on it was introduced as a state variable, usually referred to as the 'stock of knowledge'.[4] This endogenous growth idea cannot fully internalize the contribution of knowledge to growth unless the economy can do so as well. If it cannot, a fundamental non-autonomous time dependence will remain.

2.2 WELFARE MEASUREMENT IN A RAMSEY GROWTH MODEL

An example may serve to clarify our discussion so far. One of the simplest and most frequently used dynamic equilibrium models is the Ramsey model.[5] Both producers and consumers are assumed to be identical and have infinite planning horizons. To further simplify the analysis, we follow the convention in the literature on dynamic welfare measurement and disregard population growth,[6] as well as normalize the population to equal one. The representative individual's utility function (here identical to the social welfare function) is written as

$$U(0) = \int_0^\infty u(c(t))e^{-\theta t}\,dt \tag{2.6}$$

where $c(t)$ is aggregate consumption at time t and θ is the constant rate of time preference (or utility interest rate). The instantaneous utility function, $u(c(t))$, is assumed to have conventional properties; it is twice continuously differentiable, increasing, and strictly concave in its argument. The utility function is thus 'well behaved' in the sense that utility maximization, subject to a convex feasibility set, results in a unique global solution. The representative individual is here assumed to supply one unit of labor inelastically at each point in time.

Turning to the supply side of the economy, output is determined by the input of labor, $l(t)$, capital, $k(t)$, and non-autonomous technical progress, here represented by the argument t in the production function. Net output, $y(t)$, is defined by the equation

$$y(t) = f(k(t),t) = c(t) + \frac{dk(t)}{dt} \tag{2.7}$$

where $f(k(t),t)$ is the production function with constant labor input suppressed to simplify notation. Output can be used either for consumption, $c(t)$, or investments $dk(t)/dt = \dot{k}(t)$. The latter refers to net investments, thereby taking depreciation into account. The production function is assumed to be concave in the capital stock. Since labor is normalized to one, we do not have to assume that it exhibits constant returns to scale in labor and capital in order to write it as a function of the capital stock per capita. The time argument is inserted to denote non-autonomous technological progress (or regress). This will sometimes be referred to as non-attributable technological progress; that is, the progress (or regress) cannot be attributable to any production factor.

A social planner maximizes the objective function in equation (2.6) subject to the technological constraint in equation (2.7), and subject to an initial condition on the capital stock. The present value Hamiltonian of the problem, along the optimal path, is

$$H^*(x^*(t),c^*(t),\lambda^*(t),t) = u(c^*(t))e^{-\theta t} + \lambda^*(t)[f(k^*(t),t) - c^*(t)] \qquad (2.8)$$

From Proposition 2.1, after taking the partial derivative with respect to time, we obtain

$$\frac{dH^*(t)}{dt} = -\theta u(c^*(t))e^{-\theta t} + \lambda^*(t)f_t(k^*(t),t) \qquad (2.9)$$

Here f_t can be interpreted as the marginal technological progress at time t, and $\lambda^* f_t$ represents the present utility value of marginal technological progress at time t. By integrating the differential equation (2.9), we obtain

$$H^*(T) = H^*(t) - \theta \int_t^T u(c^*(s))e^{-\theta s}ds + \int_t^T \lambda^*(s)f_t(k^*(s),s)ds \qquad (2.10)$$

From results derived by Michel (1982) and Seierstad and Sydsaeter (1987),[7] we know that under certain regularity conditions, which are satisfied here, and provided that there are certain bounds on the rate of technological progress, $\lim_{T\to\infty} H^*(T) = 0$. Taking limits on both sides gives

$$H^*(t) + \int_t^\infty \lambda^*(s)f_s(k^*(s),s)ds = \theta \int_t^\infty u(c^*(s))e^{-\theta s}ds \qquad (2.11)$$

The interpretation of equation (2.11) is that the present value of the Hamiltonian at time t, plus the present utility value of future marginal technological progress along the optimal path, equals 'interest' on the present value of future utility along the optimal path.

A special case, typically treated as a standard case in much of the earlier literature, emerges if we assume that technological progress can be attributed to the capital stock. In this case the present value Hamiltonian will obviously be directly proportional to the utility value of future welfare. The proportionality factor is the inverse of the time preference. This corresponds to the classical first best result derived by Weitzman (1976), that is,

$$H^*(t) = \theta \int_t^\infty u(c^*(s))e^{-\theta s} ds \qquad (2.11a)$$

To compare the entities in equation (2.11a) at the time they are measured, it is convenient to express the result in current value. The current value Hamiltonian of the above Ramsey problem is defined as

$$H^c(\cdot) = e^{\theta t} H(t) = u(c(t)) + \lambda^c(t)[f(k(t),t) - c(t)]$$

where $\lambda^c(t) = e^{\theta t} \lambda(t)$. Using current value, equation (2.11) can be rewritten as

$$H^{c^*}(t) + \int_t^\infty \lambda^{c^*}(s) f_s(k^*(s),s)e^{-\theta(s-t)} ds = \theta \int_t^\infty u(c^*(s))e^{-\theta(s-t)} ds \quad (2.11b)$$

It is straightforward to show that the first best growth path is supported by the market solution in a perfect foresight market economy, both under and in the absence of technological progress. However, future welfare cannot be measured exactly using knowledge of current market data in the presence of non-attributable technological progress.[8] On the other hand, under non-attributable technological progress, it might be possible to estimate the growth components in future welfare using historical growth data. Such estimates, introduced by Weitzman (1997) and Weitzman and Löfgren (1997), are discussed in later chapters.

The measurement problem is rendered more difficult, however, by other kinds of time dependencies, such as externalities in production or consumption. An externality (negative) is present if the production process gives off harmful emissions. Another externality (positive) could be that the accumulation of human and/or R&D capital not only improves the productivity of the investor, but also spills over into other sectors of the economy. This kind of externality is the basis for endogenous growth theory. To model welfare measurement under these conditions we need a somewhat richer model, which enables us to model externalities in a simple manner.[9]

2.3   SOCIAL OPTIMUM AND EXTERNALITIES IN THE DECENTRALIZED ECONOMY: THE BROCK MODEL

Profit maximizing firms would not automatically be induced to engage in production with socially optimal levels of emissions. In the context of an uncontrolled market economy, a firm would typically take the shadow prices of emissions equal to zero and overproduce emissions. To mimic this we introduce a slight variation of the above growth model, which contains externalities in terms of emissions, and possibly also technological progress. The model is, apart from encompassing technological progress, identical to a growth model introduced by Brock (1977). As in the Ramsey model, there is a single homogeneous good used for consumption and investment. In order to introduce an externality, production is assumed to cause pollution which affects the welfare of society. Natural resources as potential inputs in production are suppressed, since they do not add to our principal findings. The instantaneous utility function at time t is written as

$$u(t) = u(c(t),x(t)) \tag{2.12}$$

where $u(\cdot)$ is a strictly concave, twice continuously differentiable function, which is increasing in the first argument and decreasing in its second argument. Here $x(t)$ stands for the stock of pollution at time t.

Goods are produced by capital, emissions (through the use of energy inputs) and labor. The labor endowment is fixed and normalized to one. The production function can be written as follows:

$$y(t) = f(k(t),g(t),t) \tag{2.13}$$

It is assumed to be strictly concave, twice differentiable and increasing in energy.[10] The time argument catches technological progress, and the production function is assumed to be continuously differentiable in t.

The accumulation of pollution obeys the following differential equation:

$$\dot{x}(t) = g(t) - (\gamma + \alpha)x(t) \tag{2.14}$$

where $0 < \gamma < 1$ is a parameter reflecting the assimilative capacity of the environment, and $0 \leq \alpha < 1$ is a parameter reflecting man-made additions to this capacity. The parameter α will be used later on for cost–benefit analysis. As a matter of notational convention, throughout this book we use 'α' to represent projects for which we would like to measure the costs and benefits, although the applications will differ among chapters. The input of energy may be treated in a simple way, with little loss of generality, by assuming that emissions equal the input of energy, $g(t)$. The accumulation of capital follows the equation

$$\dot{k}(t) = f(k(t),g(t),t) - c(t) - I(\alpha) \tag{2.15}$$

where $I(\alpha)$ is a strictly convex differentiable cost function which is increasing in the policy parameter α. It tells us how many units of goods are necessary to keep the man-made assimilative capacity of the environment at α. We now solve the optimization problem conditional on a given value of α, and then use the solution to derive cost–benefit rules for a project that marginally increases the assimilative capacity of the environment. This derivation has general validity for projects which can be represented by parameters.

2.3.1 The Social Optimum

The social optimum problem to be solved can now be written

$$\operatorname*{Max}_{c(t),g(t)} \int_0^\infty u(c(t), x(t))e^{-\theta t}dt \tag{2.16a}$$

subject to

(i) $\dot{k}(t) = f(k(t),g(t),t) - c(t) - I(\alpha)$

(ii) $\dot{x}(t) = g(t) - (\gamma + \alpha)x(t)$ (2.16b)

(iii) $k(0) = k_0 > 0$

                    $x(0) = x_0 > 0$

(iv) $\lim_{t \to \infty} k(t) \geq 0$

                    $\lim_{t \to \infty} x(t) \geq 0$

Neglecting the time indicator, the present value Hamiltonian of this two-state variable problem is

$$H = u(c,x)e^{-\theta t} + \lambda \dot{k} + \mu \dot{x} \tag{2.17}$$

In addition to (2.16b), the necessary conditions for optimality are[11]

(i) $\dfrac{\partial H}{\partial c} = u_c(c,x)e^{-\theta t} - \lambda = 0$

(ii) $\dfrac{\partial H}{\partial g} = \lambda f_g(k,g,t) + \mu = 0$ (2.18)

(iii) $$\dot{\lambda} = -\lambda f_k(k,g,t)$$
(iv) $$\dot{\mu} = -u_x(c,x)e^{-\theta t} + \mu(\gamma + \alpha)$$
(v) $$\lim_{t\to\infty}\lambda \geq 0 (= 0 \ \ if \lim_{t\to\infty} k > 0)$$

$$\lim_{t\to\infty}\mu \geq 0 (= 0 \ \ if \lim_{t\to\infty} x > 0)$$

where the subindices represent partial derivatives with respect to c,k and g, respectively. A little thought reveals that welfare measurement in this first best context yields a result that can be derived and expressed exactly in the same terms as in the standard Ramsey model, that is,

$$H^*(t) + \int_t^\infty \lambda^*(s)f_s(k^*(s),g^*(s),s)ds = \theta\int_t^\infty u(c^*(s),x^*(s))e^{-\theta s}ds \qquad (2.17a)$$

or in words:

Proposition 2.2 *For the model (2.16), 'interest' on the present value of future utility along the optimal path is measured by the present value Hamiltonian at time* t *plus the sum of the utility value of marginal technological progress along the future optimal path.*

In order to express the result solely in terms of a Hamiltonian, we can use a trick to elicit the shadow value of technological progress. We define an additional state variable, t_p, by setting

$$t_p = t$$
$$\frac{dt_p}{dt} = 1 \qquad (2.19)$$

In this manner we obtain a co-state variable Ω, which obeys a non-arbitrage condition

$$\dot{\Omega} = -\frac{\partial H}{\partial t_p} \qquad (2.20)$$

This means that we can rewrite equation (2.11a) in the following manner:[12]

$$H^{**}(t) = u(c^*(t),x^*(t))e^{-\theta t} + \lambda^*(t)\dot{k}^*(t) + \mu^*(t)\dot{x}^*(t) + \Omega^*(t)$$

$$= \theta\int_t^\infty u(c^*(s),x^*(s))e^{-\theta s}ds$$

where $\Omega(t) = \int_t^\infty \lambda(s) f_s(s) ds$. The trick amounts to obtaining direct proportionality between the augmented Hamiltonian at time t and the present value of future utility. The welfare measurement problem remains, however, since we cannot directly or indirectly observe Ω^* in market data at time t.

It is worthwhile examining the intuition behind Weitzman's rather surprising result. We start by observing that net investment at time t is optimally adjusted to consumption according to the first order condition (2.18i), which tells us that the present value of an extra unit of consumption at time t equals the present value of the one unit of capital invested at time $t \in [0,\infty)$. This will hold for all future $(t + s)$. The non-arbitrage (Euler) condition (2.18iii) means that, along an optimal path, it is unprofitable to move one unit of investment from $(t + s)$ to t. This is true for all kinds of investment goods in principle, including time itself (technological progress). Moreover, the use of energy at time t is optimally adjusted by equation (2.18ii), which tells us that the utility value of the last unit of energy used in production exactly equals the present value of the future disutility generated by emissions due to the use of energy. The final aspect which generates proportionality is that the time preference is constant, that is, the trade-off between the utility of consumption today and consumption tomorrow does not change over time. What remains is to solve a resulting differential equation.

2.3.2 Externalities in the Decentralized Economy

Under externalities there is, however, a measurement problem in addition to the one that we would have when estimating the future contribution of technological progress.[13] In an uncontrolled market economy, profit maximizing firms would not automatically be induced to produce the social optimal level of emissions. A firm would typically take the shadow value of emissions, μ, equal to zero and overemit, since emissions have a positive marginal product for the firm, but represent a negative externality to households.

In a decentralized economy, the consumer's maximization problem is written

$$\underset{c(t)}{\text{Max}} \int_0^\infty u(c(t), x(t)) e^{-\theta t} dt \qquad (2.21a)$$

subject to

$$\dot{k}(t) = \pi(t) + r(t)k(t) + w(t) + T(t) - c(t) - I(\alpha) \qquad (2.21b)$$

$$\lim_{t \to \infty} k(t)e^{-\int_0^t r(s)ds} \geq 0 \qquad (2.21c)$$

$$k(0) = k_0 \qquad (2.21d)$$

Equation (2.21b) is the dynamic budget constraint and emerges from the fact that in a decentralized market economy, the consumer sells one unit of labor at the given real wage, $w(t)$, and rents capital at the market rate of interest, $r(t)$, to the representative firm, which maximizes profit under perfect competition. The term $\pi(t) \geq 0$ denotes a 'possible pure profit', that is, a profit that could not be attributed to either labor or capital. Since emissions are a production factor for the firm, pure profit would, in general, be positive. The argument $T(t)$ is a time dependent lump-sum transfer to the consumer. Here, it is identically equal to zero. The condition (2.21c) is the so-called No Ponzi Game (NPG) condition, which guarantees that debt does not grow faster than the interest rate. It can be shown that the dynamic budget constraint together with the No Ponzi Game condition imply that the present value of future consumption equals the sum of human and non-human wealth[14] at time t.

In addition to (2.21b–2.21d) and a transversality condition on the shadow price of capital, the consumer obeys the following conditions (again neglecting the time argument)

(i) $u_c(c,x)e^{-\theta t} - \lambda = 0$

(ii) $\dot{\lambda} = -\lambda r$ \qquad (2.22)

To preserve notational clarity we disregard technological progress; that is, we set $f_t \equiv 0$. The representative firm would choose k and g to maximize

$$\pi = f(k,g) - rk - w \qquad (2.23)$$

and the following first order conditions emerge

(i) $f_k(k,g) - r = 0$

(ii) $f_g(k,g) = 0$ \qquad (2.24)

The first condition is standard, while the second means that input of energy (emissions) is used up to a point where its marginal productivity is zero. Inserting the pure profit expression into the dynamic budget constraint (2.21b) we obtain

$$\dot{k}^0 = f(k^0, g^0) - c^0 - I(\alpha)$$

where k^0, $\dot{k}^0$, g^0 and c^0 denote entities along the decentralized market solution. To measure welfare along the market solution we proceed in a manner analogous to the corresponding welfare measurement problem in the social optimum. The Hamiltonian corresponding to the optimization problem of the representative consumer, evaluated along the competitive path, can be written

$$H^0 = u(c^0, x^0)e^{-\theta t} + \lambda^0(f(k^0, g^0) - c^0 - I(\alpha)) \qquad (2.25)$$

Here c^0 and g^0 are optimally chosen by the consumer and the firm, respectively, and we can use Proposition 2.1 to write

$$\frac{dH^0(t)}{dt} = -\theta u(c^0(t), x^0(t))e^{-\theta t} + u_x(c^0(t), x^0(t))\dot{x}^0(t)e^{-\theta t} \qquad (2.26)$$

The second term on the RHS surfaces because the stock of pollution is not optimal from society's point of view. By integrating (2.26) forward, while letting the time horizon go to infinity, and after transforming the result into current value by multiplying by $e^{\theta t}$, we obtain

$$H^{c^0}(t) + \int_t^\infty u_x(c^0(s), x^0(s))\dot{x}^0(s)e^{-\theta(s-t)}ds = \theta \int_t^\infty u(c^0(s), x^0(s))e^{-\theta(s-t)}ds$$

$$(2.27)$$

where

$$H^{c^0}(t) = u(c^0(t), x^0(t)) + \lambda^{c^0}(t)\dot{k}^0(t)$$

is the current value Hamiltonian and $\lambda^c = \lambda e^{\theta t}$ is the current value shadow price of capital. The interpretation of (2.27) may be summed up as:

Proposition 2.3 *The correct estimate of 'interest' on the present value of future utility in a decentralized market solution under externalities is the current value Hamiltonian, plus the present value of the marginal externality measured in utilities along the competitive path.*

This should come as no surprise, since the externality, although produced within the economic system, is exogenous to the consumer. In other words, it is reminiscent of the way in which technological progress enters the production function in the preceding subsection.[15]

Except for a situation where the economy has reached a steady state, a welfare measure based solely on the Hamiltonian will result in over-(under-)estimation of future utility if there is a negative (positive) marginal externality in the economy. In a steady state, $\dot{x}^0 \equiv 0$, and the Hamiltonian welfare measure is applicable. Typically, however, market data contain no information about the value of the marginal damages along the future optimal path. Welfare measurement thus constitutes a severe practical problem. However, the ability of market data to provide welfare relevant information is likely to improve, if environmental taxes and/or emission permits are introduced. Since Pigouvian taxes[16] and permit markets are equivalent as policy means, we focus on the Pigouvian tax. In the case of a Pigouvian tax, the externality is completely internalized; that is, the economy will follow the first best (command optimum) path.

Since the firm, in this case, causes the negative externality, we introduce a unit tax, $\tau(t)$, on its emissions. The firm's maximization problem is now changed to read

$$\text{Max } \pi = \text{Max}_{k,g}[f(k,g) - rk - \tau g] \text{ for all } t \qquad (2.28)$$

The first order conditions change to

(i) $$f_k(k,g) - r = 0$$

(ii) $$f_g(k,g) - \tau = 0 \qquad (2.29)$$

The problem that remains is to choose the environmental tax in a manner such that the agents in a market economy will implement the first best solution. A reasonable guess is that the tax is related to the shadow price of the stock of pollution, $\mu^*(t)$, in the command optimum solution. This entity is negative and measures the disutility created in the future by the marginal unit emitted today. To convert this entity into money, we note that the price of consumer and investment goods is normalized to one in this problem. By rewriting (2.18i) in current value and dividing both sides by λ^{c*} we obtain the marginal willingness to pay for the last unit consumed as $u_c/\lambda^{c*} = 1 = p$. In the same spirit, the marginal willingness to pay to get rid of the last unit of pollution along the first best path would be obtained if the negative of its marginal utility, $-\mu^*$, were divided by λ^*, the marginal utility of goods. Hence an informed guess of what the Pigouvian tax looks like would be that, at each point in time, it equals this 'marginal willingness to pay' along the optimal path, that is, $\tau^*(t) = -\mu^*(t)/\lambda^*(t)$. To see what indeed does the job, we insert this tax into the optimization problem of the firm, which, after some elementary manipulations, gives

$$\lambda^* f_g(k,g) + \mu^* = 0 \qquad (2.18ii)$$

where μ^* by definition obeys the following differential equation:

$$\dot{\mu}^* = -u_x^* e^{-\theta t} + (\gamma + \alpha)\, \mu^* \qquad (2.18\text{iv})$$

$$\lim_{t \to \infty} \mu^* = 0 \qquad (2.18\text{v})$$

Inserting the expression for pure profits into the intertemporal budget constraint, and redistributing the tax revenues from the emission tax as a lump-sum transfer, yields the expression

$$\dot{k} = f(k,g) - c - I(\alpha) \qquad (2.16\text{bi})$$
$$k(0) = k_0$$

By using the first order condition for the allocation of capital within the firm, (2.29i), in the non-arbitrage condition corresponding to the optimization problem of the consumer, we obtain

$$\dot{\lambda} = -\lambda f_k(k,g) \qquad (2.18\text{iii})$$
$$\lim_{t \to \infty} \lambda = 0 \qquad (2.18\text{iv})$$

Moreover, the consumer chooses according to

$$u_c(c,x)e^{-\theta t} - \lambda = 0 \qquad (2.18\text{i})$$

where x by definition obeys the differential equation

$$\dot{x} = g - (\gamma + \alpha)x \qquad (2.16\text{bii})$$
$$x(0) = x_0$$

In other words, by reproducing the necessary conditions for the social optimum under the dynamic tax, we have shown:

Proposition 2.4 *If* $\tau^*(t) = -\mu^*(t)/\lambda^*(t)$, *where* $\lambda^*(t)$ *is the shadow price of capital, and* $\mu^*(t)$ *is the shadow price of the stock of pollution in the social planner's optimal solution, and if the tax revenues* $T(t) = \tau^*(t)g(t)$ *are redistributed in a lump-sum fashion, then the decentralized solution will coincide with the social optimum.*

The dynamic tax, which contains information about the present value of the marginal externality along the socially optimal path, is the dynamic analogue of the atemporal Pigouvian tax. It has the virtue that welfare can now be measured by using the 'Hamiltonian' that supports the perfectly controlled market economy. The reason why current market data are now sufficient is that we are on a first best path, since the externality has been fully adjusted for by the dynamic Pigouvian tax.

It is instructive to solve the differential equations for the two co-state variables along the optimal path, (2.18iii–iv), using the transversality conditions. We can write

$$\lambda^*(t) = \lambda(0)e^{-\int_0^t f_k^*(s)ds} \qquad (2.30\text{i})$$

$$\mu^*(t) = \int_t^\infty u_x^*(s)e^{-\theta s}e^{-(\gamma+\alpha)(s-t)}ds \qquad (2.30\text{ii})$$

where $u_x(t) = u_x(c(t),x(t))$ and $f_k(t) = f_k(k(t),g(t))$.

Two comments are in order. First, welfare measurement may seem superfluous in a Panglossian world, that is, on the first best growth path. Second, the economy cannot reach this path without solving a, to say the least, non-trivial information problem. It is necessary to find out the real value (the quotient of (2.30i) and (2.30ii) of the marginal externality along the first best growth path. In theory, this can be achieved by solving for the social optimum. As a practical exercise, however, it cannot be done, since we would have to estimate entities only available far into the future.

This implies that, for practical welfare accounting, we need good approximations of entities not available in the market economy at time t. This will be high on our agenda in subsequent chapters. In order to prepare for these analyses, we consider cost–benefit analysis in a dynamic framework.

Let us once again return to the welfare measure corresponding to the social optimum, given by equation (2.17a), and for simplicity assume that $f_t(\cdot) \equiv 0$ for all t. For a better understanding of how market data can be used to obtain a money-metric measure of welfare at time t we introduce a first order approximation of the utility function to obtain

$$u(c^*,x^*) \approx u_c(c^*,x^*)c^* + u_x(c^*,x^*)x^* = \lambda^* c^* + u_x(c^*,x^*)x^* \qquad (2.31)$$

where the second equality follows of the first order conditions. Substituting the approximation for the utility function into the current value Hamiltonian of the optimally corrected market solution, and dividing through by the marginal utility of consumption, results in the following approximation of welfare in real terms:

$$RAW = c^* + \dot{k}^* + \frac{u_x^*}{\lambda^c}x^* - \tau^*\dot{x}^* \qquad (2.17\text{b})$$

where the third term is the monetary cost of the marginal environmental damage at time t, while the fourth term measures the monetary costs of the future damage caused by an additional unit of pollution. The first two terms, of course, measure traditional NNP (consumption plus investment). The third term can, in practice, be measured by asking what an individual would be willing to pay to get rid of one unit of pollution during the time interval $(t,t + dt)$. The fourth term is more problematic to estimate, since it contains forward-looking components. The error in welfare measurement generated by imprecise estimation of this term is estimated numerically in Chapter 4.

Unfortunately we know little about the empirical accuracy of the linear approximation (2.17b). The question of deciding whether welfare has improved from one period to the next by looking at real term entities (defined as all-inclusive NNP) is addressed in Chapter 3.

2.3.3 Cost–Benefit Analysis

An optimal value function can be defined according to static theory, as well as in a dynamic context. For the particular dynamic problem (2.16) we define the optimal value function in the following manner:

$$V(t,\Theta,k_t,x_t) = \underset{c(s),g(s)}{\text{Max}} \int_t^\infty u(c(s),x(s))e^{-\theta s}ds = \int_t^\infty u(c^*(s),x^*(s))e^{-\theta s}ds$$

$$(2.32)$$

subject to (2.16b). Here $\Theta = (\theta,\alpha,\gamma)$ is a parameter vector, and t is the lower bound of integration. A project may be represented by one or more parameters, and a cost–benefit rule is the partial derivative of the optimal value function with respect to the parameter(s). In order to use a heuristic argument in the derivation we introduce a vector of artificial state variables, $y = \Theta$, with $\dot{y} \equiv 0$, and a co-state vector $P(t)$. To start with, we will keep the time horizon finite and equal to T. Following an idea in Léonard (1987), the value function can be rewritten as

$$V(t,T,\Theta,k_t,x_t) = \int_t^T \{u(c^*(s),x^*(s))e^{-\theta s} + \lambda(s)[f(k^*(s),g^*(s)) - c^*(s) - I(\alpha) - \dot{k}^*(s)] +$$

$$\mu(s)[(\alpha + \gamma)x^*(s) - g^*(s) - \dot{x}^*(s)] + P(t)\dot{y}^*(s)\}ds$$

$$= \int_t^T [u^*(\cdot)e^{-\theta s} + \lambda(s)\dot{k}^*(s) + \mu(s)\dot{x}^*(s) + P(s)\dot{y}^*(s)]ds - \int_t^T \lambda(s)\dot{k}^*(s)ds - \int_t^T \mu(s)\dot{x}^*(s)ds$$

$$= \int_t^T H(k^*(s),x^*(s),y^*(s),c^*(s),g^*(s),\lambda(s),\mu(s),P(s))ds$$

$$-\lambda(T)k^*(T) - \mu(T)x^*(T) + \lambda(t)k^*(t) + \mu(t)x^*(t) + \int_t^T \dot{\lambda}(s)k^*(s)ds + \int_t^T \dot{\mu}(s)x^*(s)ds$$

Here, the functions $\lambda(t)$, $\mu(t)$ and $P(t)$ are arbitrary differentiable functions of time. The first equality follows because we have only added terms that are identically equal to zero, and the second because we have only split up the integral. The third is true by the definition of the Hamiltonian, and since partial integration yields the remaining terms.

Differentiation with respect to the lower integration limit t now gives

$$\frac{\partial V}{\partial t} = -H(t) + \dot{\lambda}(t)k^*(t) + \lambda(t)\dot{k}^*(t) - \dot{\lambda}(t)k^*(t) + \dot{\mu}(t)x^*(t) + \mu(t)\dot{x}^*(t) - \dot{\mu}(t)x^*(t)$$

(2.33)

Since $k(t) = k_t$ and $x(t) = x_t$, it follows that the above expression, measured along the optimal path where $\lambda(t) = \lambda^*(t)$ and $\mu(t) = \mu^*(t)$, reduces to

$$\frac{\partial V}{\partial t} = -H^*(t) \qquad (2.34a)$$

Applying a similar argument to the derivative of the upper limit of integration yields[17]

$$\frac{\partial V}{\partial T} = H^*(T) \qquad (2.34b)$$

We can also differentiate the value function with respect to the initial conditions (they are parameters) to obtain

$$\frac{\partial V}{\partial k_t} = \lambda^*(t) \qquad (2.34c)$$

$$\frac{\partial V}{\partial x_t} = \mu^*(t) \qquad (2.34d)$$

It remains to be shown how a change in a parameter (a project) affects the optimal value function. Since we have treated parameters as state variables, we can use the non-arbitrage condition for state variables to obtain

$$\dot{P}^*(t) = -\frac{\partial H^*(t)}{\partial y} \qquad (2.35)$$

Integrating the differential equation forward yields

$$P^*(T) = P^*(t) - \int_t^T \frac{\partial H^*(s)}{\partial y} ds \qquad (2.36)$$

After letting T approach infinity, recalling that $\lim_{T \to \infty} P^*(T) = 0$ according to the transversality conditions, we now obtain

$$P^*(t) = \int_t^\infty \frac{\partial H^*(s)}{\partial y} ds \tag{2.37}$$

From (2.34a–b) we know that

$$\frac{\partial V}{\partial y_t} = P^*(t) = \frac{\partial V}{\partial \Theta} \tag{2.38}$$

The total effect of an infinitesimally small change in a parameter on the optimal value function is thus obtained by taking the partial derivative of the present value Hamiltonian with respect to the parameter, and then integrating along the optimal path over the planning horizon, which here is taken to be infinite. Equation (2.36) combined with the relevant transversality condition for a problem with a finite planning horizon gives us the corresponding derivative under a finite time horizon.[18]

2.3.4 Applications

Let us now apply the above results to a project represented by a change in the parameter α, which can be interpreted as a project that improves the assimilative capacity of the environment. The outcome of this exercise hinges, of course, on the regime under which it is conducted. We begin by carrying out the analysis under first best principles. Partially differentiating the Hamiltonian of the command optimum problem with respect to α yields

$$\frac{\partial H^*(t)}{\partial \alpha} = -\mu^*(t)x^*(t) - \lambda^*(t)I_\alpha(\alpha) \tag{2.39}$$

The first term denotes the revenues in terms of utility over the interval $(t, t + dt)$ from a marginal increase in the assimilate capacity of the environment, and the second term is the marginal cost in terms of the utility value of consumption foregone when additional resources are spent on environmental policy.

According to the result in equation (2.38), the cost–benefit rule can be written

$$\frac{\partial V}{\partial \alpha} = \int_t^\infty [-\mu^*(s)x^*(s) - \lambda^*(s)I_\alpha(\alpha)]ds \tag{2.40}$$

Equation (2.38) measures the value of the project in terms of utility. By using the formula for the Pigouvian tax, we can rewrite (2.40) in the following manner:

$$\frac{\partial V}{\partial \alpha} = \int_{t}^{\infty} [\tau^*(s)x^*(s) - I_\alpha(\alpha)]\bar{\lambda}^*(s)ds = \int_{t}^{\infty} [\tau^*(s)x^*(s) - I_\alpha(\alpha)]\lambda^{c^*}(s)e^{-\theta s}ds$$

(2.41)

The above equation measures the discounted value of the sum of the difference between the discounted value of the marginal benefit and the marginal cost of the project in real terms times the current value of the shadow price of capital. Note that the latter is measured in utilities and, hence, that a positive present value in real terms does not seem to be sufficient for the project to be welfare improving, contrary to what is taught in standard textbooks on investment theory. However, using the non-arbitrage condition along an optimal path

$$\dot{\lambda}^{c^*}(s) = (\theta - \int_{0}^{t} f_k^*(s))\lambda^{c^*}(s)$$

(2.42)

we obtain

$$\lambda^{c^*}(t) = \lambda(0)\exp\left(\theta t - \int_{0}^{t} f_k^*(s)ds\right)$$

Since $r(s) = f_k(s)$, the cost–benefit rule can now be rewritten

$$\frac{\partial V}{\partial \alpha} = \lambda(0)\int_{0}^{\infty} [\tau^*(t)x^*(t) - I_\alpha(\alpha)]e^{-\int_{0}^{t} r(s)ds} dt$$

(2.43)

which corresponds, except for a positive constant, to the traditional present value criterion.

It is instructive to compare this result with the corresponding cost–benefit rule under the uncontrolled market solution, where the environmental tax equals zero. The present value 'Hamiltonian' along the uncontrolled market solution corresponds to equation (2.25), which, with an explicit time argument, can be written

$$H^0(t) = u(c^0(t),x^0(t))e^{-\theta t} + \lambda^0(t)[f(k^0(t),g^0(t)) - c^0(t) - I(\alpha)] \quad (2.25a)$$

The (sub)optimal value function is obtained if the market solution is substituted into the objective funtion of the representative consumer to obtain

$$V^0(t, \Theta) = \int_t^\infty u(c^0(s), x^0(s))e^{-\theta s} ds \qquad (2.32a)$$

where the initial stocks have been suppressed in the value function. As the 'Hamiltonian' is written here, the parameter α seems to enter the problem solely through the cost function. In our notation we have, in general, suppressed the fact that control and state variables depend on the parameter vector Θ. One reason for this omission is that the indirect effects of changes in the parameter vector vanish along the first best path. As we have indicated by quotation marks around the word Hamiltonian, there is, in general, an important difference between the Hamiltonian of the first best problem and the pseudo-Hamiltonian that is obtained by inserting the market solution into the Hamiltonian corresponding to the dynamic optimization problem of the consumer. In the latter problem the stock of pollution is no longer treated as a state variable, but as an exogenous variable affecting the utility of the consumer. Its development over time is governed by the differential equation

$$\dot{x}^0(s) = g^0(s) - (\alpha + \gamma)x^0(s) \qquad (2.44)$$
$$x(t) = x_t$$

where g^0 is determined in the firm's optimization problem from the first order condition that the marginal productivity from emissions equals zero. Solving equation (2.44) we obtain[19]

$$x^0(T, \alpha) = x_t e^{-(\alpha+\gamma)T} + \int_t^T g^0(s, \alpha)e^{-(\alpha+\gamma)(T-s)} ds \qquad (2.45)$$

In other words, the stock of pollution is a function of the parameter α, both directly through its impact on the depreciation rate, and indirectly through the emission function. The latter relationship follows since $g^0(s)$ is a function of the capital stock at time s, and the differential equation for the capital stock contains the cost function $I(\alpha)$. The partial derivative with respect to α, $x_\alpha(s, \alpha)$, is presumably negative. The depreciation effect obviously works in this direction, and an increase in α leads to less capital accumulation, since the marginal cost $I_\alpha(\alpha) > 0$. If capital and energy are technical complements in production, the output of emissions will decrease for all s.

Under these conditions it can be shown that the derivative of the value function equals[20]

$$\frac{\partial V^0(t, \Theta)}{\partial \alpha} = \int_t^\infty \frac{\partial H^0(s)}{\partial \alpha} ds = \int_t^\infty [u_x(c^0(s), x^0(s))x_\alpha(s)e^{-\theta s} - \lambda^0(s)I_\alpha(\alpha)]ds$$

$$(2.46)$$

The first term in the last component denotes the benefits of the project in utility units, and the second term is the corresponding costs of the project. Clearly, $u_x x_\alpha > 0$, since both terms are negative.

Again the project cannot be evaluated correctly unless we know the development over time of state, control and exogenous variables. These information requirements are, of course, demanding, but in principle not less demanding in the first best optimum case. The magnitude of the Pigouvian tax can be determined by solving the command optimum problem. Here, without market data on the marginal disutility of the stock of pollution, we have to determine the net willingness to pay for the project. The willingness to pay for getting rid of one unit of the pollution stock over the interval $(s, s+ds)$ equals

$$wtp(s) = -u_x(s)/\lambda^c(s) \tag{2.47}$$

We can then rewrite the cost–benefit rule in the following manner

$$\frac{\partial V}{\partial \alpha} = \lambda(0) \int_t^\infty \{wtp^0(s)[-x_\alpha^0(s)] - I_\alpha(s)\} e^{-\int_t^s r(\tau)d\tau} \, ds \tag{2.46a}$$

The second term on the RHS, the (marginal) cost of the project, can be estimated from technical knowledge about the physical processes involved, while the first term requires both technical knowledge and data on willingness to pay. A major practical problem is that we need information on future willingness to pay. A not far-fetched idea would be to approximate future willingness to pay by the current one, that is, to use $u_x^0(t)/\lambda^{c^0}(t) = constant$ in the first term in equation (2.46a). We return to the feasibility of this and similar ideas in subsequent chapters.

2.4   WELFARE MEASUREMENT IN A UTILITY METRICS OR MONEY METRICS

The cost–benefit rules studied in the preceding section show that it does not matter whether we use a utility metrics or a money metrics. The non-arbitrage condition that connects the utility and money discount rates enables us to move from one metrics to another. The money metrics, however, exhibits a practicable advantage in that it is observable.

In the next chapter we show that Weitzman's welfare theorem in terms of a utility metrics can be converted into a money metrics under first best conditions. This simplifies the welfare measurement, since money values are typically observable in markets. It turns out, however, that the money values required are not easily accessible, even under perfect markets. The main reason is that, except in the case of marginal projects, we typically need measures of consumer surpluses.

Welfare measurement in a utility metrics is a good substitute for a money metrics as long as the context concerns theoretical efficiency considerations and the qualitative aspects of policy reform. In traditional static general equilibrium theory consumer preferences are represented by an ordinal utility function. Utility levels are thus arbitrary, since consumer rankings are independent of monotone transformations of the utility function. However, this does not prevent us from comparing two states, which are evaluated with the same utility function but with different underlying parameters. The absolute difference in utility has no clear meaning, but its sign tells us whether the change in the underlying parameter improves the situation or not.

Under discounted utilitarianism, the additive separability of the value function over time adds a cardinal dimension, but absolute utility differences are not well defined. The reason is that the optimal path is invariant to linear transformations of the instantaneous utility function. Suppose that $\{c^*(t)\}_0^\infty$ solves the problem

$$V(0, k_0) = \underset{c(t)}{\text{Max}} \int_0^\infty u(c(t))e^{-\theta t} dt \qquad (2.48a)$$

subject to

$$\dot{k}(t) = f(k(t)) - c(t) \qquad (2.48b)$$

$$k(0) = k_0$$

Thus, for a constant, $a > 0$ it will also solve

$$\tilde{V}(0, k_0) = \underset{c(t)}{\text{Max}} \int_0^\infty au(c(t))e^{-\theta t} dt \qquad (2.49)$$

under the same restrictions. Moreover, $\tilde{V}(0, k_0) = aV(0, k_0)$ and $H^{a*}(t) = aH^*(t)$ where $H^{a*}(t)$ is the optimized Hamiltonian corresponding to the problem in (2.49). The explanation is that the first order conditions for utility maximization will be scaled by the constant. In other words, the relative magnitude of the optimal value function and the corresponding Hamiltonian will be independent of the scale parameter. This implies also that relative comparisons in a utility metrics are invariant to a scaling of the utility function, that is,

$$\frac{H^*(t)}{V(0, k_0)} = \frac{H^{a*}(t)}{\tilde{V}(0, k_0)} \qquad (2.50)$$

We will make frequent use of this fact when comparing the deviation between welfare measured by a (pseudo-)Hamiltonian and the true welfare measure in Chapters 4 and 7. These deviations are measured relative to the optimal value function.

Of course, we could add any constant to the above linear transformation of the utility function, that is, choose a utility function $au + b$, and still have the same solution. But this would violate (2.50) because the marginal utility of income (money) is independent of b. With respect to Weitzman's welfare theorem, nothing would happen. We would get a constant on both sides of equation (2.11a), which is independent of any economic behavior. The resulting equality can be written

$$\theta \tilde{V}(0,k_0) = \theta a V(0,k_0) + b = aH^*(t) + b + atp \qquad (2.51)$$

where atp is shorthand for the sum of marginal technological progress along the optimal path measured in the transformed utility metrics. The relative welfare contribution of technological progress in the new and the old metrics would be, respectively

$$\frac{atp}{aV(0,k_0)+b} \neq \frac{tp}{V(0,k_0)} \qquad (2.52)$$

Letting b approach infinity, the contribution from technological progress in the LHS would approach zero, which seems both arbitrary and meaningless. Moreover, b is unobservable in both a utility metrics and a money metrics (indirectly so). The latter result follows since it is independent of consumption behavior and, therefore, cannot be priced.

The bottom line is that we do not allow any welfare measure to contain terms that are independent of economic behavior. Although unimportant for the theoretical analysis, this approach is necessary for the numerical applications to be meaningful. In fact from a practical point of view, this is the best we can do, since an additive constant cannot be measured on the basis of economic behavior. Setting $b = 0$ means that equation (2.52) is transformed into an equality, and the relative importance of technological progress is invariant with respect to the choice of linear transformation.

NOTES

1.   The original reference is Pontryagin et al. (1962). A rigorous and good presentation of the theory is given by Seierstad and Sydsaeter (1987). For a slightly less technical presentation, see Chiang (2000).

2. The first two conditions follow from the necessary conditions for an optimal path, and the third is a consequence of the shape of the Hamiltonian.

3. Also called a Most Rapid Approach, MRA, solution; see, for example, Spence and Starrett (1975).

4. For comprehensive coverage of modern endogenous growth theory, invented in Romer (1986a) and Lucas (1988), see Barro and Sala-i-Martin (1995) and Aghion and Howitt (1998).

5. This model was first introduced by Frank Plumpton Ramsey (1928).

6. A growing population would also introduce non-autonomous time dependence. We address population growth in later chapters.

7. See Chapter 3, pp. 244–245. Note also that if the time horizon is endogenous, the necessary conditions for an optimal path contain the condition $H^*(T^*) = 0$.

8. Kemp and Long (1982) were the first to point out the consequences for welfare measurement of non-autonomous time dependencies. See also Aronsson et al. (1997. ch. 3).

9. See Aronsson and Löfgren (1996).

10. Note that the production function is net of capital depreciation, so that the marginal productivity of capital becomes negative for large capital stocks.

11. Details may be found in Seierstad and Sydsaeter (1987, Theorem 3.16). The transversality conditions are necessary provided that certain growth conditions are fulfilled. The growth conditions serve as upper bounds for the influence of the state variables on the functions involved.

12. To see this, integrate (2.20) forwards and use the transversality condition $\Omega^*(T) = 0$.

13. Such estimations for the US economy have been carried out by Weitzman (1997) and Weitzman and Löfgren (1997). See also Chapters 4 and 7 below.

14. Here human wealth is the discounted future value of wage income, and non-human wealth is the capital stock at time t.

15. Obviously, if $f_t \neq 0$, equation 2.27 would be augmented with a term representing the present value of marginal technological progress along the competitive path.

16. See Pigou (1920). The first to understand how to correct for externalities by taxing the polluter was Warming (1911). Crocker (1965) introduced markets for tradable permits.

17. Note that if $x(T)$ is free $\lambda^*(T) = 0$. (We assume that the terminal conditions on k and x do not bind.)

18. In the strict mathematical problem with the above derivation, we have assumed differentiability, rather than proved it. Theorems on the differentiability of the value function are provided in Seierstad (1982).

19. For clarity, we suppress all parameters except the project parameter.

20. These calculations will be frequently carried out in the subsequent chapters.

3. A money-metrics version of Weitzman's welfare theorem

Weitzman's (1976) fundamental result on welfare measurement introduced in Chapter 2 was obtained in a first best setting with one aggregate consumption good, m capital goods, and a utility function equal to aggregate consumption. Hence, by normalizing the price of the consumption good to one, the Hamiltonian will coincide with real NNP and, consequently, the money and utility metrics will coincide. However, in a more general setting this is no longer true. Since utility is not observable, a practical problem arises, at least if we want an observable measure of the static welfare equivalent. We attempted to deal with this problem in Chapter 2 by linearizing the utility function as in equation (2.17b). In a first best setting, with no externalities and one consumption good, this would give us an approximate relation between current NNP and future wealth. However, the approximation will be poor if the utility function deviates strongly from linearity. In addition, more than one consumption good will give rise to a price index problem.

To simplify as much as possible, and since Weitzman's (1976) result constitutes a natural starting point, we carry out the analysis in a first best framework. As such, the most important result is Proposition 3.2, which provides a money-metric analogue to the first best welfare theorem in a utility metrics. It shows exactly what information is required for measuring welfare at a given point in time, as well as explaining why the traditional approach of linearizing the Hamiltonian might be misleading.

3.1   THE WELFARE THEOREM

To illustrate the shortcomings of a linear approximation of the utility function, let us assume that we are dealing with a spaceship economy[1] with utility function $u = (1/\beta)c(t)^{\beta}$, and in which the resource stock dynamics is given by the differential equation $\dot{f}(t) = -c(t)$, with a limited food supply, $f(0) = f_0$, at the outset. The maximization problem is

$$\underset{c(t)}{\text{Max}} \frac{1}{\beta} \int_0^\infty c(t)^\beta e^{-\theta t} dt \tag{3.1}$$

subject to

$$\dot{f}(t) = -c(t), \quad f(0) = f_0$$
$$0 < \beta < 1$$

The maximized current value Hamiltonian can be written

$$H^{c*}(t) = \beta^{-1} c^*(t)^\beta - \lambda^{c*}(t) c^*(t) \tag{3.2}$$

Linearizing by taking the first differential of the utility function, the Hamiltonian and, hence, future welfare can be approximated by the expression

$$H^{c*}(t) \approx u_c(c^*(t)) c^*(t) - \lambda^{c*}(t) c^*(t) = \lambda^{c*}(t)(c^*(t) - c^*(t)) \equiv 0 \tag{3.3}$$

The second equality in equation (3.3) follows from the first order conditions for an optimal path. Hence, NNP defined as the value of consumption plus net investment is zero for the spaceship economy, independent of the size of the 'packed lunch', f_0. In other words, a linear money-metricized index will in general be misleading as a welfare index, even if the spaceship economy is a somewhat extreme example. The utility metrics, of course, still works, and it is also straightforward to show that the size of the packed lunch matters. The first order condition yields $c(t) = \lambda^c(t)^{1/\beta-1}$ and the co-state equation reads $\dot{\lambda}^c(t) = \theta \lambda^c(t)$ or, equivalently, $\dot{c}(t) = (\theta/(\beta - 1)) c(t)$. The solution of this differential equation is

$$c^*(t) = c_o e^{\frac{\theta t}{\beta - 1}} = \frac{\theta f_0}{1 - \beta} e^{\frac{\theta t}{\beta - 1}} \tag{3.4}$$

Substituting this expression into the objective function yields the value function

$$V(f_0) = \frac{1}{\theta} \left[\frac{1-\beta}{\beta} \left(\frac{\theta f_0}{1-\beta} \right) \right] = \frac{1}{\theta} H^{c*}(f_0) \tag{3.5}$$

Clearly, $\partial V / \partial f_0 > 0$; that is, food supply matters for welfare, but it will not be captured by a linear index. The reason is that, at the margin, an extra unit of food will be allocated so that the marginal utility from consuming today equals what it would yield in terms of future utility, if stored. Since the storage of food does not yield any extra services as a capital stock, $\partial H^{c^*}(t)/\partial f \equiv 0$ along the optimal path. The utility of non-marginal units of food is, however, greater than their marginal storage values, and would then account for a positive value function. The problem here is that consumer surplus is not properly accounted for by money NNP. In this example we have consumer surplus, $cs^*(t)$, equal to

$$cs^*(t) = \frac{1-\beta}{\beta} c^*(t)^\beta$$

which for $\beta = 1/2$ reduces to $\sqrt{c^*(t)}$.

There is, however, a very general sense in which a comprehensive measure of money NNP in a perfect market economy can serve as a static equivalent of future utility along the competitive path of the economy. The formulation of the Ramsey–Brock problem implies, since we are adding utilities over time, that the optimal solution will not be independent of monotone transformations of the utility function. It is, however, as shown in Chapter 2, independent of linear (affine) transformations of the utility function. Suppose that we have an economy with n consumption goods, $\mathbf{c}(t) = (c_1(t),...,c_n(t))$, and m capital goods, $\mathbf{k}(t) = (k_1(t),...,k_m(t))$, where the vector of capital goods is comprehensive in the sense that it contains all goods that are relevant for the productive capacity of the economy. Moreover, let $\mathbf{p}(t) = (p_1(t),...,p_n(t))$ be the nominal prices of consumption goods, including the rental prices of the services rendered by capital goods at time t, and $\mathbf{q}(t) = (q_1(t),...,q_m(t))$ be the corresponding prices of capital goods. In this economy NNP at time t is defined as $NNP(t) = \mathbf{p}^*(t)c^*(t) + \mathbf{q}^*(t)\mathbf{k}^*(t)$. The top indices denote that the economy follows an optimal path. Given that technological progress can be attributed to the capital stocks, and if we disregard externalities, it is straightforward to prove the following result:

Proposition 3.1 (Weitzman, 2000) *When the instantaneous utility function is money-metricized by the transformation* $u_{ab}(\mathbf{c}(t)) = a(0)u(\mathbf{c}(t)) + b(0)$, *where* $b(0) = \mathbf{p}^*(0)\mathbf{c}(0) - a(0)u(\mathbf{c}(0))$, $a(0) = 1/\lambda_0^m$ *and* λ_0^m *is the marginal utility of money (income) at time zero, then*

$$NNP(0) \int_0^\infty e^{-\theta t} dt = \int_0^\infty u_{ab}(\mathbf{c}(t))e^{-\theta t} dt$$

Proof: *From equation (2.11) we have for the original utility function that*

$$\int_0^\infty H(0)e^{-\theta t} dt = \int_0^\infty [u(\mathbf{c}^*(0)) + \lambda_0^m \mathbf{q}^*(0)\dot{\mathbf{k}}^*(0)]e^{-\theta t} dt = \int_0^\infty u(\mathbf{c}(t))e^{-\theta t} dt.$$

Expressed in terms of the transformation $u(\mathbf{c}(t)) = u_{ab}(\mathbf{c}(t))a(0)^{-1} + u(\mathbf{c}(0))$ $- \mathbf{p}(0)\mathbf{c}(0)a(0)^{-1}$, we can rewrite this expression as

$$\int_0^\infty [\mathbf{p}^*(0)\mathbf{c}^*(0)a^{-1} + \lambda_0^m \mathbf{q}^*(0)\dot{\mathbf{k}}^*(0)]e^{-\theta t}dt = a^{-1}\int_0^\infty u_{ab}(\mathbf{c}^*(t))e^{-\theta t}dt$$

Setting $a = 1/\lambda_0^m$ and *dividing through by* λ_0^m *proves the claim.*

The transformation of the utility function is, of course, arbitrary and the formula is of very limited practical value. In particular, the transformation cannot handle changes from one period to another, and comparisons over time become meaningless. It nevertheless shows that in a first best situation, most of what we want to measure will be captured by present NNP, as long as it is sufficiently comprehensive and accurately calibrated.

If we take a closer look at the transformation, it is clear that the constant $a(0) = 1/\lambda_0^m$ measures the inverse of the marginal utility income and, as a multiplier, it takes utility into money. The constant $b(0) = \mathbf{p}^*(0)\mathbf{c}(0) - a(0)u(0)$ is the difference between the 'marginal money value of consumption' and the 'total money value of consumption' (the negative of a 'consumer surplus'). It shifts total money utility downwards to equal the money-metricized Hamiltonian, *NNP*(0).

However, even if the consumer surplus problem can be handled, we have to find a method that endogenously handles the path from one affine transformation to another. Otherwise intertemporal index comparisons will not be meaningful. We also need means of distinguishing nominal price changes from changes in relative prices. The first problem requires a result that shows how the anchor, the marginal utility of money, develops over time. The second is an index number problem.

As regards the first problem, we need a general multisector growth model, and we have one; the Brock model introduced in Chapter 2 is an example. There, the production technology is specified in terms of a neoclassical production function and the emission technology is also explicitly defined. Here, following Weitzman (1976), we introduce the technology in terms of a multidimensional production possibility set. The model was also used in Weitzman (2001) to compare the money-metrics welfare levels in two countries at a given point in time. It is the workhorse in his recent book.[2] Hence, a consumption–investment pair $[\mathbf{c}(t), \dot{\mathbf{k}}(t)]$ is attainable at time t from the capital stock $\mathbf{k}(t)$ if and only if

$$\mathbf{c}(t), \dot{\mathbf{k}}(t), \mathbf{k}(t) \in \mathbf{A}$$

where $\mathbf{A}$ is a convex attainable production possibility set.

The general multisector growth problem can now be formulated as follows;

$$\text{Max}_{c(t),i(t)} \int_0^\infty u(\mathbf{c}(t))e^{-\theta t}dt \qquad (3.6)$$

subject to the constraints

$$\mathbf{c}(t),\dot{\mathbf{k}}(t),\mathbf{k}(t) \in \mathbf{A} \qquad (3.7)$$

and the differential equations

$$\dot{\mathbf{k}}(t) = \mathbf{i}(t) \qquad (3.8)$$

with initial conditions

$$\mathbf{k}(0) = \mathbf{k}_0 \qquad (3.9)$$

The maximum principle is valid and it requires that the current value Hamiltonian

$$H^c = u(\mathbf{c}(t)) + \boldsymbol{\lambda}^c(t)\mathbf{i}(t) \qquad (3.10)$$

be maximized with respect to $[\mathbf{c}(t),\mathbf{i}(t)]$ subject to the restrictions (3.7)–(3.9). Here $\boldsymbol{\lambda}^c$ is an n-dimensional vector of utility shadow prices of capital goods (co-state variables) which satisfies

$$\dot{\boldsymbol{\lambda}}^c(t) = \theta\boldsymbol{\lambda}^c(t) - H_{\mathbf{k}}^c(t) \qquad (3.11)$$

where $H_{\mathbf{k}}^c$ is the gradient of the Hamiltonian with respect to the capital stocks. In the Ramsey (1928) growth model the nominal interest rate is determined by the marginal productivity of capital. Here, matters are somewhat more complicated since the technology is very general and there are many capital stocks. A non-arbitrage argument is available, however. If the consumer, along an optimal path, abstained from one dollar at time t, she would abstain from $\lambda^m(t)$ units of utility. At time $t + \Delta t$, she would enjoy $(1 + \theta\Delta t)\lambda^m(t)$ units of utility. This is equivalent to consuming, in period $t + \Delta t$, the dollar amount

$$\frac{(1 + \theta\Delta t)\lambda^m(t)}{\lambda^m(t + \Delta t)} = (1 + r(t))\Delta t \qquad (3.12)$$

where $r(t)$ is the nominal interest rate. Rewriting the above equation by multiplying both sides by $\lambda^m(t + \Delta t)/\Delta t$ and taking limits yields

$$\dot{\lambda}^m(t) = [\theta - r(t)]\lambda^m(t) \tag{3.13}$$

which is the differential equation for the marginal utility of income along the optimal path. It has the same form as equation (2.42), which was used to transfer the utility value of a project into a money metrics in Chapter 2. The solution is

$$\lambda^m(s)e^{-\theta(s-t)} = \lambda^m(t)e^{-\int_t^s r(\tau)d\tau} \tag{3.14}$$

Equation (3.14) will be used to transfer the utility discount factor into a money discount factor. It is also instrumental for decomposing utility along an optimal path into a monetary component and a component measuring marginal utility of income. To avoid notational clutter, we do not introduce a top index to denote that the marginal utility of income is measured along an optimal path. Obviously, the formula is valid for any economy where the above arbitrage argument holds. Such an economy does not have to be governed solely by first best principles.

Our next project is to come up with a measure of consumer surplus in a money metrics. To this end we use an ingenious observation in Weitzman (2001). Conditional on the market prices along the first best path of the economy, one can represent consumer choice at time t by the solution to the following optimization problem

$$\underset{[\mathbf{c}(t),\kappa(t)]}{\text{Max}}\ H^c(t) = u(\mathbf{c}(t)) + \lambda^m(t)\kappa(t) \tag{3.15}$$

subject to

$$\mathbf{p}^*(t)\mathbf{c}(t) + \kappa(t) = y^*(t) \tag{3.16}$$

where $\kappa(t) = \mathbf{q}^*(t)\mathbf{i}(t)$ is the total aggregate money value of net investments in the n capital stocks. The marginal utility of income is treated as a constant during the period, as is money NNP, $y^*(t)$. Since the objective function in (3.15) is quasi-linear, the solution for current consumption is $\mathbf{c}^*(t) = \mathbf{d}(\mathbf{p}^*(t),\lambda^m(t))$, where $\mathbf{d}(\cdot)$ is the m-dimensional vector of demand functions. The corresponding net investment value is $\kappa^*(t) = y^*(t) - \mathbf{p}^*(t)\mathbf{c}^*(t)$.

Hence, along an optimal path, we can represent the utility function by

$$u(\mathbf{c}^*(t)) = \int_0^{\mathbf{c}^*(t)} u_\mathbf{c}(\mathbf{c})d\mathbf{c} = \lambda^m(t)\left[\mathbf{p}^*(t)\mathbf{c}^*(t) + \int_{\mathbf{p}^*(t)}^{\bar{\mathbf{p}}} \mathbf{d}(\mathbf{p},\lambda^m(t))d\mathbf{p}\right] \quad (3.17)$$

Here, $\bar{\mathbf{p}}$ denotes a vector of choke-off prices.[3] It is straightforward to use (3.17) to rewrite the current value Hamiltonian as

$$H^{\mathbf{c}^*}(t) = \lambda^m(t)[y^*(t) + cs^*(t)] \quad (3.18)$$

where $y^*(t)$ is given in equation (3.16) and

$$cs^*(t) = \int_{\mathbf{p}^*(t)}^{\bar{\mathbf{p}}} \mathbf{d}(\mathbf{p},\lambda^m(t))d\mathbf{p} \quad (3.19)$$

is the consumer surplus. It may seem tempting to integrate (3.18) over time, so as to end up with the Weitzman foundation. This does not result in any additional information, however. The welfare measure in (3.18) is decomposed in money and utility components, but still embedded in a utility metrics. We need an anchor in order to move the marginal utility of income outside the resulting integral.

To solve this problem we introduce a price index that is independent of the market basket in the economy. In the same spirit as Weitzman (2001), we define an ideal consumer price index

$$\pi(t) = \frac{\mathbf{p}(t;\mathbf{c})\mathbf{c}}{\mathbf{p}(t_0;\mathbf{c})\mathbf{c}} \quad (3.20)$$

The notation on the left hand side, π depends only on time, indicates that the index is independent of the marker basket – benchmark independent. The reason is that $\mathbf{p}(t,\mathbf{c})$ and $\mathbf{p}(t_0,\mathbf{c})$ denote the 'imputed' market clearing prices that would be observed at the two points in time if the market basket of goods being consumed in the economy were $\mathbf{c}$. The name 'ideal measure' is chosen by Weitzman (2001) to denote the direction toward which the formulators of a CPI- or PPP-type index strive when they try to select a representative market basket straddling two economies at a given point in time, or the same economy at two points in time. The imputation problem is difficult in both cases. The scalar $\pi(t)$ measures the price level at time t relative to that at time t_0. To show that the index is independent of the market basket $\mathbf{c}$, that is, benchmark independent, we note that since the utility function is stationary over time, it holds that

$$u_\mathbf{c}(\mathbf{c}) = \lambda^m(t_0)\mathbf{p}(t_0;\mathbf{c}) = \lambda^m(t)\mathbf{p}(t;\mathbf{c}) \quad (3.21)$$

Multiplying through by the market basket **c**, and solving for the marginal utility of income at time t_0, yields

$$\lambda^m(t_0) = \pi(t)\lambda^m(t) \tag{3.22}$$

which is a constant.

This property makes the index consistent with or, perhaps better, a mix of the two approaches in Francis Ysidro Edgeworth's pioneer work[4] on index numbers, called the 'aggregative approach'[5] and the 'stochastic approach', respectively. The former refers to any group or applies to any set of circumstances. The reference can, as here, be to the aggregate expenditure of all consumers with the object of saying something about the standard of living of the group. According to the latter approach, which Edgeworth prefers, the objective is the 'determination of an index irrespective of quantities of commodities; upon the hypothesis that there is a numerous group of articles whose prices vary after the manner of perfect market, with changes affecting the supply of money'.[6]

We can now re-scale equation (3.18) to read

$$H^{c^*}(t) = \lambda^m(t)\pi(t)\left[\frac{y^*(t) + cs^*(t)}{\pi(t)}\right] = \lambda^m(t_0)[y_r^*(t) + cs_r^*(t)] \tag{3.23}$$

where $y^*_r(t) = y^*(t)/\pi(t) = \mathbf{p}^*_r(t)\mathbf{c}^*(t) + \mathbf{q}^*_\mathbf{r}(t)\mathbf{i}^*(t)$ is the real comprehensive NNP and $cs^*_r(t) = cs^*(t)/\pi(t)$ the consumer surplus, both expressed in real terms (in the prices of period t_0). The real prices for consumer and investment goods are $\mathbf{p}^*_r(t) = \mathbf{p}^*(t)/\pi(t)$ and $\mathbf{q}^*_\mathbf{r}(t) = \mathbf{q}^*(t)/\pi(t)$, respectively. The consumer surplus in real terms can be written

$$cs^*_r(t) = \int_{\mathbf{p}^*(t)}^{\bar{\mathbf{p}}} \mathbf{d}(\mathbf{p}, \lambda^m(t))d\mathbf{p}/\pi(t) = \int_{\mathbf{p}^*_r(t)}^{\bar{\mathbf{p}}_r} \mathbf{d}(\mathbf{p}_r, \lambda^m(t_0))d\mathbf{p}_r \tag{3.24}$$

Again the demand functions are time invariant, since the utility function does not change over time, that is,

$$u_\mathbf{c}(\mathbf{c}(t)) = \lambda^m(t)\pi(t)\mathbf{p}(t)/\pi(t) = \lambda^m(t_0)\mathbf{p}_r(t) \tag{3.25}$$

We can thus simplify the notation by writing $\mathbf{d}_0 = \mathbf{d}_0(\mathbf{p}_r(t))$ for a given time t, where the index denotes that the base year is t_0. Now define the generalized comprehensive net national product (GCNNP) as follows

$$H^{c^*}_r(t) = \frac{H^{c^*}(t)}{\lambda^m(t_0)} = y_r^*(t) + cs_r^*(t) \tag{3.26}$$

Weitzman's (1976) fundamental theorem in a utility metrics can now be used to derive the following proposition, due to Li and Löfgren (2002):

Proposition 3.2 *The generalized comprehensive net national product (GCNNP) in (3.26) is a stationary equivalent of the future value of consumption plus the consumer surplus in real terms such that*

$$\int_t^\infty H_r^{c^*}(t)\exp(-\theta(s-t))ds = \int_t^\infty \left[\mathbf{p}_r^*(s)\mathbf{c}^*(s) + \int_{\mathbf{p}_r^*(s)}^{\bar{\mathbf{p}}_r} \mathbf{d}_0(\mathbf{p_r})d\mathbf{p_r} \right]\exp(-\theta(s-t))ds$$

or equivalently

$$H_r^{c^*}(t) = \theta M_r^*(t)$$

where

$$M_r^*(t) = \int_t^\infty \left[\mathbf{p}_r^*(s)\mathbf{c}^*(s) + \int_{\mathbf{p}_r^*(s)}^{\bar{\mathbf{p}}_r} \mathbf{d}_0(\mathbf{p_r})d\mathbf{p_r} \right]\exp(-\theta(s-t))ds$$

can be interpreted as the generalized welfare (wealth) in real terms.

The proof is available in Li and Löfgren (2002). It follows from (3.17), (3.18) and the definitions (3.22)–(3.26). The key to the result is already in Weitzman (2001), where welfare levels in two different economies are ranked at a given point in time. Proposition 3.2 shows that a money-metrics static equivalent to future welfare along the first best path of the economy will in general exist, but that it is more demanding than the traditional NNP concept, which will only work under special circumstances. One such situation is an economy with one aggregate consumption good, and a linear utility function. Another is when the instantaneous utility function is linear homogenous. The reason that NNP works as a welfare indicator in the latter situation is that the linear approximation becomes exact. It is also worth noting that the discount rate in Proposition 3.2 is the utility discount rate.

3.2 COST–BENEFIT RULES

The cost–benefit rule (2.41) in Chapter 2 does not have a consumer surplus component. Why? The answer is that a perfect intertemporal market economy with equality between supply and demand entails envelope properties that will net out all indirect effects if a project is assumed to be small enough.[7] Note that the projects in Chapter 2 were evaluated at the ruling market prices, although almost any project would imply price changes. This indicates that the present value of the direct change in NNP is the relevant cost–benefit rule for any small project in a first best setting. This is indeed the case. To see this, let us represent a small project by a change in a parameter (vector) α. The maximized Hamiltonian can be written

$$H^{c^*}(\cdot) = H^c[(\mathbf{c}^*(\mathbf{k}^*(t,\alpha),\alpha,t), \mathbf{i}^*(\mathbf{k}^*(t,\alpha),\alpha,t), \boldsymbol{\lambda}^c(\mathbf{k}^*(t,\alpha),t)] \quad (3.27)$$

Here, following Li and Löfgren (2002), the consumption vector may be regarded as parameterized in the following manner: $\mathbf{c}^* = \mathbf{c}^*(\mathbf{k}(t,\alpha),t) + \alpha$, with the parameter vector α equal to zero initially. The same parameter vector also has an independent influence on the vector of net inestments. The envelope theorem derived in Chapter 2 tells us that the welfare improvement from the reform $d\alpha$ is measured in a utility metrics by the following partial derivative

$$\frac{\partial V(t,\alpha)}{\partial \alpha} = \int_t^\infty \frac{\partial H^{c^*}(s)}{\partial \alpha} e^{-\theta(s-t)} ds = \int_t^\infty \lambda^m(s)[\mathbf{p}^*(s)\mathbf{c}_\alpha^*(s) + \mathbf{q}^*(s)\mathbf{i}_\alpha^*(s)] e^{-\theta(s-t)} ds$$

$$(3.28)$$

where the partials c_α^* and i_α^* are the derivatives measuring the direct impact from the project $d\alpha$.

Expression (3.28) may easily be transferred into a money metrics by making use of equation (3.14) to obtain

$$\frac{\partial V(t,\alpha)}{\partial \alpha} = \lambda^m(t) \int_t^\infty [\mathbf{p}^*(s)\mathbf{c}_\alpha^*(s) + \mathbf{q}^*(s)\mathbf{i}_\alpha^*(s)] e^{-\int_t^s r(\tau)d\tau} ds \quad (3.29)$$

$$= \lambda^m(t) \int_t^\infty \left[\frac{\partial y^*(s)}{\partial \alpha} e^{-\int_t^s r(\tau)d\tau} \right] ds$$

where the marginal utility of income at time t is a constant which can be set equal to one without changing the rankings between projects. The value of the project in a money metrics thus equals the present value of the change in money NNP. Clearly, if the project only lasts a finite period of time, $[t,T]$, then $c_\alpha^* = i_\alpha^* = 0$ for all $s > T$, and it suffices, under first best, to integrate (3.29) between $[t,T]$.[8]

3.3 REAL NNP GROWTH AND WELFARE

According to conventional wisdom, real NNP growth is equivalent to a welfare improvement. This view is not generally correct, however. As we are about to show, the choice of consumer price index matters for the answer. Differentiating equation (3.26) with respect to time yields[9]

$$\dot{H}_r^{c^*}(t) = \dot{y}_r^*(t) + c\dot{s}_r^*(t) = \dot{y}_r^*(t) - \dot{\mathbf{p}}_r^*(t)\mathbf{c}^*(t) \tag{3.30}$$

Obviously, as long as the last term on the right hand side of equation (3.30) is different from zero, we cannot conclude that NNP growth, $\dot{y}_r^*(t) > 0$, indicates a welfare improvement. The reason is that changes in relative prices will take place along the endogenously determined growth path of the economy.

The conventional wisdom is wrong because it incorrectly and implicitly assumes that real comprehensive NNP is a static equivalent of future welfare. Obviously, GCNNP growth, $\dot{H}_r^{c^*}(t) > 0$, indicates a welfare improvement.

There is a special case, or rather a special index formula, under which real NNP growth indicates a welfare improvement. As shown by Asheim and Weitzman (2001), when real NNP is defined in terms of a Divisa price index[10] its growth will always indicate a welfare improvement. The reason is that this index satisfies

$$\frac{\dot{\pi}^d(t)}{\pi^d(t)} = \frac{\dot{\mathbf{p}}(t)\mathbf{c}(t)}{\mathbf{p}(t)\mathbf{c}(t)} \tag{3.31}$$

implying that $\dot{\mathbf{p}}_{\mathbf{d}}^*(t)\mathbf{c}^*(t) \equiv 0$, where $\mathbf{p}_d^* = \mathbf{p}^*/\pi^d$.

As we saw above, in connection with the derivation of the cost–benefit rule, the present value of the change in (real) NNP measures the welfare change. The underlying reason is that, at the margin, there is no consumer surplus involved.

Our next task is to investigate what GCNNP can tell us about sustainable development. For this reason we introduce a new concept, 'genuine saving', coined by Hamilton (1994) and Hamilton and Clemens (1999).

3.4 GENUINE SAVING

It is tempting to assume that if the value of the comprehensive net investment vector along the first best path of the economy is positive at time t, then the productive capacity of the economy is kept intact and the economy will be 'sustainable'. By now, however, it is well known that this is not the case. Asheim (1994a) and Pezzey (1995) have shown that a positive net investment value typically means not only that aggregate consumption in a resources dependent economy goes to zero along the optimal path, but also, more surprisingly, that the current consumption level cannot be sustained even if one deviates from the optimal path to avoid the 'curse of discounting' that governs the optimal path.

More specifically, following Aronsson et al. (1997, p. 93), we can start from Weitzman's (1976) result on the proportionality between the maximized Hamiltonian and the present value of future utility, that is,

$$u(\mathbf{c}^*(t))e^{-\theta t} + \boldsymbol{\lambda}^*(t)\mathbf{i}^*(t) = \theta \int_t^\infty u(\mathbf{c}^*(s))e^{-\theta s} ds \tag{3.32}$$

By partially integrating the right hand side and canceling terms, and after moving to current value, we obtain

$$\boldsymbol{\lambda}^{c^*}(t)\mathbf{i}^*(t) = \int_t^\infty u_c(\mathbf{c}^*(s))\dot{\mathbf{c}}^*(s)e^{-\theta(s-t)} ds \tag{3.33}$$

Written in terms of efficiency prices, equation (3.33) transfers into

$$\boldsymbol{\lambda}^m(t)[\mathbf{q}^*(t)\mathbf{i}^*(t)] = \int_t^\infty \boldsymbol{\lambda}^m(s)[\mathbf{p}^*(s)\dot{\mathbf{c}}^*(s)]e^{-\theta(s-t)} ds \tag{3.34}$$

To transform this into a money metrics we use the benchmark invariant price index in the same manner as in section 3.1 to end up with the following result:[11]

Proposition 3.3 *Along the first best path of the economy it holds that*

$$\mathbf{q}_r^*(t)\mathbf{i}^*(t) = \int_t^\infty \mathbf{p}_r^*(s)\dot{\mathbf{c}}^*(s)e^{-\theta(s-t)} ds$$

that is, the value of comprehensive net investment at time t (genuine saving in a money metrics) equals the present value of the changes in consumption along the future path of the economy evaluated at real efficiency prices. The deflator is the benchmark invariant price index $\pi(t)$.

The market value of comprehensive net investment is often referred to as 'genuine saving'.[12] Proposition 3.3 provides an exact money-metrics explanation for the information content of genuine saving in a first best context. Note, however, that in order to rely on genuine saving as a precise indicator of the sign of the sum of weighted future consumption changes, either the economy has to be on a first best path, or we have reason to believe that the deviations from first best do not matter.

Our next task is to determine the relationship between growth and genuine saving.

3.5   THE RELATIONSHIP BETWEEN GCNNP GROWTH AND GENUINE SAVING

There is clearly a relationship between growth in GCNNP as expressed in equation (3.30) and the result in Proposition 3.3. Both measure the change in future welfare in money terms. We will now specify this relationship in more detail.

Starting from the current value Hamiltonian and using the necessary conditions for an optimal path, it can be shown that

$$\frac{dH^{c^*}(t)}{dt} = \theta[H^{c^*}(t) - u(\mathbf{c}^*(t))] = \theta\boldsymbol{\lambda}^{c^*}(t)\mathbf{i}^*(t) = \theta\boldsymbol{\lambda}^m(t)\mathbf{q}^*(t)\mathbf{i}^*(t) \quad (3.35)$$

which measures the welfare change along an optimal path at time t in a utility metrics. Again, invoking the price index, equation (3.30) and Proposition 3.3 yield

$$\dot{H}_r^{c^*}(t) = \dot{y}_r^*(t) - \dot{\mathbf{p}}_r^*(t)\mathbf{c}^*(t) = \theta\mathbf{q}_r^*(t)\mathbf{i}^*(t) = \theta\int_t^\infty \mathbf{p}_r^*(s)\dot{\mathbf{c}}^*(s)e^{-\theta(s-t)}ds \quad (3.36)$$

Since $\dot{H}_r^{c^*} = dGCNNP/dt$, then after simplifying the notation by setting $GCNNP = G^C$ and defining genuine saving $I = \mathbf{q}_r^*\mathbf{i}^*$, we can sum up the relationship between growth and genuine saving as:

Proposition 3.4 *Along an optimal path it holds that*

$$g^c(t) = \frac{\dot{G}^C(t)}{G^C(t)} = \frac{I(t)}{G^C(t)\theta^{-1}} = \frac{I(t)}{M_r(t)}$$

that is, the rate of growth in GCNNP equals the ratio between total comprehensive investment and money welfare.

Note that $G^C\theta^{-1}$ equals M_r (generalized welfare) in Proposition 3.2.

It is clear that welfare theorems in a money metrics is much more practical than the corresponding theorems in a utility metrics. However, the road to a practical implementation of the insights in Propositions 3.2–3.4 is still bumpy. One problem is the estimation of the benchmark independent price index. Another, and perhaps more fundamental, is that we do not know how good first best theory is as an approximation in an imperfect market economy.

The choice of metrics should of course depend on the objective of the analysis. If the purpose is to provide a framework for practical applications, then the choice of metrics is obviously important. If, on the other hand, an analysis serves to characterize the welfare measure and/or analyze the relative welfare contributions of different parts of the welfare measure, the choice between utility and money metrics is less important. Since we, in particular, will be concerned with welfare measurements in imperfect market economies, where a complete set of general equilibrium prices does not exist, we will mainly use the analytically more convenient utility metrics in subsequent chapters.

NOTES

1. The term was introduced by Boulding (1966). He conducted an insightful inquiry into the planet earth's sustainability problem. An economy with a similar problem of defining comprehensive NNP would be Kuwait, which is extremely dependent on its oil resources.
2. Weitzman (2003).
3. We have to assume that such finite prices exist, or, if not, that the intergral converges.
4. This work was done in the 1880s; see Edgeworth (1925).
5. This term is, in fact, due to Frisch (1936). The other approach is called the stochastic approach.
6. See Edgeworth (1925, p. 233).
7. Equality between supply and demand means that the sum of consumer and producer surpluses is maximized.
8. See Li and Löfgren (2002).
9. Note that typically the choke-off price vector changes. However, this change cancels out, since consumption at choke-off prices is zero by definition.
10. See Allen (1986, p. 178).
11. The marginal utility of income at time $t_0 < t$ has in the proposition been normalized to one.
12. See, for example, Hamilton and Clemens (1999).

4. An almost practical step towards green accounting?

The valuation problems implicit in green accounting are, to a large extent, related to environmental externalities. As explained in Chapter 2, if it were possible to design and implement Pigouvian taxes such that the external effects would become fully internalized, these taxes might also be used to value the depletion of environmental capital. In practice, however, little consensus has yet been reached regarding methods to measure the future welfare consequences of using environmental resources. Some of the early literature on social accounting[1] suggested using the willingness-to-pay technique as a means of collecting information. This is clearly a challenging topic for social accounting in the sense that the willingness-to-pay technique is widely used in economics to capture the values of non-market goods. To our knowledge, the only attempt to reconcile the willingness-to-pay approach to collecting information with the growth theoretical approach to social accounting is Aronsson and Löfgren (1999a). This chapter is largely based on their analysis.

The Pigouvian emission tax plays two important roles in the context of Chapter 2: it brings the economy to the socially optimal path, and it provides useful information for accounting purposes by measuring the social opportunity cost of emissions. However, since Pigouvian taxes are generally forward looking, their informational content is not easily recovered in practice. The main reason is that Pigouvian taxes, in part, reflect the preferences of future generations, whereas willingness-to-pay studies, by necessity, have to focus on the preferences of those currently alive. What would happen if we tried to design emission taxes on the basis of the willingness-to-pay to reduce pollution today? Such a study would not only provide a basis for evaluating the willingness-to-pay technique as a means of collecting policy-relevant information; it would also help in evaluating the usefulness of willingness-to-pay information for accounting purposes. Of course, since the more or less static willingness-to-pay approach is not able to capture the preferences of future generations, it will not provide enough information to construct Pigouvian taxes in the general case. At best, we could hope to design 'non-Pigouvian' taxes that closely resemble their Pigouvian counterparts. Two questions immediately come to mind. First, would the approximations of Pigouvian taxes improve the welfare in comparison with the uncontrolled market economy? Second, if these taxes were used to value additions to the stock of pollution in the accounting system, would the resulting green NNP in utility terms provide a reasonable approximation of the correct welfare measure?

Following Aronsson and Löfgren (1999a), the main purpose of this chapter is to address these two questions by using the model set out in Chapter 2. We also complement the theoretical analysis with numerical simulations. The numerical analysis is motivated by the fact that static approximations of the Pigouvian taxes will, in general, differ from the correct Pigouvian taxes. Therefore, it is important to try to assess the empirical relevance of this bias. The numerical analysis is intended to compare the welfare of the market equilibrium controlled by the approximation of the Pigouvian tax with the welfare in the first best optimum, as well as to measure the relative welfare contribution of external effects in a situation where the economy is controlled by the approximation of the Pigouvian tax.

4.1   A BRIEF RECAPITULATION OF THE MODEL

The model set out in Chapter 2 is here applied in the context of an imperfectly controlled market economy. Suppose that an emission tax, $\tau^0(t)$, is imposed on the firm at each point in time, and that the tax revenues, $\tau^0(t)g(t)$, are redistributed to the consumer in the form of a lump-sum transfer. The optimization problems of the representative consumer and firm are given by problems (2.21) and (2.28) in Chapter 2. For the reader's convenience, we briefly recapitulate the necessary conditions, since they will be useful in the subsequent analysis. Recall that, in addition to the equations of motion for k and x, as well as to the initial and No Ponzi Game (NPG) conditions, the necessary conditions are

$$u_c(c^0(t), x^0(t))e^{-\theta t} - \lambda^0(t) = 0 \tag{4.1}$$

$$f_g(k^0(t), g^0(t)) - \tau^0(t) = 0 \tag{4.2}$$

$$\dot{\lambda}^0(t) = -\lambda^0(t)f_k(k^0(t), g^0(t)) \tag{4.3}$$

for all t, where the superindex 0 denotes the solution in the decentralized economy, which is defined conditional on the emission tax path $\{\tau^0(t)\}_0^\infty$. Note that equations (4.1)–(4.3) are general equilibrium conditions; that is, they are obtained by combining the necessary conditions for the consumer and the firm. The problem is assumed to be well behaved in the sense that the transversality condition, $\lim_{t\to\infty}\lambda^0(t) = 0$, is fulfilled.

Before proceeding with the analysis, two aspects are worth noting. First, the production function does not contain a separate time argument, as seen from equations (4.2) and (4.3). Contrary to the analysis in Chapter 2, therefore, we refrain from discussing the implications of disembodied technological change. Second, we disregard the possibility of 'abatement' policies that increase the rate of decay of pollution. Such abatement policies were addressed in Chapter 2. The fact that these two issues are neglected here does not affect the principal findings below. Compared with the more general version of the model, the suggested simplifications imply that, in the general equilibrium, the equations of motion for the physical capital stock and the stock of pollution can be written as follows:

$$\dot{k}^0(t) = f(k^0(t), g^0(t)) - c^0(t)$$
$$\dot{x}^0(t) = g^0(t) - \gamma x^0(t)$$

4.2   WELFARE-IMPROVING NON-PIGOUVIAN TAXES

The purpose of this section is to examine whether a market economy controlled by certain non-Pigouvian taxes is welfare superior to the uncontrolled market economy. To accomplish this task, we start by deriving a cost–benefit rule for a small increase in the emission tax. This rule may then be used to determine the conditions under which a market economy controlled by (non-Pigouvian) emission taxes is welfare superior to an uncontrolled market economy.

To begin with, suppose the emission tax is increased from $\tau^0(t)$ to $\tau^0(t) + \alpha$ for all t, where α is a small positive constant. The additional tax revenues are redistributed in a lump-sum fashion to the consumer. This policy is interpretable in terms of a small permanent increase in the emission tax.[2] If the resource allocation obeys equations (4.1)–(4.3), together with the other necessary conditions[3], the optimal value function may be written as

$$V^0(0; \xi) = \int_0^\infty u(c^0(t; \xi), x^0(t; \xi)) e^{-\theta t} dt \qquad (4.4)$$

where ξ is a parameter vector with α as one of its elements. In the pre-reform equilibrium defined by equations (4.1)–(4.3) and the other necessary conditions, $\alpha = 0$. If the optimal value function is differentiable with respect to α, which is assumed throughout this section, we can follow the approach outlined in Chapter 2 and derive the cost–benefit rule by applying the dynamic envelope theorem. We show in Appendix A that the cost–benefit rule for α takes the form

$$\frac{\partial V^0(0;\xi)}{\partial \alpha} = \int_0^\infty \left[u_x(c^0(t), x^0(t))e^{-\theta t} \frac{\partial x^0(t)}{\partial \alpha} + \lambda^0(t)\tau^0(t) \frac{\partial g^0(t)}{\partial \alpha} \right] dt \qquad (4.5)$$

in which the vector ξ has been suppressed for notational convenience. Note that equation (4.5) is evaluated in the pre-reform equilibrium, where $\alpha = 0$. The second term in brackets is the cost of increasing α in terms of forgone consumption and is clearly negative, since $\tau^0 > 0$ and $\partial g^0(\cdot)/\partial \alpha < 0$. The first term is the utility value of a reduction in the stock of pollution and is positive, since $u_x(c^0, x^0) < 0$ and $\partial x^0(\cdot)/\partial \alpha < 0$.[4]

Note that, for a small change in the emission tax to affect the welfare level, it must be the case that the initial emission tax is suboptimal from society's point of view. Otherwise, the welfare change measured by equation (4.5) would be equal to zero. In the present context, this means that the initial emission tax does not fully internalize the external effect. In other words, the initial emission tax does not provide an exact measure of the present value of future reductions in the stock of pollution (if it did, then the external effect would have become fully internalized). Therefore, it is convenient to write the emission tax at each point in time as if it is a biased estimate of the marginal utility of pollution at that time. This is done by assuming that the initial, or pre-reform, emission tax takes the following form:

$$\tau^0(t) = -\left[\int_t^\infty (u_x(c^0(s), x^0(s)) + \beta(s))e^{-(\theta+\gamma)(s-t)} ds \right] / \lambda^{c^0}(t) \qquad (4.6)$$

for all t, where $\lambda^{c^0}(t) = \lambda^0(t)e^{\theta t}$ is the current value shadow price of physical capital at time t. The expression $u_x(c^0(t), x^0(t)) + \beta(t)$ can be interpreted as our incorrect estimate of the marginal utility of pollution at time t, implying that $\beta(t)$ is interpretable in terms of a bias: it measures the extent to which the estimate of the marginal utility of pollution at time t deviates from the valuation made by the consumer, $u_x(c^0(t), x^0(t))$. In addition, note that if $\beta(t) = 0$ for all t, equation (4.6) will fully internalize the external effect, so that the outcome of the controlled market economy discussed here would coincide with the socially optimal resource allocation discussed in Chapter 2.[5] With equation (4.6) at our disposal, we can derive a useful result:

Proposition 4.1 *If the pre-reform emission tax takes the form of equation (4.6) for all* t, *the cost–benefit rule for* α *can be written as*

$$\frac{\partial V^0(0;\xi)}{\partial \alpha} = -\int_0^\infty \beta(t)e^{-\theta t} \frac{\partial x^0(t)}{\partial \alpha} dt \qquad (4.7)$$

Proof: The differential equation $\dot{x}^0(t;\xi) = g^0(t;\xi) - \gamma x^0(t;\xi)$ implies

$$\frac{\partial^2 x^0(t)}{\partial t \partial \alpha} = \frac{\partial g^0(t)}{\partial \alpha} - \gamma \frac{\partial x^0(t)}{\partial \alpha} = \frac{\partial^2 x^0(t)}{\partial \alpha \partial t} \qquad (4.8)$$

where the vector ξ has been suppressed for notational convenience and the last equality follows from Young's theorem. By solving equation (4.8) for $\partial g^0(t)/\partial \alpha$ and substituting into equation (4.5), we obtain

$$\frac{\partial V^0(0;\xi)}{\partial \alpha} = \int_0^\infty \left[u_x^0(t)e^{-\theta t}\frac{\partial x^0(t)}{\partial \alpha} + \lambda^0(t)\tau^0(t)\left(\frac{\partial^2 x^0(t)}{\partial \alpha \partial t} + \gamma\frac{\partial x^0(t)}{\partial \alpha} \right) \right]dt \quad (4.9)$$

where $u_x^0(t) = u_x(c^0(t),x^0(t))$. Integrating the second term on the right-hand side by parts, we obtain

$$\int_0^\infty \lambda^0(t)\tau^0(t)\frac{\partial^2 x^0(t)}{\partial \alpha \partial t}\,dt = \lambda^0(t)\tau^0(t)\frac{\partial x^0(t)}{\partial \alpha}\bigg|_0^\infty - \int_0^\infty (\dot{\lambda}^0(t)\tau^0(t) + \lambda^0(t)\dot{\tau}^0(t))\frac{\partial x^0(t)}{\partial \alpha}\,dt$$

$$= -\int_0^\infty (\dot{\lambda}^0(t)\tau^0(t) + \lambda^0(t)\dot{\tau}^0(t))\frac{\partial x^0(t)}{\partial \alpha}\,dt$$

$$(4.10)$$

where the last equality follows because $x(0)$ is fixed and $\lim_{t\to\infty}\lambda^0(t) = 0$. Using equations (4.3) and (4.10), equation (4.9) can be rewritten as

$$\frac{\partial V^0(0;\xi)}{\partial \alpha} = \int_0^\infty [u_x^0(t)e^{-\theta t} + \lambda^0(t)\tau^0(t)\{f_k^0(t) + \gamma\} - \lambda^0(t)\dot{\tau}^0(t)]\frac{\partial x^0(t)}{\partial \alpha}\,dt \quad (4.11)$$

with $f_k^0(t) = f_k(k^0(t),g^0(t))$. The final step is to differentiate equation (4.6) with respect to time:

$$\dot{\tau}^0(t) = \frac{[u_x^0(t) + \beta(t)]e^{-\theta t}}{\lambda^0(t)} + \tau^0(t)(f_k^0(t) + \gamma) \qquad (4.12)$$

Substituting equation (4.12) into equation (4.11) gives equation (4.7). ∎

Let us denote the marginal disutility of pollution at time t by $-u_x^0(t) > 0$. Proposition 4.1 provides a framework for analyzing the welfare effects of non-Pigouvian taxes and, therefore, comparing the imperfectly controlled market economy with the uncontrolled market economy. Note that if $\beta(t) > 0\ (< 0)$ for all t, then $\partial V^0(0;\xi)/\partial\alpha > 0(< 0)$. This suggests that, if the emission tax is based on an underestimation of the marginal disutility of pollution at each point in time (that is, $\beta(t) > 0$ for all t), a permanent increase in the emission tax is always welfare improving. Similarly, reducing the emission tax permanently will always reduce the welfare level. The following result is a direct consequence of Proposition 4.1:

Corollary 4.1 *If the emission tax is given by equation (4.6), and with $0 < \beta(t) < -u_x^0(t)$ for all* t, *the controlled market economy is always welfare superior to the uncontrolled market economy.*

The result in Corollary 4.1 is important in the sense of suggesting that emission taxes may play an important allocative role, even if they do not bring the economy to the socially optimal path. The upper limit for β is used to ensure that we are dealing with a tax and not a subsidy. One potential member of the family of tax paths in Corollary 4.1 is a tax based on static willingness-to-pay information reflecting the marginal disutility of pollution. Its welfare effect and potential usefulness for green accounting are discussed in the next section.

4.3 CLOSE TO PIGOUVIAN TAXES – A PRACTICAL RESULT?

According to Chapter 2, if external effects remain uninternalized in the general equilibrium, then welfare measurement requires more information than is provided by the current value Hamiltonian. To extend this argument, we begin with a general discussion of the welfare measurement problem in a situation where the emission tax is a biased estimate of the marginal disutility of pollution. Consider the following potential welfare measure:

$$H_p^0(t) = u(c^0(t), x^0(t))e^{-\theta t} + \lambda^0(t)\dot{k}^0(t) - \lambda^0(t)\tau^0(t)\dot{x}^0(t) \qquad (4.13)$$

where $H_p^0(t)$ is a 'pseudo-Hamiltonian' in the sense that the necessary conditions in Section 4.1 look as if they are derived from $H_p^0(t)$. If evaluated in the first best, $H_p^0(t)$ is equivalent to the maximized present value Hamiltonian corresponding to the social optimization problem. The form of the implicit shadow price of pollution at time t, $-\lambda^0(t)\tau^0(t)$, is explained by the fact that if $-\tau^0(t)$ is the shadow price of pollution in real terms at time t, then $-\lambda^0(t)\tau^0(t)$ transforms this value into utility units. Differentiating the pseudo-Hamiltonian with respect to time and using equations (4.1)–(4.3) gives

$$\frac{dH_p^0}{dt} = -\theta u(c^0, x^0)e^{-\theta t} + [u_x^0 e^{-\theta t} + \lambda^0 \tau^0 (f_k^0 + \gamma) - \lambda^0 \dot{\tau}^0] \dot{x}^0 \qquad (4.14)$$

in which the time indicator has been suppressed for notational convenience. According to equation (4.14), time has a direct effect on the pseudo-Hamiltonian in addition to its effect via the utility discount factor. This additional non-autonomous time dependence is represented by the second term on the right-hand side. With equation (4.6) at our disposal, and along the lines of the analysis in Section 4.2, we see that the terms in brackets of equation (4.14) are equal to $-\beta(t)e^{-\theta t}$, that is,

$$u_x^0(t)e^{-\theta t} + \lambda^0(t)\tau^0(t)(f_k^0(t) + \gamma) - \lambda^0(t)\dot{\tau}^0(t) = -\beta(t)e^{-\theta t}$$

This expression measures the extent to which the emission tax is based on a biased estimate of the marginal disutility of pollution at time t. In other words, it represents a discrepancy between the marginal disutility of pollution and the marginal cost of pollution control, so that part of the welfare effect associated with emissions remains uninternalized in the equilibrium. If we use the methods developed in Chapter 2 to solve equation (4.14), and assume that $\lim_{t \to \infty} H_p^0(t) = 0^6$, the welfare measure can be written as follows:

$$\theta V^0(t) = H_p^{c^0}(t) + \int_t^\infty \Omega^0(s)e^{\theta t}ds \qquad (4.15)$$

where $V^0(t) = \int_t^\infty u(c^0(s), x^0(s))e^{-\theta(s-t)}ds$ is the optimal value function at time t, $H_p^{c^0}(t) = H_p^0(t)e^{\theta t}$ the current value pseudo-Hamiltonian and $\Omega^0(t) = -\beta(t)e^{-\theta t}\dot{x}^0(t)$.

Equation (4.15) suggests that the current value pseudo-Hamiltonian – which is our 'best estimate' of green NNP in utility terms – does not constitute an exact welfare measure. Instead, welfare is measured by the sum of the current value pseudo-Hamiltonian and the value of the uninternalized part of the marginal external effect, where the latter is represented by the second term on the right-hand side of equation (4.15). The value of the uninternalized part of the marginal external effect is, in turn, interpretable in terms of the bias of the estimate of the marginal disutility of pollution. If, on the other hand, the external effect is fully internalized, the second term on the right-hand side of equation (4.15) vanishes. Therefore, implementation of Pigouvian taxes implies that the current value Hamiltonian constitutes an exact welfare measure. This is why Pigouvian taxes are so useful in the context of social accounting.

In general, it is not altogether clear how non-Pigouvian taxes might be useful in social accounting. Under certain conditions, however, they may be closely related to their Pigouvian counterpart and, as such, provide close enough approximations of the value of depletion of environmental capital. Here, we consider a static approximation of the Pigouvian tax based on currently available (or at least collectable) willingness-to-pay information.[7] The concept of static approximations of Pigouvian taxes refers to an emission tax path that would support the first best optimum in the case where the marginal utility of pollution is constant.[8] On the other hand, it is important to recognize that Pigouvian taxes are, in general, forward looking. Therefore, in an attempt to avoid at least some of the bias that is likely to ensue when the emission tax is calculated as if the marginal utility of pollution were constant, we assume that the emission tax is revised repeatedly as new willingness-to-pay information becomes available. This implies that new willingness-to-pay studies are carried out repeatedly. The market economy controlled by the resulting tax path is welfare superior to the uncontrolled market economy under the general condition stated in Corollary 4.1. In addition, as shown below, the controlled market economy and the social optimum will have the same steady state.

To be more specific, suppose we were to ask the consumer how much he/she is willing to pay to reduce the stock of pollution temporarily by one unit at time t. In other words, we are considering the instantaneous willingness-to-pay for a marginal unit. This question is then repeated as time passes. The consumer is also assumed to reveal his/her true willingness to pay; that is, the answer at time t will be $-u_x^0(t)/\lambda^{c^0}(t)$. Let us consider welfare measurement at a given point in time, t, and assume that, until new information becomes available, $u_x(\cdot)$ is treated as a constant, which means that $u_x^0(t)/(\theta + \gamma)$ is the implicit approximation of the current value shadow price of pollution in utility terms. The latter would be the correct formula for the shadow price in a steady state.[9]

In order for the approximation of the Pigouvian tax to provide a reasonably accurate estimate of the shadow price of pollution at each point in time, the lengths of the time intervals between which we collect new willingness-to-pay information are likely to be important. We explore the practical importance of the time frequency of the revisions numerically in Section 4.4. For the time being, we assume that it takes Δt units of time until new information becomes available. Then, consider

$$\tau_a^0(t) = -\frac{\bar{u}_x^0(t)}{(\theta + \gamma)\lambda^{c^0}(t)}$$

as a possible approximation of the Pigouvian tax on the time interval $(t, t + \Delta t)$, where $\bar{u}_x^0(t)$ is constant and equal to $u_x(c^0(t), x^0(t))$. Note the intuitive interpretation of $\tau_a^0(t)$ in an intergenerational context: it is an estimate of the value of additions to the stock of pollution based solely on preferences at time t. In terms of the preceding analysis, this implies a biased estimate of the marginal disutility of pollution, with the bias equal to $\beta(s) = u_x^0(t) - u_x^0(s)$ for $s \in [t,\infty)$. Therefore, the static approximation of the Pigouvian tax is welfare improving in comparison with the uncontrolled market economy, provided the marginal disutility of pollution, $-u_x^0(\cdot)$ does not decrease over time.

In general, it is not possible to show that the approximation of the Pigouvian tax is welfare improving. Except for two special cases where the bias is either positive at each point in time or negative at each point in time, the welfare effect of introducing the approximation of the Pigouvian tax in an otherwise uncontrolled market economy is ambiguous from a theoretical point of view. The fact that we discount future utility emphasizes the importance of the exact time path of the marginal disutility of pollution. If the marginal disutility of pollution is expected to rise in the near future and decline in the distant future, discounting future utilities is likely to imply that the tax increases the welfare level. If, on the other hand, the marginal disutility of pollution is expected to decrease in the near future and increase in the distant future, the welfare effect of introducing the approximation of the Pigouvian tax may go the other way. In practice, such expectations are presumably based on the projected development of the stock. In addition, and irrespective of the path of pollution, the controlled market economy and the social optimization problem have the same steady state solution in this case. Therefore, provided the tax policy brings the economy to a (unique) steady state, we will eventually approach the social optimum, in the neighborhood of which the tax policy is always welfare improving for future generations. The welfare effect measured at an arbitrary point in time depends on what happens before the steady state is reached.

Let us now analyze the approximation of the Pigouvian tax from the point of view of social accounting. If this tax is used to value additions to the stock of pollution, will the resulting pseudo-Hamiltonian be a reasonable approximation of the correct welfare measure? The pseudo-Hamiltonian is given by

$$H_p^0(t) = u(c^0(t), x^0(t))e^{-\theta t} + \lambda^0(t)\dot{k}^0(t) + \frac{\bar{u}_x^0(t)}{\theta + \gamma}e^{-\theta t}\dot{x}^0(t) \qquad (4.16)$$

where the present value shadow price of additions to the stock of pollution is measured as the marginal utility value of physical capital in present value terms times $\tau_a^0(t)$. The difference between equations (4.13) and (4.16) is that the latter is based on the approximation of the Pigouvian tax as a measure of the shadow price of pollution in real terms, whereas equation (4.13) is based on an arbitrary emission tax. Differentiating equation (4.16) with respect to time, and rearranging, we show in Appendix B that

$$\frac{dH_p^0(t)}{dt} = -\theta u(c^0(t), x^0(t))e^{-\theta t} \quad \text{on} \quad (t, t + \Delta t) \tag{4.17}$$

At first glance, equation (4.17) seems to be the differential equation we are looking for. It takes the same general form as its counterpart in the first best equilibrium, since the only direct effect of time that remains originates from the utility discount factor. Integrating over each short time interval and summing these integrals up to time T gives

$$H_p^0(T) = H_p^0(t) - \theta \sum_{s=t}^{T} \int_s^{s+\Delta s} u(c^0(\varsigma), x^0(\varsigma))e^{-\theta \varsigma} d\varsigma \tag{4.18}$$

Although equation (4.18) is quite similar to measures derived earlier, one important problem remains. To prove the welfare equivalence of the pseudo-Hamiltonian – which would provide an analogue to the first best welfare measure derived in Chapter 2 – it would have to be assumed that $H_p^0(T)$ approaches zero when T goes to infinity. However, this assumption does not apply here, because equation (4.17) only holds on the time interval $(t, t + \Delta t)$. To see this more clearly, note that the value of utility at the upper limit of the interval $(s, s + \Delta s)$ is, in general, different from the value of utility at the lower limit of the next interval, $(s + \Delta s, s + 2\Delta s)$, and so on, since the emission tax changes discretely at the beginning of each such time interval. Every such point of discontinuity may contribute to make the limit of $H_p^0(T)$ different from zero. An interpretation is that the ensuing loss of information when the data collection involves a discrete element may invalidate the welfare interpretation of the current value pseudo-Hamiltonian.

Only if the sum of the welfare contributions of the discontinuities is zero are we able to derive the following exact welfare measure:

$$\theta V^0(t) = H_p^{c^0}(t) \tag{4.19}$$

where $H_p^{c^0}(t) = H_p^0(t)e^{\theta t}$ and $V^0(t)$ is the sum of integrals in equation (4.18). At the same time, even if the welfare contributions of the discontinuities do not sum to zero, they are not necessarily important from a practical point of view. If the sum of their welfare contributions is small relative to the welfare contribution of the current value pseudo-Hamiltonian, the current value pseudo-Hamiltonian might still provide a useful approximation of the correct welfare measure. Consider the following:

Proposition 4.2 *If the equilibrium is defined conditional on the static approximation of the Pigouvian tax, $\tau_a^0(t)$, for all t, and if $\lim_{T \to \infty} H_p^0(T) \approx 0$,* *welfare at time t is closely approximated by the pseudo-Hamiltonian in current value terms. The approximation of the Pigouvian tax would, in this case, play the same general role in social accounting in the decentralized economy as the correct Pigouvian tax in the first best equilibrium.*

This result enhances our efforts to establish a close connection between the growth theoretical approach to social accounting and the willingness-to-pay method as a means of capturing the values of non-market goods. If the welfare effects of discontinuities are small on average, Proposition 4.2 reconciles the growth theoretical approach to social accounting with the (static) willingness-to-pay approach to environmental services in the sense that the only additional information which has to be collected at time t is the marginal willingness-to-pay for a reduction in the stock of pollution at that time. Note also that, with the appropriate additivity and linearity assumptions, $\tau_a^0(t)$ is the Pigouvian tax at time t. Formally:

Proposition 4.3 *If willingness-to-pay information can be collected continuously, and if* $u(c,x) = \phi(c) + \kappa x$, *where* κ *is a constant, then* $\tau_a^0(t) = \tau^*(t)$.

This result follows because $\tau_a^0(t) = -\kappa/[(\theta + \gamma)\lambda^{c^0}(t)]$ is the Pigouvian tax at time t, if $u_x(t) = \kappa$ for all t. Proposition 4.3 provides a sufficient condition for the tax to be Pigouvian and for the economy to follow the socially optimal path.[10] It is not a necessary condition, since $\tau_a^0(t)$ and $\tau^*(t)$ are the same in a steady state.

4.4   ON THE STEP FROM THEORY TO PRACTICAL APPLICATION

Turning now to some practical implications of the theory of social accounting, two questions immediately come to mind. First, are the additional complications associated with imperfect market economies (some of which were addressed above) practically relevant, or can we use the first best accounting practice as a reasonable approximation in a more or less imperfect market economy? Second, is the approximation of the Pigouvian tax discussed in Section 4.3 useful in practice? The second question is closely related to Proposition 4.2: if the welfare contributions of the discontinuities become small on average, the approximation of the Pigouvian tax will be a reasonably accurate estimate of the shadow price of pollution. For the model set out above, this means, in turn, that the current value pseudo-Hamiltonian may provide a close approximation of the correct welfare measure. These issues will be addressed by means of numerical simulations as a complement to the theoretical analysis.

4.4.1 Are the Imperfections Practically Relevant?

A large amount of empirical work has been concerned with augmenting traditional national accounts with different kinds of 'natural capital': reviews include Sheng (1995), Hamilton and Lutz (1996), Vincent and Hartwick (1997), Nordhaus and Keppelenberg (1999) and Heal and Kriström (2001). According to Vincent and Hartwick (1997), this research has grown more or less steadily since Repetto et al. (1989), which is one of the most cited studies on natural resources and national accounts. Vincent and Hartwick list a dozen studies since 1996, and review about 30 studies covering accounts for 20 countries (most of which pertain to Asia). A majority of studies covered are devoted to augmenting the national accounts with the benefits and/or costs of more than one natural resource. The most predeterminant resource is the forest[11]. The pollution concept includes nitrogen and sulfur.[12] Other studies have focused on the estimation of the true output from the educational sector, that is, the value of net investments in human capital. The first of these studies was Jorgensen and Fraumeni (1992) for the USA, which was followed by Ahlroth et al. (1997) and Aronsson et al. (1999) for Sweden.

Without going into detail, it seems fair to say that most of these studies attempt to follow, either explicitly or implicitly, the theory of social accounting in the first best, as described in Chapter 2. This means that they add estimates of the value of consumption of 'non-market goods' and/or the value of net investment in, for example, natural and environmental capital to the conventional NNP. In many instances, however, the authors do not address the complications generated by uninternalized external effects and/or other deviations from the first best. As should be clear from the analysis so far, such omissions imply that a green NNP measure based on the Hamiltonian concept provides a biased welfare indicator. An important question is whether this bias is empirically relevant in the context of social accounting. A complete answer to this question would require information about the value of the marginal external effects in a dynamic economy. For obvious reasons, such information is very difficult (if not impossible) to obtain in practice.

On the other hand, a few studies have tried to assess the potential importance of external effects in the context of social accounting by means of numerical analysis. Aronsson et al. (1997) analyze a numerical general equilibrium model with an externality related to the influence of the stock of human capital on output. In their study, both the instantaneous utility and production functions are of Cobb–Douglas type. Three production factors – effective labor, physical capital and human capital – produce output, and the production technology is assumed to exhibit constant returns to scale. Human capital is, in turn, assumed to affect output through two channels: (i) the use of effective labor,[13] where the influence of human capital is internalized through the wage formation system, and (ii) a direct effect of the total stock of human capital in the production function. The latter is interpretable as a spillover effect of each individual's human capital stock in terms of the productivity of other individuals, which is what causes the external effect in an uncontrolled market economy (that is, when no attempt is made to control the accumulation of human capital).

In addition to the obvious conclusion that welfare is greater in the first best than in the distorted market economy, the results presented by Aronsson et al. (1997) imply that the current value Hamiltonian underestimates welfare in the decentralized version of the model. The reason is that the external effect arising from human capital is positive. Of course, the importance of the externality depends on the weight assigned to the separate human capital argument, in comparison with the weights on the other factors of production, in the production function. In the baseline simulation, the weights attached to effective labor, physical capital and human capital are 0.45, 0.30 and 0.25, respectively. The results of the baseline simulation show that the current value Hamiltonian underestimates welfare – measured as the present value of future utility times the utility discount rate – by 33 percent. This figure also represents the relative contribution of the external effect to the welfare measure, since there are no other market failures in the model. When the weight assigned to the separate human capital argument was changed to 0.15 and 0.35, respectively, while adjusting the weight assigned to effective labor accordingly, the relative welfare contribution of the external effect changed to 24 percent and 45 percent, respectively. This means that the greater the weight assigned to the separate human capital argument in the production function, which is what causes the external effect, the less accurate the current value Hamiltonian becomes as a welfare measure in an uncontrolled market economy. The percentages also indicate that the welfare contribution of the external effect may be considerable.

The human capital example is also relevant from another point of view: it introduces technological change into the welfare analysis. In Chapter 2 it was shown how the welfare measure has to be adjusted to reflect the value of disembodied technological change. However, the reader should note that technological change need not necessarily be exogenous for the results to apply. In the literature on endogenous growth[14], technological change at the firm level is often related to economy-wide measures of capital formation. To the extent that all welfare effects of capital formation are not internalized, endogenous technological change will influence the welfare measures in a way that resembles the effect of disembodied, exogenous technological change. An attempt to estimate the effects of technological progress on future welfare can be based on the fact that green NNP in utility terms, under ideal conditions, is an annuity equivalent of future utility at the prevailing rate of time preference. By assuming that technological progress proceeds at a constant (average historical) rate, one obtains an estimate of the downward bias of a green NNP measure which neglects technological progress. Estimates[15] using available US historical data imply that this bias can be as high as 40–50 percent; that is, the 'true' annuity equivalent is obtained by scaling current NNP by 1.4–1.5. In other words, omitting technological progress may bias the estimates of future consumption possibilities to a considerable extent.

Externalities caused by a stock of pollution have been addressed numerically by Backlund (2000, 2003) in the context of social accounting. The production side of his model is based on the Swedish Energy and Environmental Policy (SEEP) model developed by Nordhaus (1993). Backlund extends this model by adding an accumulation equation for the stock of sulfur (the pollution concept he considers), where emissions of sulfur are related to the use of energy in production. Backlund assumes that the instantaneous utility function facing the representative consumer depends on the consumption and the stock of sulfur. The model used in the simulations may be interpreted as a numerical, and much more elaborated, version of the model analyzed in previous sections of this chapter and in Chapter 2. Since the externality associated with pollution is negative, the current value Hamiltonian implicit in the uncontrolled market economy will overestimate the welfare level (measured as interest on the present value of future utility). The results from the simulations suggest, not surprisingly, that the degree of overestimation of welfare depends on the extent to which the instantaneous utility function is non-linear in the stock of pollution. The reason is that the stock of pollution increases substantially during the first part of the simulation period. Therefore, the more the marginal disutility of pollution rises for a given increase in the stock of pollution, the greater the social welfare cost of pollution that is not captured by the current value Hamiltonian. We shall return to Backlund (2000, 2003) below and discuss some of the other results in greater detail.

At this point, it should be kept in mind that although the examples based on externalities and technological change are suggestive, in the sense of showing that the current value Hamiltonian may be a seriously biased welfare measure, they do not provide realistic descriptions of real world economies. In the real world, there are both positive and negative external effects. Some of them are (imperfectly) controlled by means of, for example, emission taxes and subsidies to human capital. However, even if there are both positive and negative externalities, there is no reason to believe that the welfare effects of these externalities typically cancel out, and that the current value Hamiltonian provides an unbiased estimate of welfare. Therefore, there is a need for practical tools that can gauge the welfare consequences of externalities.

4.4.2 Are Approximations of Pigouvian Taxes Useful in Practice?

Does the approximation of the Pigouvian tax discussed in Section 4.3 constitute a reasonably accurate estimate of the shadow price of pollution in real terms? If it does, the bias arising from discrete collection of information will be of minor importance, and the green NNP in utility terms based on the Hamiltonian concept will provide a close enough approximation of the correct welfare measure. Here, we return to the basic questions addressed earlier in this chapter by studying (i) whether the approximation of the Pigouvian tax is welfare improving in comparison with the uncontrolled market economy, and (ii) whether the approximation of the Pigouvian tax can be used to measure the shadow price of pollution in the same way as in a first best framework, where the Pigouvian tax constitutes an exact measure of this shadow price.

Backlund (2000, 2003) applies the theory of social accounting by means of numerical methods and, in particular, uses the numerical model to address the two questions mentioned above. As such, his results provide a natural complement to the theoretical analysis, since none of the questions can be fully answered in a theoretical context. We begin by a brief presentation of the numerical model. Unless indicated otherwise, the notations are the same as above. The instantaneous utility function is assumed to take the form

$$u(t) = c(t)^{\beta_1} z(t)^{(1-\beta_1)} \tag{4.20}$$

where β_1 is the utility weight attached to consumption, and $z(t)$ refers to an indicator of environmental quality at time t. The indicator of environmental quality is measured by $z(t) = \beta_2 - \beta_3 x(t)^{\beta_4}$, where $\beta_2 > 0$, $\beta_3 > 0$ and $\beta_4 > 0$. This means that environmental quality depends negatively on the stock of pollution. The parameter β_4 measures the degree of non-linearity of this relationship and will play a key role in the analysis below. The stock of pollution accumulates according to

$$\dot{x}(t) = x^E(t) - \beta_5 x(t) \tag{4.21}$$

where $x^E(t)$ measures the sum of emissions from using gas, oil and coal (which are all related to the use of transportation and electricity) as well as from uses other than transportation and electricity. These emissions are, in turn, related to the use of energy in production. The parameter β_5 refers to the rate of depreciation.

The production side originates from the SEEP model, which is primarily concerned with the use of energy. The production function is written as

$$f(\cdot) = \beta_6 k(t) \left[\frac{e^l(t)}{e^l(0)} \right]^{\beta_7} \left[\frac{e^n(t)}{e^n(0)} \right]^{\beta_8} \left[\frac{e^{tr}(t)}{e^{tr}(0)} \right]^{\beta_9} \tag{4.22}$$

where e^l, e^n and e^{tr} represent energy consumption in the electricity, non-electricity and transportation sectors, respectively, whereas β_6, β_7, β_8 and β_9

are parameters that characterize the production function. The parameter β_6 reflects productivity and is related to the use of production factors other than physical capital and energy. Contrary to the SEEP model, net investments are endogenous. Net investments in physical capital are given by

$$\dot{k}(t) = f(\cdot) - I(t) - c(t) \qquad (4.23)$$

The function $I(t)$ denotes the total cost of producing energy and is measured by $I(t) = \Sigma_i g^i(t)(mc)^i$, where g^i is the energy produced by source i, which is multiplied by the corresponding constant marginal cost, $(mc)^i$.

The parameters β_1 and β_4 are varied between the simulations, whereas the other parameters are fixed. They are given by $\beta_2 = 10000$, $\beta_3 = 0.7$, $\beta_5 = 0.00001$, $\beta_6 = 1319$, $\beta_7 = 0.0218$, $\beta_8 = 0.0715$ and $\beta_9 = 0.049$. These parameter values are chosen to reproduce, as closely as possible, the relevant characteristics of the Swedish economy in 1995. The rate of time preference is 0.05, which corresponds to the original SEEP model, and the model is simulated for 75 years. The simulations are based on the program package GAMS.

Based on these simulations, we can now compare the first best resource allocation (social optimum), the uncontrolled market economy and the market economy controlled by the approximation of the Pigouvian tax with respect to the relative welfare contribution of the current value (pseudo-)Hamiltonian.[16] Recall from Section 4.3 that the approximations of Pigouvian taxes are revised repeatedly as new information about the marginal utility of pollution becomes available. The simulations for the controlled market economy were conducted under the assumption that this information is revised every year, every second year, every fifth year and every tenth year, respectively. This allows us to study how the frequency of the revisions affects the results. We begin by analyzing the model for the case where the estimate of the marginal utility of pollution is revised every tenth year, so as to ascertain how the results depend on the extent to which the instantaneous utility function is nonlinear in the stock of pollution. Consider Table 4.1, where V represents the value function, or the present value of future utility, measured at the beginning of the simulation period, $x(75)$ is the stock of pollution during the terminal year and $\mu(2)$ is the shadow price of the stock of pollution during year 2 measured in utility terms. This is the correct shadow price in a situation where the resource allocation is socially optimal. In the imperfectly controlled market economy, it is measured by the approximation of the Pigouvian tax times the shadow price of physical capital. Both the value function and the stock of pollution are normalized in the sense that they are measured relative to the outcome of the social optimum. The term HI is written

$$HI = \frac{H(0) - H(T)}{\theta V(0)} 100$$

where $\lim_{T \to \infty} H(T) = 0$, except possibly in the market economy controlled by the approximation of the Pigouvian tax. We can interpret *HI* as an indicator of how accurately the current value Hamiltonian measures welfare, defined as interest on the present value of future utility at time 0. Since $H(0) - H(T)$ is an exact finite time analogue to the first best welfare measure, this indicator is expected to equal 100 in the social optimum; see Chapter 2. Outside the social optimum, if *HI* > 100 (< 100), negative (positive) external effects influence the welfare measure, and their welfare contribution can be quantified in percent by calculating |100–*HI*|. However, although *HI* is constructed in this way, we find that it deviates slightly from 100 even if the resource allocation is a social optimum. This is because the step from continuous to discrete time introduces an approximation error. The measures we would like to evaluate by using the discrete numerical model are derived in a continuous time framework. At the same time, this approximation error does not seem to be particularly important since the magnitude by which *HI* diverges from 100 in the social optimum is very small.

Table 4.1 The social optimum and the market economy for different values of β_4

	β_4	*V*	*x*(75)	μ(2)	*HI*
	1.0				
Soc. opt.		100.0000	100.00	–2.30	100.14
Approx. 10		99.9862	102.59	–2.28	100.15
UC Market		97.9792	283.82	0	104.73
	1.03				
Soc. opt.		100.0000	100.00	–2.79	100.18
Approx. 10		99.9792	105.03	–2.56	100.29
UC Market		96.2597	348.32	0	107.12
	1.06				
Soc. opt.		100.0000	100.00	–3.35	100.19
Approx. 10		99.9530	107.43	–2.85	100.48
UC Market		93.9340	422.04	0	110.54
	1.3				
Soc. opt.		100.0000	100.00	–10.72	100.36
Approx. 10		98.8295	131.27	–5.23	102.98
	1.5				
Soc. opt.		100.0000	100.00	–21.13	100.44
Approx. 10		94.6466	176.10	–6.51	109.88

Source: Backlund (2000, 2003).

The simulations in Table 4.1 are based on the assumption that $\beta_1 = 0.5$. The numbers in the table suggest that the market economy controlled by the approximation of the Pigouvian tax is welfare superior to the uncontrolled market economy. Since the stock of pollution increases over the simulation period, and since the choices of functional form and parameters of the instantaneous utility function mean that the marginal disutility of pollution, $-u_x(\cdot) = -u_z(\cdot)z_x(\cdot)$, increases with the stock of pollution, this result is expected; see Section 4.2. It suggests that the approximation of the Pigouvian tax is likely to be based on an underestimation of the marginal disutility of pollution. This is also the condition under which the market economy controlled by the approximation of the Pigouvian tax is welfare superior to the uncontrolled market economy. Backlund shows that the qualitative picture provided by Table 4.1 is not particularly sensitive to (minor) changes in the parameter β_1, which represents the weight attached to consumption in the instantaneous utility function. By increasing (reducing) β_1 to 0.55 (0.45), implying that lower (higher) weight is attached to environmental quality in the instantaneous utility function, the welfare level of the uncontrolled market economy will slightly increase (decrease) relative to those of the other two regimes. Note also that the simulation program for the uncontrolled market economy did not converge in the cases where β_4 takes the values 1.3 and 1.5, respectively, which explains why the numbers corresponding to these cases are not included in Table 4.1.

A noteworthy result in Table 4.1 is that if β_4 is equal to or close to one – in which case the environmental quality function is linear or almost linear in the stock of pollution – the approximation of the Pigouvian tax provides a relatively accurate estimate of the shadow price of pollution. As a consequence, the current value pseudo-Hamiltonian corresponding to the market economy controlled by the approximation of the Pigouvian tax becomes a reasonable approximation of the correct welfare measure. This result applies even if the estimate of the marginal utility of pollution is only revised every tenth year. The intuition is that it takes time to build up a stock of pollution. The less sensitive the marginal utility of pollution to changes in the stock of pollution, the smaller the future welfare costs of building up a higher stock of pollution, which explains why the approximation method may work well even when the time interval between the revisions is very long.

If, on the other hand, the parameter β_4 takes values as high as 1.3 or 1.5, implying that the environmental quality function exhibits a substantial degree of non-linearity in the stock of pollution, the approximation of the Pigouvian tax is based on considerable underestimation of the marginal disutility of pollution. As a consequence, the current value pseudo-Hamiltonian corresponding to the market economy controlled by the approximation of the Pigouvian tax will be a less accurate welfare indicator here than when β_4 is equal to or close to one. This outcome is partly a consequence of the way in which the approximations are done: they are calculated as if the marginal utility of pollution is constant and then revised repeatedly as new information is assumed to become available. Therefore, given the frequency of revisions, the bias is likely to be greater, the more the marginal disutility of pollution increases in the near future. At the same time, the bias is likely to be reduced, if the estimate of the marginal disutility of pollution is revised more often. The potential importance of the frequency of revisions is shown in Table 4.2, where all of the numbers are based on the assumptions that $\beta_1 = 0.5$ and $\beta_4 = 1.5$.

Table 4.2 A comparison between revision frequencies when $\beta_4 = 1.5$

	V	x(75)	μ(2)	HI
Soc. opt.	100.0000	100.00	−21.13	100.44
Approx. 1	99.8213	109.78	−7.17	103.11
Approx. 2	99.3259	116.11	−6.98	103.21
Approx. 5	98.1620	128.81	−6.76	104.83
Approx. 10	94.6466	176.10	−6.51	109.88

Source: Backlund (2000, 2003).

The results in Table 4.2 suggest that the more often the estimate of the marginal utility of pollution is revised, the higher the welfare level, and the better the current value pseudo-Hamiltonian as an approximation of the correct welfare measure in the market economy controlled by the approximation of the Pigouvian tax. This is particularly interesting from the point of view of social accounting, and it confirms what we have expected: the estimate of the shadow price of pollution and, therefore, the accuracy of the current value pseudo-Hamiltonian as a welfare measure in the controlled market economy can be improved by collecting willingness-to-pay information more often. At the same time, it should be noted that even if the estimate of the marginal utility of pollution is revised every year, the current value pseudo-Hamiltonian appears to be a biased estimate of the correct welfare measure. Therefore, although the approximation of the welfare measure becomes more accurate if willingness-to-pay information is collected more frequently, the non-linearity of the environmental quality function makes it impossible to eliminate all the bias. This may appear to be a negative result, as the (more or less static) willingness-to-pay technique is often regarded as a sophisticated method of capturing the value of a non-market good. At the same time, much more research is required to fully evaluate this method in the context of social accounting. However, the results do suggest that the entities of an extended accounting system, whose values are measured by the willingness-to-pay technique, should be interpreted carefully.

4.5 SUMMARY

This chapter has addressed welfare measurement in a general equilibrium growth model, in which pollution gives rise to a consumption externality. A basic idea has been to evaluate an argument proposed in the early literature on social accounting, whereby the willingness-to-pay technique is used to collect information relevant for social accounting. We examined whether emission taxes based on static willingness-to-pay information are welfare improving in comparison with the uncontrolled market economy, and if they can be used to value depletion of environmental capital in an extended accounting system.

The results suggest that 'non-Pigouvian' taxes are always welfare improving, provided they do not overestimate the marginal disutility of pollution over time. Given some strong information requirements, it is possible to construct a (non-Pigouvian) emission tax on the basis of current willingness-to-pay information. This tax implies that the controlled market economy and the social optimum have the same steady state solution. Therefore, even if the tax overestimates the marginal disutility of pollution during some time intervals, it is always welfare improving in the long run, provided the controlled market economy approaches the steady state. For the special case where the marginal utility of pollution is nearly constant over time, this tax closely approximates the correct Pigouvian tax. The numerical simulations that supplement the theoretical analysis suggest that the market economy controlled by the approximation of the Pigouvian tax is welfare superior to the uncontrolled market economy for different combinations of parameters.

If the 'predictions errors' implicit in the approximation of the Pigouvian tax to a large extent cancel out over time, the first best accounting principles can be extended to apply in the imperfectly controlled market economy. Here, the numerical simulations are less conclusive. If the instantaneous utility function exhibits a moderate degree of non-linearity with respect to the stock of pollution, the approximation of the Pigouvian tax constitutes a relatively accurate estimate of the value of additions to the stock of pollution. As a consequence, the current value pseudo-Hamiltonian implicit in the controlled market economy may become a reasonable approximation of the correct welfare measure. This holds even if the estimate of the marginal utility of pollution, which is used to construct the approximation of the Pigouvian tax, is revised infrequently. If, on the other hand, the marginal disutility of pollution increases substantially when the stock of pollution increases, the approximation of the Pigouvian tax will provide a less accurate estimate of the value of additions to the stock of pollution. As a consequence, the numerical results imply that the current value pseudo-Hamiltonian implicit in the market economy controlled by the approximation of the Pigouvian tax tends to overestimate the correct welfare measure. In addition, this problem does not seem to be fully solved by more frequent revisions of the information that is used to construct approximations of Pigouvian taxes. Having reached this stage of the analysis, the reader is better able to understand the question mark in the title of this chapter.

NOTES

1. See, for example, Peskin and Peskin (1978).
2. Extensions of this technique to analyze the welfare effects of temporary parameteric changes in optimal control problems are discussed by Léonard (1987) and, in the context of emission taxation, by Aronsson (2001).
3. The 'other necessary conditions' are, in this case, the equations of motion for the stock of physical capital and the stock of pollution, the initial conditions, the NPG condition and the transversality condition. See Section 4.1 above or Chapter 2.
4. By solving the differential equation for $x^0(t;\xi)$ defined above, we obtain

$$x^0(t;\xi) = x(0)e^{-\gamma t} + \int_0^t g^0(s;\xi)e^{-\gamma(t-s)}ds$$

   which means that

$$\frac{\partial x^0(t;\xi)}{\partial \alpha} = \int_0^t \frac{\partial g^0(s;\xi)}{\partial \alpha} e^{-\gamma(t-s)}ds < 0$$

   since $\partial g^0(t;\xi)/\partial \alpha < 0$ for all t.
5. If the formula for the actual emission tax coincides with the formula for the Pigouvian emission tax – as will be the case if $\beta(t) = 0$ for all t – the first order conditions that characterize the resource allocation in the controlled market economy are identical to the first order conditions of the socially optimal resource allocation.
6. See Michel (1982). See also Seierstad and Sydsaeter (1987, p. 245) for an extension to the situation where both the instantaneous objective function and the equations of motion are non-autonomously time dependent.
7. For a thorough survey of the willingness-to-pay technique as a means of capturing values, see Hanemann (1994).
8. One can conceive of similar methods to approximate the marginal value of external effects in production. We will return to external effects in production in Chapter 7.
9. A current value analogue to equation (2.18iv) can be written as

$$\dot{\mu}^c - \theta\mu^c = -u_x + \mu^c\gamma$$

   since we disregard man-made additions to the rate of depreciation. If $\dot{\mu}^c = 0$, the shadow price becomes

$$\mu^c = u_x / (\theta + \gamma).$$

10. Note that, if the utility function is non-linear in the stock of pollution, continuous information collection does not imply that the tax path is Pigouvian, since the instantaneous shadow price of pollution is not correctly estimated in this case.
11. See Hultkrantz (1992) for an application to the Swedish forest sector. See also Hartwick (1992) for a theoretical analysis of deforestation in the context of social accounting.

12. Ahlroth (2001) augments the NNP in Sweden with the value of the additions to the stocks of nitrogen and sulfur.
13. The concept of effective labor here means that an individual becomes more productive as his/her endowment of human capital increases.
14. See Barro and Sala-i-Martin (1995) for an overview.
15. See Weitzman (1997) and Weitzman and Löfgren (1997). In the former paper, future growth is driven by a time-dependent residual shift factor that increases productivity, although it does not show up anywhere in national income accounts. In the latter paper, future growth is driven by labor-augmenting technological progress. The technological premium is of approximately the same magnitude in both cases.
16. The relative welfare contribution of the current value Hamiltonian is independent of a multiplicative transformation of the instantaneous utility function. On the other hand, it is affected if a constant is added to the instantaneous utility function; see Section 2.4 of Chapter 2.

5.   Green accounting and distortionary taxation

The decentralized economy analyzed so far contains a single distortion: an external effect associated with environmental damage. Within such a framework, one of the main purposes of Chapter 2 was to derive exact welfare measures in an uncontrolled or imperfectly controlled market economy and compare them with the first best welfare measure. However, although market failures have important implications for welfare measurement, our previous analysis was based on the assumption that the first best can (in principle) be attained by means of a properly designed policy rule. This basic idea was further explored in Chapter 4, where we argued that such policy rules are difficult to implement in practice, which may necessitate a 'practical approach' to social accounting. On the other hand, if we were to relax the assumption that the government has the appropriate policy instruments for implementation of the first best, the concept of social optimum would also change. One example – thoroughly addressed in other areas of welfare economics – is that the public revenues have to be raised by distortionary taxes. This is clearly relevant for welfare measurement, since distortionary taxation gives rise to a welfare cost. In Section 5.1, we consider green accounting under distortionary taxes and explain why the green NNP in utility terms derived earlier may fail to measure welfare in this case, as well as derive a second best analogue to the green NNP in utility terms.

Although the step from the first best to the second best resource allocation has practical value in the sense of adding realism to the description of the policy instruments, practical implementation is very difficult (if not impossible). As a consequence, even if the government wants to combine revenue objectives and environmental goals, and is aware of the fact that the choice of policy mix will influence both environmental distortions and the welfare cost of taxation, it is not likely to be able to choose the optimal program. This makes it important to consider the situation where the second best has not become fully implemented. In addition, going beyond the second best is of interest not only in the context of social accounting; it is also interesting in the sense of providing a natural framework for studying the welfare effects of policy reform. This framework constitutes the starting point for Section 5.2, in which we consider cost–benefit analysis of a change in the tax mix when the preexisting policy has not been optimally chosen from the point of view of society.

5.1 WELFARE MEASUREMENT UNDER DISTORTIONARY TAXES

Most earlier studies on social accounting, where the first best constitutes a natural reference case, imply that public revenues (if any) are raised by lump-sum taxes. To our knowledge, the only study which addressed how distortionary taxes influence social accounting is Aronsson (1998a), who uses a slightly modified version of the model set out in Chapter 2. The modifications are that leisure is an argument in the utility function, and that the government uses labor income taxation and emission taxation to finance a publicly provided good. This section is based on Aronsson (1998a), although we extend his model by including capital income taxation in addition to the taxes on labor income and emissions.

We begin by introducing the model and briefly describing the first best welfare measure. Although the first best welfare measure itself is not of major concern in this chapter, it is useful from the point of view of comparison with the welfare measures to be derived later on. We then introduce distortionary taxes and analyze the welfare measurement problem in the case where neither the taxes nor the publicly provided good are optimally chosen from the point of view of society. Finally, we consider the situation where the government chooses the taxes and the publicly provided good in an optimal way and derive a second best analogue to the green NNP in utility terms.

5.1.1 The Model and the First Best Welfare Measure

To simplify the analysis as much as possible, we disregard the possibility that the government has distributional objectives.[1] Distributional objectives are incorporated into the analysis in Chapters 7 and 8. Let us also neglect population growth and, for the time being, normalize the population to equal one. The instantaneous utility function takes the form

$$u(t) = u(c(t), h(t), G(t), x(t))$$

As before, c is consumption of a privately provided good and x the stock of pollution, while h is leisure and G consumption of a publicly provided good. Leisure is, in turn, defined as a time endowment, T, less the time in market work, l. We assume that $u(\cdot)$ is increasing in c, h and G, decreasing in x and strictly concave.

Net output is produced by labor, capital and energy. The production function is written

$$y(t) = f(l(t), k(t), g(t))$$

where k is the physical capital stock and g energy input. The production function is assumed to be increasing in l and g as well as strictly concave. Net investments in physical capital are determined by

$$\dot{k}(t) = f(l(t), k(t), g(t)) - c(t) - I(g(t)) - G(t) \qquad (5.1)$$

in which $I(g)$ is an increasing and strictly convex function representing the cost of the resources used to produce energy. Recall that in Chapter 2, this private production cost was set equal to zero. We introduce this cost here to facilitate distinguishing between a 'final goods producer' and an 'energy producer'. This distinction is convenient from the point of view of the optimal tax problem; it is not important for the qualitative results to be derived.

We again assume that the emission production function is linear in g, implying a one-to-one relationship between energy use and emissions. The equation of motion for the stock of pollution is written

$$\dot{x}(t) = g(t) - \gamma x(t) \qquad (5.2)$$

where γ is the rate of depreciation.

In order to derive the first best welfare measure for the model set out above, we start by characterizing the first best resource allocation. Following our earlier approach, suppose that the resource allocation is decided on by a social planner. The social planner chooses $c(t)$, $l(t)$, $g(t)$ and $G(t)$ to maximize the present value of future utility

$$U(0) = \int_0^\infty u(c(t), h(t), G(t), x(t)) e^{-\theta t} dt$$

subject to the equations of motion for k and x, initial conditions $k(0) = k_0$ and $x(0) = x_0$, and the terminal conditions $\lim_{t \to \infty} k(t) \geq 0$ and $\lim_{t \to \infty} x(t) \geq 0$. The present value Hamiltonian is written

$$H(t) = u(c(t), h(t), G(t), x(t)) e^{-\theta t} + \lambda(t) \dot{k}(t) + \mu(t) \dot{x}(t) \qquad (5.3)$$

Note that the model presented here is only a slight extension of the model used in Chapters 2 and 4, so that several of the first order conditions will coincide with those derived previously. For the reader's convenience we write the full set of first order conditions here. They will be useful below when we compare the implications of the first best and second best resource allocations. In addition to equations (5.1) and (5.2), as well as to the initial and terminal conditions, the necessary conditions are[2] (neglecting the time indicator for notational convenience)

$$u_c(c^*, h^*, G^*, x^*)e^{-\theta t} - \lambda^* = 0 \tag{5.4}$$

$$-u_h(c^*, h^*, G^*, x^*)e^{-\theta t} + \lambda^* f_l(l^*, k^*, g^*) = 0 \tag{5.5}$$

$$\lambda^*[f_g(l^*, k^*, g^*) - I_g(g^*)] + \mu^* = 0 \tag{5.6}$$

$$u_G(c^*, h^*, G^*, x^*)e^{-\theta t} - \lambda^* = 0 \tag{5.7}$$

$$\dot{\lambda}^* = -\lambda^* f_k(l^*, k^*, g^*) \tag{5.8}$$

$$\dot{\mu}^* = -u_x(c^*, h^*, G^*, x^*)e^{-\theta t} + \mu^* \gamma \tag{5.9}$$

$$\lim_{t \to \infty} \lambda^* \geq 0 \, (= 0 \, \text{if} \lim_{t \to \infty} k^* > 0) \tag{5.10}$$

$$\lim_{t \to \infty} \mu^* \geq 0 \, (= 0 \, \text{if} \lim_{t \to \infty} x^* > 0) \tag{5.11}$$

As before, the superindex * is used to denote the first best equilibrium, and the subindices denote partial derivatives. Equations (5.4), (5.8), (5.9), (5.10) and (5.11) are identical to their counterparts in Chapter 2 and need no further explanation. The first order condition for energy, given by equation (5.6), is a slightly extended version of equation (2.18ii), since we now explicitly recognize the private marginal cost associated with energy production. Since $\mu^* < 0$, we can interpret equation (5.6) such that the marginal product of energy exceeds the private marginal cost. The reason is, of course, that the use of energy gives rise to emissions, so that the social marginal cost of energy exceeds the private marginal cost. The remaining two first order conditions have no counterparts in Chapter 2. Equation (5.5) is the first order condition for the hours of work, and implies that the marginal utility of leisure equals the utility value of the marginal product of labor. Finally, equation (5.7) is the first order condition for the publicly provided good. A comparison of equations (5.4) and (5.7) suggests that the marginal utilities of the privately and publicly provided goods are equal in the first best equilibrium.

The appropriate methodology for measuring welfare in the first best was explained in Chapter 2. By applying Proposition 2.1, together with the result that the present value Hamiltonian approaches zero when time goes to infinity, the welfare measure for the model set out here can be written as

$$\theta V^*(t) = u(c^*(t), h^*(t), G^*(t), x^*(t)) + \lambda^{c^*}(t)\dot{k}^*(t) + \mu^{c^*}(t)\dot{x}^*(t) \qquad (5.12)$$

where

$$V^*(t) = \int_t^\infty u(c^*(s), h^*(s), G^*(s), x^*(s))e^{-\theta(s-t)}ds$$

is the optimal value function, and the right-hand side of equation (5.12) is the current value Hamiltonian evaluated in the first best equilibrium. Although this general result is well known, it is instructive to analyze the components of green NNP for the model set out above a bit more thoroughly. Therefore, we follow Hartwick (1990) and Mäler (1991) once again by linearizing the instantaneous utility function and replacing the instantaneous utility function by the linear approximation. The linearized welfare measure in real terms is given by

$$\frac{\theta V^*(t)}{\lambda^{c^*}(t)} \approx c^*(t) + G^*(t) + \dot{k}^*(t) + w^*(t)h^*(t) + \frac{u_x^*(t)}{\lambda^{c^*}(t)}x^*(t) \qquad (5.12a)$$
$$- \tau^*(t)\dot{x}^*(t)$$

where $u_x^* = u_x(c^*, h^*, G^*, x^*)$, $w^* = f_l(l^*, k^*, g^*)$ and $\tau^* = -\mu^*/\lambda^*$.

Equation (5.12a) is not a complete welfare measure in real terms because it neglects the consumer surplus part. However, the right-hand side can be interpreted as representing an important aspect of such a welfare measure; that is, the green NNP in money metrics for the model set out above. The first three terms comprise the conventional NNP: consumption of privately and publicly provided goods and net investments in physical capital. The fourth term is the value of leisure time and stems from the assumption that leisure is an argument in the utility function. Since the labor market is competitive, the marginal value of leisure can be measured by the real wage rate. As we show in Chapter 8, this does not necessarily apply in case of imperfect competition in the labor market. The fifth and sixth terms are, respectively, the social value of the stock of pollution at time t and the social value of additions to the stock of pollution at time t. These two terms are identical to their counterparts in equation (2.17b) and will not be discussed further here.

It should be pointed out that in order to interpret the first best equilibrium as the outcome of a controlled market economy, we would need two important assumptions about the government: (i) that it has access to lump-sum taxation and (ii) that it can fully internalize external effects by means of Pigouvian taxes. Some of the consequences for welfare measurement of relaxing the latter assumption were analyzed in Chapter 4. We are now concerned with the consequences of relaxing the first assumption, by deriving an analogue to green NNP in a second best world with distortionary labor income and capital income taxation.

5.1.2 Introducing Distortionary Taxes in the Decentralized Economy

When characterizing the agents in the decentralized economy, we distinguish between three types of private agents: the consumer, the producer of final goods and the energy producer. Starting with the consumer, the utility maximization problem is

$$\underset{c(t),l(t)}{Max} \int_0^\infty u(c(t),h(t),G(t),x(t))e^{-\theta t}\,dt$$

subject to an asset accumulation equation. The consumer holds two assets, physical capital, k, and government bonds, b. Since there is no uncertainty, these two assets are perfect substitutes and have the same rate of return. By defining $a = k + b$, the asset accumulation equation is written

$$\dot{a}(t) = \pi(t) + r(t)a(t)[1 - \tau_k(t)] + w(t)l(t)[1 - \tau_l(t)] - c(t) \qquad (5.13)$$

with $k(0) = k_0$ and $b(0) = b_0$, where w is the wage rate, r the interest rate, $\pi = \pi_f + \pi_g$ possible profit income from final goods production and energy production, respectively, τ_l the labor income tax rate and τ_k the capital income tax rate. In addition to equation (5.13), the consumer also obeys a No Ponzi Game (NPG) condition:

$$\lim_{t\to\infty} a(t)\exp(-\int_0^t r(s)ds) \geq 0$$

We assume that the consumer treats the paths of the factor prices, the profit income, the two income tax rates, the publicly provided good and the stock of pollution as exogenous during optimization.

Turning to the production side of the economy, the (representative) producer of final goods uses labor, capital and energy to produce a homogeneous good. Given competitive behavior, the objective function can be written as

$$\pi_f(t) = f(l(t),k(t),g(t)) - w(t)l(t) - r(t)k(t) - q(t)g(t) \qquad (5.14)$$

where q is the energy price. The producer of final goods treats the factor prices as exogenous.

The (representative) energy producer also acts competitively. If we simplify the analysis by disregarding the use of labor and capital, the objective function of the energy producer is given by

$$\pi_g(t) = q(t)g(t) - I(g(t)) - \tau(t)g(t) \tag{5.15}$$

where τ is the emission tax.

There is also a fourth agent in the decentralized economy: the government. The stock of government bonds accumulates according to

$$\dot{b}(t) = r(t)b(t) + G(t) - \tau_l(t)w(t)l(t) - \tau_k(t)r(t)[k(t) + b(t)] \tag{5.16}$$
$$- \tau(t)g(t)$$

Following the literature on optimal taxation, we assume that the government acts as a Stackelberg leader in the sense of recognizing how the private sector responds to its policy decisions, whereas the private sector acts as a follower. The private sector thus treats the tax rates and the publicly provided good as exogenous. Let $\tau_l^0(t)$, $\tau_k^0(t), \tau^0(t)$ and $G^0(t)$ for all t represent the levels of the three tax rates and the publicly provided good chosen by the government. The government announces these paths, while the consumer and the two types of firms then make their optimal choices.

We start by characterizing the outcome of private optimization conditional on the tax rates and the publicly provided good. Let us also simplify the notations by defining the net wage rate, the net interest rate and the net energy price as

$$w_n = w(1 - \tau_l), \quad r_n = r(1 - \tau_k) \text{ and } q_n = q - \tau$$

respectively. In addition to the initial and NPG conditions, the necessary conditions characterizing the private sector are[3] (neglecting the time indicator)

$$u_c(c^0, h^0, G^0, x^0)e^{-\theta t} - \phi^0 = 0 \tag{5.17}$$

$$-u_h(c^0, h^0, G^0, x^0)e^{-\theta t} + \phi^0 w_n^0 = 0 \tag{5.18}$$

$$\dot{\phi}^0 = -\phi^0 r_n^0 \tag{5.19}$$

$$q_n^0 - I_g(g^0) = 0 \tag{5.20}$$

$$\dot{k}^0 = f(l^0, k^0, g^0) - I(g^0) - G^0 - c^0 \tag{5.21}$$

$$\dot{b}^0 = r^0 b^0 + G^0 - (w^0 - w_n^0)l^0 - (r^0 - r_n^0)(k^0 + b^0) - (q^0 - q_n^0)g^0 \qquad (5.22)$$

$$\lim_{t \to \infty} \phi^0 = 0 \qquad (5.23)$$

where ϕ is the consumer's present utility value of additional wealth. The superindex 0 denotes that the equilibrium is defined conditional on $\tau_l^0(t)$, $\tau_k^0(t)$, $\tau^0(t)$ and $G^0(t)$ for all t. Note that the gross prices, w^0, r^0 and q^0, are endogenous and determined by $w^0 = f_l(l^0, k^0, g^0)$, $r^0 = f_k (l^0, k^0, g^0)$ and $q^0 = f_g(l^0, k^0, g^0)$, respectively. Equations (5.17)–(5.23) may, therefore, be interpreted as general equilibrium conditions. The accumulation equation for private wealth is not included among the necessary conditions; it is redundant in view of equations (5.21) and (5.22). Equation (5.21) is derived by combining equations (5.13), (5.14), (5.15) and (5.16).

5.1.3 Distortionary Taxes and the First Best Welfare Measure

To analyze the complications for welfare measurement arising from distortionary taxes, we begin by reexamining the relationship between welfare, as measured by the present value of future utility, and the Hamiltonian concept of Subsection 5.1.1. The purpose is to explain why green NNP in utility terms – as we have come to know it from the first best equilibrium – cannot be used as a welfare measure in the presence of distortionary taxes.

So as to enable comparisons with Subsection 5.1.1, consider the measure

$$H_p^0(t) = u(c^0(t), h^0(t), G^0(t), x^0(t))e^{-\theta t} + \phi^0(t)\dot{k}^0(t) - \phi^0(t)\tau^0(t)\dot{x}^0(t) \qquad (5.24)$$

Equation (5.24) is analogous to equation (4.13) in Chapter 4. We may interpret $H_p^0(t)$ as a present value 'pseudo-Hamiltonian': it would be equivalent to the present value Hamiltonian if evaluated in the first best. It is also the green NNP in utility terms discounted to present value and evaluated in the decentralized equilibrium for the model set out above. This follows because $H_p^0(t)$ measures the utility value of consumption at time t, $u(\cdot)e^{-\theta t}$, plus an estimate of the utility value of the net investments in physical capital and pollution, which are the capital concepts of the model. Note that the way in which we have written the shadow price of pollution at time t, $-\phi^0(t)\tau^0(t)$, is also analogous to the corresponding shadow price in equation (4.13). The interpretation is that if $-\tau^0(t)$ is an estimate of the real value of additions to the stock of pollution at time t, then $-\phi^0(t)\tau^0(t)$ transforms this value into utility units. Differentiating equation (5.24) with respect to time and using equations (5.17)–(5.20) gives (neglecting the time indicator)

$$\frac{dH_p^0}{dt} = -\theta u(c^0, h^0, G^0, x^0)e^{-\theta t} + [u_G^0 e^{-\theta t} - \phi^0]\dot{G}^0$$

$$+ \phi^0 \tau_l^0 f_l^0 \dot{l}^0 + \phi^0 \tau_k^0 f_k^0 \dot{k}^0 \qquad (5.25)$$

$$+ [u_x^0 e^{-\theta t} + \phi^0 \tau^0 (f_k^0 (1 - \tau_k^0) + \gamma) - \phi^0 \dot{\tau}^0]\dot{x}^0$$

in which $u_x^0 = u_x(c^0, h^0, G^0, x^0)$, $u_G^0 = u_G(c^0, h^0, G^0, x^0)$, $f_l^0 = f_l(l^0, k^0, g^0)$ and $f_k^0 = f_k(l^0, k^0, g^0)$.

The direct effect of time on the pseudo-Hamiltonian can be divided into five parts. The first term on the right-hand side of equation (5.25) represents the direct effect of time associated with the utility discount factor. This effect is well known from the welfare measures derived previously. The second term is due to the fact that we have not yet assumed that the publicly provided good is optimally chosen, whereas the third and fourth terms originate from distortionary labor income taxation and capital income taxation, respectively. Note that the second, third and fourth terms would all vanish in the first best equilibrium, where $\phi^0 = \lambda^*$, $u_G^0(\cdot)e^{-\theta t} - \phi^0 = 0$, $\tau_l = 0$ and $\tau_k = 0$. Finally, the fifth term is analogous to its counterpart in equation (4.14). In the first best optimum, this term would also vanish due to the form of the differential equation for the Pigouvian emission tax.[4] By solving equation (5.25), assuming that $\lim_{t \to \infty} H_p^0(t) = 0$, and transforming the solution into current value terms, we have

$$\theta \int_t^\infty u(c^0(s), h^0(s), G^0(s), x^0(s))e^{-\theta(s-t)}ds = H_p^{c^0}(t) + \int_t^\infty \Omega^0(s)e^{\theta t}ds \qquad (5.26)$$

where $H_p^{c^0}(t) = H_p^0(t)e^{\theta t}$ is the current value pseudo-Hamiltonian and $\Omega^0(t)$ is the sum of the last four terms on the right-hand side of equation (5.25). It is evident that the pseudo-Hamiltonian does not provide an exact welfare measure in this case. Welfare at time t cannot be measured without considering the future welfare consequences associated with the tax system, the publicly provided good and the pollution, respectively.

In order to relate equation (5.26) explicitly to the use of distortionary taxes, it is instructive to analyze this welfare measure in the special case where the publicly provided good and the emission tax are chosen in the same general way as their first best counterparts in Subsection 5.1.1. This would make it possible to isolate the effects of distortionary taxes from the effects of time via the public good and the stock of pollution in equation (5.25). Consider Proposition 5.1:

Proposition 5.1 *To isolate the effect of distortionary taxation, suppose that the publicly provided good and the emission tax are chosen in such a way that*

$$u_G^0 e^{-\theta t} - \phi^0 = 0 \text{ and } u_x^0 e^{-\theta t} + \phi^0 \tau^0 (f_k^0 (1 - \tau_k^0) + \gamma) - \phi^0 \dot{\tau}^0 = 0$$

for all t. *In this case, by assuming that* $\phi^0(t)$, $f_l^0(t)$, $f_k^0(t)$, $\tau_l^0(t)$ *and* $\tau_k^0(t)$ *are positive for all* t, *the pseudo-Hamiltonian in current value terms will overestimate (underestimate) welfare at time* t *if, and only if,*

$$\int_t^\infty \phi^{c^0}(s)[\tau_l^0(s)f_l^0(s)\dot{l}^0(s) + \tau_k^0(s)f_k^0(s)\dot{k}^0(s)]e^{-\theta(s-t)}ds < 0 \, (> 0)$$

Since distortionary taxes on labor income and capital income imply that l and k are not optimally chosen from the point of view of society, future changes in l and k will affect the welfare measure. We can also interpret Proposition 5.1 such that a weighted sum of future changes in tax revenues from the labor income tax and the capital income tax affects the welfare measure, where the weights are equal to the marginal utility value of wealth at each point in time. If this sum is positive (negative), it contributes to making the pseudo-Hamiltonian underestimate (overestimate) welfare. This is reminiscent of the consequences for welfare measurement of uninternalized external effects; cf. Chapters 2 and 4.

5.1.4 A Green NNP Analogue in a Second Best Environment

Although the necessity of collecting tax revenues by means of distortionary taxes implies that the first best resource allocation is unattainable, the way in which these taxes are chosen still matters for welfare measurement. So far, we have not made any assumptions about the behavior of the government. The previous section only focused on showing how the traditional Green NNP in utility terms fails as a welfare measure when the government uses distortionary taxes. We now turn to deriving a second best analogue to the welfare measure in Subsection 5.1.1.

We begin by formulating the optimization problem facing the government. In the second best problem, the necessary conditions of the private sector appear as restrictions faced by the government. For our purposes here, it is convenient to express the necessary conditions of the private sector in current value terms. This is accomplished by multiplying equations (5.17) and (5.18) by $e^{\theta t}$, in which case these two equations can be written as follows:

$$u_c(c^0(t), h^0(t), G^0(t), x^0(t)) - \phi^{c^0}(t) = 0 \qquad (5.17a)$$

$$-u_h(c^0(t), h^0(t), G^0(t), x^0(t)) + \phi^{c^0}(t)w_n^0(t) = 0 \qquad (5.18a)$$

In equations (5.17a) and (5.18a), $\phi^{c^0}(t) = \phi^0(t)e^{\theta t}$ is the consumer's marginal utility of wealth in current value terms, where

$$\dot{\phi}^{c^0}(t) - \theta\phi^{c^0}(t) = -\phi^{c^0}(t)r_n^0(t) \tag{5.19a}$$

is a restatement of equation (5.19). Solving equations (5.17a) and (5.18a) for c^0 and l^0 as functions of w_n^0, ϕ^{c^0}, G^0 and x^0 and equation (5.20) for g^0 as a function of q_n^0 gives

$$c^0(t) = c(w_n^0(t), \phi^{c^0}(t), G^0(t), x^0(t)) \tag{5.27}$$

$$l^0(t) = l(w_n^0(t), \phi^{c^0}(t), G^0(t), x^0(t)) \tag{5.28}$$

$$g^0(t) = g(q_n^0(t)) \tag{5.29}$$

Since tax rates and net prices are equivalent policy instruments, the optimization problem facing the government[5] is to choose the control variables, $w_n^0(t)$, $r_n^0(t)$, $q_n^0(t)$ and $G^0(t)$, to maximize the consumer's utility function subject to the equations of motion for the state variables as well as subject to equations (5.27), (5.28) and (5.29). The state variables are the capital stock, k, the stock of pollution, x, the private marginal utility of wealth, ϕ^c, and the stock of government bonds, b. Since the differential equation for ϕ^c is part of the necessary conditions facing the consumer, it provides an intertemporal constraint subject to which the government chooses the second best program. This means that ϕ^c is a state variable in the government's optimization problem. Formally, the optimization problem of the government can be written as (neglecting neglect the time indicator):

$$\underset{w_n^0, r_n^0, q_n^0, G^0}{\text{Max}} \int_0^\infty u(c^0, h^0, G^0, x^0)e^{-\theta t}\, dt \tag{5.30}$$

s.t.

$$\dot{k}^0 = f(l^0, k^0, g^0) - c^0 - I(g^0) - G^0 \tag{5.31}$$

$$\dot{x}^0 = g^0 - \gamma x^0 \tag{5.32}$$

$$\dot{\phi}^{c^0} = \phi^{c^0}(\theta - r_n^0) \tag{5.33}$$

$$\dot{b}^0 = r^0 b^0 + G^0 - (w^0 - w_n^0)l^0 - (r^0 - r_n^0)(k^0 + b^0) - (q^0 - q_n^0)g^0 \tag{5.34}$$

$$r_n^0 \geq 0 \tag{5.35}$$

where c^0, l^0 and g^0 are given by equations (5.27), (5.28) and (5.29). In addition, the gross factor prices are endogenous, which means that $w^0 = f_l(l^0,k^0,g^0)$, $r^0 = f_k(l^0,k^0,g^0)$ and $q^0 = f_g(l^0,k^0,g^0)$. We also impose the initial conditions $k(0) = k_0$, $x(0) = x_0$ and $b(0) = b_0$, terminal conditions on k and x of the form discussed in Subsection 5.1.1 as well as an NPG condition on b. The government does not face any explicit constraint on the initial value of the private marginal utility of wealth, $\phi^c(0)$; this variable is chosen by the private sector and depends on the equilibrium path taken by the economy in the future. The latter is, in turn, influenced by the decisions of the government.

The constraint (5.35) is a minimum restriction on the net interest rate: it is written such that the net interest rate must be non-negative, although a positive lower bound could have been considered. In the absence of a lower bound on the net interest rate, the optimal policy would be to implement a capital income tax such that the net interest rate becomes negative with an arbitrarily large absolute value during an infinitesimal time interval. The reason is that the capital stock is fixed initially. Such a policy is equivalent to lump-sum taxation. The constraint (5.35) is used to avoid this situation and ensures that the optimization problem facing the government is, indeed, a second best problem. This has been pointed out by Chamely (1986), who analyzes optimal taxation of labor income and capital income in a dynamic general equilibrium model without environmental external effects.

By defining the indirect utility function as

$$v(w_n,\phi^c,G,x) = u(c(w_n,\phi^c,G,x), T - l(w_n,\phi^c,G,x), G, x)$$

the present value Hamiltonian can be written

$$H^0 = v(w_n^0,\phi^{c^0},G^0,x^0)e^{-\theta t} + \lambda^0 \dot{k}^0 + \mu^0 \dot{x}^0 + v^0 \dot{\phi}^{c^0} + \psi^0 \dot{b}^0 \quad (5.36)$$

The Lagrangean will then become $L^0 = H^0 + \zeta^0 r_n^0$, where ζ is the Lagrange multiplier. The necessary conditions are

$$\frac{\partial L^0}{\partial w_n^0} = v_{w_n}^0 e^{-\theta t} + \lambda^0 [f_l^0 l_{w_n}^0 - c_{w_n}^0] + \psi^0 \dot{b}_{w_n}^0 = 0 \quad (5.37)$$

$$\frac{\partial L^0}{\partial r_n^0} = -v^0 \phi^{c^0} + \psi^0 \dot{b}_{r_n}^0 + \zeta^0 = 0 \quad (5.38)$$

$$\frac{\partial L^0}{\partial q_n^0} = [\lambda^0 (f_g^0 - I_g^0) + \mu^0]g_{q_n}^0 + \psi^0 \dot{b}_{q_n}^0 = 0 \quad (5.39)$$

$$\frac{\partial L^0}{\partial G^0} = v_G^0 e^{-\theta t} + \lambda^0 [f_l^0 l_G^0 - c_G^0 - 1] + \psi^0 \dot{b}_G^0 = 0 \tag{5.40}$$

$$\dot{\lambda}^0 = -\lambda^0 f_k^0 - \psi^0 \dot{b}_k^0 \tag{5.41}$$

$$\dot{\mu}^0 = -v_x^0 e^{-\theta t} - \lambda^0 [f_l^0 l_x^0 - c_x^0] + \mu^0 \gamma - \psi^0 \dot{b}_{\phi^c}^0 \tag{5.42}$$

$$\dot{v}^0 = -v_{\phi^c}^0 e^{-\theta t} - \lambda^0 [f_l^0 l_{\phi^c}^0 - c_{\phi^c}^0] - v^0(\theta - r_n^0) - \psi^0 \dot{b}_\phi^0 c \tag{5.43}$$

$$\dot{\psi}^0 = -\psi^0 \dot{b}_b^0 \tag{5.44}$$

supplemented by transversality conditions (which are necessary provided that certain growth conditions are fulfilled) and a non-negativity constraint on the Lagrange multiplier. Since $\phi^c(0)$ is free in the government's optimization problem, we also have to impose the initial transversality condition $v(0) = 0$; see Seierstad and Sydsaeter (1987, p. 185). The intuition is the same as for transversality conditions corresponding to the terminal state. If there is no restriction associated with the initial state, the costate variable is zero. The subindices on $v^0(\cdot), f^0(\cdot), l^0, c^0, g^0$ and $\dot{b}^0$ in equations (5.37)–(5.44) are partial derivatives.

Equations (5.37)–(5.40) are efficiency conditions for the control variables, whereas equations (5.41)–(5.44) are equations of motion for the costate variables. We return to interpretations of some of the necessary conditions in detail below. Let

$$(\tilde{w}_n^0(t), \tilde{r}_n^0(t), \tilde{q}_n^0(t), \tilde{G}^0(t)) \; \forall t$$

be the control variables that solve the government's optimization problem, where a tilde (~) is used to indicate that the government has made an optimal choice. Since we focus on the implications of the second best resource allocation throughout this subsection, we simplify the notations and suppress the tilde symbol in what follows. The second best resource allocation can be interpreted as a decentralized equilibrium. The government first solves the second best problem in order to find the optimal paths for the tax rates and the publicly provided good, and the private sector then solves its own optimization problems subject to these paths. Such a decentralized equilibrium would, of course, support the second best resource allocation, because all aspects of private optimization are taken into consideration by the government.

Since all policy instruments are optimally chosen subject to the relevant constraints, we would expect some similarities between the second best welfare measure and the first best welfare measure derived in Subsection 5.1.1. Substituting the optimal solution into the present value Hamiltonian, differentiating with respect to time and using the necessary conditions given by equations (5.37)–(5.44), we obtain[6]

$$\frac{dH^0(t)}{dt} = -\theta v(w_n^0(t), \phi^{c^0}(t), G^0(t), x^0(t))e^{-\theta t} \tag{5.45}$$

since the only non-autonomous time dependence arises via the utility discount factor. By solving equation (5.45), and assuming that $\lim_{t\to\infty}H^0(t) = 0$, the welfare measure can be written as

$$\theta \int_t^\infty v(w_n^0(s), \phi^{c^0}(s), G^0(s), x^0(s))e^{-\theta(s-t)}ds = v(w_n^0(t), \phi^{c^0}(t), G^0(t), x^0(t))$$

$$+ \lambda^{c^0}(t)\dot{k}^0(t) + \mu^{c^0}(t)\dot{x}^0(t) + v^{c^0}(t)\dot{\phi}^{c^0}(t) + \psi^{c^0}(t)\dot{b}^0(t)$$

$$\tag{5.46}$$

where the right-hand side of equation (5.46) is the current value Hamiltonian implicit in the government's optimization problem, $H^{c^0}(t) = H^0(t)e^{\theta t}$. Equation (5.46) may be interpreted as follows:

Proposition 5.2 *In a second best economy, the current value Hamiltonian corresponding to the government's optimization problem is a static equivalent of future utility.*

In other words, the present value of future utility is proportional to the sum of the utility value of current consumption and the discounted utility value of the current net investments, where the factor of proportionality is the utility discount rate. As a consequence, equations (5.12) and (5.46) have the same general interpretation. Meanwhile, there are some important differences between the second best welfare measure derived here and the first best welfare measure in Subsection 5.1.1. By analogy to our previous analyses, if the current value Hamiltonian of the first best optimization problem is interpreted as the green NNP welfare measure in utility terms, a prerequisite for welfare measurement in the second best is that the green NNP in utility terms be augmented by the fourth and fifth terms on the right-hand side of equation (5.46). The fourth term is included in the welfare measure, since the equation of motion for the private marginal utility of wealth imposes a restriction on the government. The fifth term is the marginal utility value of government bonds times the accumulation of government bonds at time t. An alternative interpretation is that $-\psi^0(t)$ measures the marginal excess burden at time t.

There are also other differences between the first best and the second best welfare measures. In our context, it is particularly interesting to compare the two resource allocations with respect to the procedures associated with accounting for pollution. To begin with, consider equation (5.39), which is the necessary condition for the emission tax. In the first best, the final term on the right-hand side is zero, and equation (5.39) coincides with the necessary condition for emissions given by equation (5.6). Therefore, in the first best, the optimal emission tax is determined by the value of additions to the stock of pollution. Indeed, this is what makes the emission tax valuable for social accounting. However, in the second best, the final term on the right-hand side of equation (5.39) is generally non-zero. As a consequence, the emission tax becomes a less accurate predictor of the value of additions to the stock of pollution in the second best than in the first best. Therefore, the emission tax becomes less useful for social accounting in the second best.

Note that the first best and second best situations also differ with respect to the principles of calculating the shadow price of additions to the stock of pollution. This is easily verified by solving equation (5.42) subject to the appropriate transversality condition and then comparing the results with the solution to equation (5.9), which is the shadow price in the first best equilibrium. By observing that $v_x = u_c c_x - u_h l_x + u_x$, and using the short notation

$$\Lambda = (u_c e^{-\theta t} - \lambda)c_x + (-u_h e^{-\theta t} + \lambda f_l)l_x$$

the solution to equation (5.42) is written[7]

$$\mu^0(t) = \int_t^\infty [u_x^0(s)e^{-\theta s} + \Lambda^0(s) + \psi^0(s)\dot{b}_x^0(s)]e^{-\gamma(s-t)}ds \qquad (5.47)$$

In the first best, $\phi = \lambda$ and the second and third terms on the right-hand side are equal to zero. This is seen by solving equation (5.9) subject to the appropriate transversality condition

$$\mu^*(t) = \int_t^\infty u_x^*(s)e^{-\theta s}e^{-\gamma(s-t)}ds \qquad (5.48)$$

A comparison of equations (5.47) and (5.48) suggests that the connection between the consumer's willingness to pay to reduce the stock of pollution and the social value of a reduction in the stock of pollution is weaker in the second best than in the first best model. In the first best, the marginal utility of pollution along the optimal path, the rate of depreciation and the utility discount rate constitute, combined, the information required to calculate the shadow price of additions to the stock of pollution. In the second best, it is also necessary to explicitly consider that changes in this stock will affect consumption and the labor supply. In general, the second best model requires more information than the first best model to calculate the value of additions to the stock of pollution. This also means that the (almost) practical approach to green accounting discussed in Chapter 4 loses some of its appeal, since the first best and second best differ with respect to the informational content of the shadow price of pollution.

5.2   A COST–BENEFIT RULE FOR THE ENVIRONMENTAL TAX

The second best model clearly requires a great deal of information, which makes it difficult (or impossible) to implement in practice. The consequences for welfare measurement of relaxing the second best assumption were hinted at in Subsection 5.1.2, where no specific assumptions about the behavior of the government were imposed. However, relaxing the second best assumption also provides a framework for studying policy reform. Following Aronsson (1999), the purpose of this section is twofold. Given that the initial policy is suboptimal, the first is to derive a cost–benefit rule for evaluating the welfare effect of a change in the tax mix. This would enable us to relate the welfare effect to changes in employment, the capital stock, emissions and the stock of pollution along the whole general equilibrium path. The second is to study the conditions under which an emission tax, which is set slightly above or below the value of the marginal damage of pollution, is welfare superior to an emission tax that fully internalizes the external effect, when other distortionary taxes affect the resource allocation.

Suppose the private sector obeys equations (5.17)–(5.23). This equilibrium may be suboptimal from the point of view of society, since the fiscal variables are not necessarily at their optimal levels. Part of this resource allocation problem is due to the external effect arising from pollution. In such a framework, a green tax reform might be one means of improving the resource allocation. By analogy to the analysis carried out in Section 4.2, consider a permanent increase in the emission tax such that the new tax rate becomes $\tau^0(t) + \alpha$ for all t, where α is a small positive constant. Since the purpose is to study the welfare effect associated with a change in the tax mix, we make two additional assumptions that simplify the analysis: (i) the government balances its budget at each point in time, implying that $b(t) = 0$ for all t, and (ii) the reform does not affect the public good. This means that the government can use the additional tax revenues to reduce the labor income tax rate or the capital income tax rate (or possibly both). Either the labor income tax rate or the capital income tax

rate must be endogenous in the sense of allowing the government to balance its
budget at each point in time. However, in either case, the general equilibrium
solution for the private control variables can be written in terms of general
functions of the parameters of the model, among which α is included. The
only difference is that the form of the functional relationship between α and
the private decision variables depends on how the government balances its
budget. Since our primary purpose is to characterize the cost–benefit rule, the
way the government achieves this is not of major concern. In addition, since
the path for the publicly provided good is not affected by the reform, we can
assume that $G^0(t) = \bar{G}$ for all t.

The optimal value function is written

$$V^0(0;\xi) = \int_0^\infty u(c^0(t;\xi), h^0(t;\xi), \bar{G}, x^0(t;\xi))e^{-\theta t} dt \qquad (5.49)$$

where $\xi = [k_0, x_0, \gamma, \theta, \alpha]$ is a parameter vector with α as one of its elements.
The cost–benefit rule we are looking for can be derived by differentiating the
value function with respect to α and evaluating the resulting derivative at the
point where $\alpha = 0$. To simplify the notation, we suppress the time indicator
and the vector ξ, while using the same short notation for marginal utility and
product as above;

$$u_x^0(\cdot) = u_x(c^0, h^0, \bar{G}, x^0), \; f_l^0(\cdot) = f_l(l^0, k^0, g^0) \text{ and } f_k^0(\cdot) = f_k(l^0, k^0, g^0)$$

The cost–benefit rule derived by Aronsson (1999) is presented in Proposition
5.3:

Proposition 5.3 *If the value function is differentiable, and the path for the
public good remains unaffected by the reform, the cost–benefit rule for α can
be written as*

$$\frac{\partial V^0(0;\xi)}{\partial \alpha} = \int_0^\infty \left[\phi^0 \left\{ \tau_l^0 f_l^0(\cdot)\frac{\partial l^0}{\partial \alpha} + \tau_k^0 f_k^0(\cdot)\frac{\partial k^0}{\partial \alpha} + \tau^0 \frac{\partial g^0}{\partial \alpha} \right\} + u_x^0(\cdot)e^{-\theta t}\frac{\partial x^0}{\partial \alpha} \right] dt$$

$$(5.50)$$

The derivation of equation (5.50) is analogous to the derivation of equation
(4.5), and the proof of Proposition 5.3 is, therefore, omitted. The first three
terms on the right-hand side of equation (5.50) are due to the preexisting tax
system. Erosion of the tax bases, as represented by the effects of α on l, k and
g, depends on the properties of the utility function and production function as
well as on whether the additional tax revenues are used to cut the labor income

tax, the capital income tax or both. In general, it is not clear which option is preferable. As long as the indirect effects via the other tax rates are never strong enough to dominate; that is if the direct effects on the tax bases of increasing the emission tax dominate the indirect effects following due to adjustments of other taxes, the choice between using the additional tax revenues in one way or another does not affect the qualitative results.

Note that raising the emission tax increases the marginal cost of releasing emissions. Therefore, given the assumptions underlying the model, and if the direct effects on the tax bases owing to increased emission taxation dominate the indirect effects due to the adjustments of the other taxes, it is reasonable to assume that $\partial g^0/\partial \alpha < 0$ for all t. Then, by using equation (5.2) to solve for x^0 as a function of past emissions, it follows that $\partial x^0/\partial \alpha < 0$. In terms of equation (5.50), this means that $u_x^0(\cdot)e^{-\theta t}(\partial x^0/\partial \alpha) > 0$ represents the instantaneous benefit of a reduction in the stock of pollution or, equivalently, the instantaneous benefit of a better environment.

An increase in the emission tax may change both l and k in either direction. However, with an upward sloping labor supply, and if labor and emissions are complements in production, it is reasonable to assume that $\partial l^0/\partial \alpha < 0$, at least during certain time intervals. The interpretation is that the existing tax system, in part, determines the costs of an increase in the emission tax. In this case, the higher the preexisting taxes, the higher the cost of the reform. This assumption also seems to be in line with results from numerical analyses. By simulating a numerical general equilibrium model for the USA, in which agents optimize intertemporally, Goulder (1995) found that an increase in carbon taxation tends to augment the existing tax distortions, even if the additional revenues are used to lower other taxes. The preexisting capital income tax influences the cost–benefit rule in a similar way: if $\partial k/\partial \alpha < 0(>0)$, an increase in the emission tax augments (tends to diminish) the preexisting tax distortion.

Let us extend the analysis of preexisting tax distortions by asking the following question: if the equilibrium is characterized by distortionary taxes, is it welfare improving to set the emission tax above or below the value of additions to the stock of pollution instead of fully internalizing the external effect? More specifically, if the pre-reform emission tax is set equal to the value of additions to the stock of pollution at each point in time along the general equilibrium path, under what conditions will a small permanent increase or decrease in the emission tax improve the welfare level? Assume that the pre-reform emission tax is equal to the value of additions to the stock of pollution at each point in time. This implies that emission taxation is governed by the same general principles as in the first best, in the sense of serving as an intertemporal measure of the willingness to pay to reduce the stock of pollution, and suggests that the formula for the emission tax should read

$$\tau^0(t) = -\frac{\int\limits_t^\infty u_x(c^0(s), h^0(s), \bar{G}, x^0(s))e^{-\theta s}e^{-\gamma(s-t)}ds}{\phi^0(t)} \tag{5.51}$$

Differentiating equation (5.51) with respect to time and using equation (5.19), we obtain (neglecting the time indicator)

$$\dot{\tau}^0 = \frac{u_x^0(\cdot)e^{-\theta t}}{\phi^0} + \tau^0[f_k^0(\cdot)(1 - \tau_k^0) + \gamma] \tag{5.52}$$

If the equation of motion for the emission tax takes the form of equation (5.52), then the third and fourth terms on the right-hand side of equation (5.50) cancel out. We have derived the following result:

Proposition 5.4 *If the prereform emission tax evolves according to equation (5.52), the cost–benefit rule for α reduces to*

$$\frac{\partial V^0(0;\xi)}{\partial \alpha} = \int\limits_0^\infty \phi^0 \left[\tau_l^0 f_l^0(\cdot) \frac{\partial l^0}{\partial \alpha} + \tau_k^0 f_k^0(\cdot) \frac{\partial k^0}{\partial \alpha} \right] dt \tag{5.53}$$

Proof: see Appendix C.

The intuition behind this proposition is, of course, that the marginal benefit of a reduction in the stock of pollution is equal to the direct marginal cost of emissions at each point in time. As a consequence, only the welfare effects via the changes in labor and capital remain in the cost–benefit rule. We can interpret Proposition 5.4 as follows: if the (prereform) emission tax is chosen such that the welfare effects via g and x cancel out, then a small permanent reduction in the emission tax increases the welfare level if, and only if, a weighted sum of instantaneous responses in the tax bases for l and k over the whole planning period is positive. The weights are, in turn, given by the marginal utility value of wealth at each point in time (discounted to present value). It is important to emphasize the time dimension involved, because there are no particular restrictions on the labor market and/or the capital market at a given point in time. Instead, the welfare effect of a permanent decrease in the emission tax below the marginal damage of pollution depends on a weighted sum of behavioral responses over the whole general equilibrium path. In addition, both the sign and magnitude of behavioral responses may vary over time, suggesting that the magnitude or sign of the welfare effect depends on the utility weights in equation (5.53). The higher the utility discount rate and, as a consequence, the lower the present value of future shadow prices of wealth, the greater the importance of the behavioral responses in the near future, in relation to those in the distant future, for the welfare effect. Similarly, the lower the utility discount rate, the greater the importance of the responses in the distant future.

On the basis of a static model, Bovenberg and de Mooij (1994) argue that if emission taxes reduce employment, it is welfare improving to reduce the emission tax below the level corresponding to the marginal damage of pollution. In the special case with no capital income taxation, Proposition 5.4 would imply that welfare increases if, and only if, a weighted sum of instantaneous responses in the labor income tax bases over the planning period is positive. This is essentially a dynamic analogue of Bovenberg and de Mooij's result. The main difference is that the relationship between the welfare effect and changes in employment is weaker in the dynamic case, since no particular restrictions are imposed on the employment effects at a given point in time (or in a steady state, if it exists).

5.3 DISCUSSION

This chapter has addressed two issues related to the public sector; green accounting under distortionary labor income and capital income taxation, and the welfare effects associated with a change in the policy mix. Distortionary taxes invalidate the welfare interpretation of the Hamiltonian concept as defined in a first best setting. In other words, what we normally refer to as green NNP in utility terms is no longer sufficient for measuring welfare. This result is hardly surprising, considering that distortionary taxes are associated with a loss for society. We have also shown what the exact welfare measure looks like. In a second best optimum, welfare is appropriately measured by the current value Hamiltonian corresponding to the government's optimization problem. This current value Hamiltonian is interpretable as an analogue to the (first best) green NNP in utility terms: it is a static equivalent to future utility, although based on different valuation principles than those corresponding to the first best optimum.

If the public policy is not chosen in an optimal way from the point of view of society, it becomes imperative to consider the welfare effect of a change in the policy mix. We have studied the welfare effect of a change in the tax mix using cost–benefit analysis. More specifically, the reform considered was an increase in the emission tax accompanied by a decrease in the other taxes. Part of the cost–benefit rule is related to the preexisting tax system. In general, the higher the preexisting taxes, the greater the importance of the welfare contributions of the responses in labor and capital. In addition, we found that it is welfare superior to set the emission tax slightly below the value of the marginal damage caused by emissions, instead of fully internalizing the external effect, if higher emission taxation tends to reduce a weighted sum of tax bases over the whole planning horizon. Interestingly, the latter condition is weaker than the corresponding condition derived in the context of static models.

NOTES

1. It is well known that distributional objectives and distortionary taxes are difficult to separate. In fact, it may well be the combination of distributional objectives and asymmetric information that necessitates the use of distortionary taxes; see Stiglitz (1982). Here, we limit ourselves to analysing the complications for welfare measurement associated with the use of distortionary taxes, and do not explain why distortionary taxes are used. This allows us to concentrate on distortionary taxes here and return to distributional objectives later on.
2. The transversality conditions are necessary, provided that certain growth conditions are fulfilled; see footnote 11 in Chapter 2 and Seierstad and Sydsaeter (1987, Theorem 16 of Chapter 3).
3. Note that the NPG condition imposes a restriction on the limit of $a(t) \exp(-\int_0^t r(s)ds)$, and not on the limit of $a(t)$, which means that the transversality condition takes the form of equation (5.23).
4. In the first best optimum, $\phi^0(t) = \lambda^*(t)$ and the emission tax is given by $\tau^*(t) = -\mu^*(t) / \lambda^*(t)$. Differentiating with respect to time and using equations (5.8) and (5.9) gives

$$\dot{\tau}^*(t) = u_x^*(t)e^{-\theta t}/\lambda^*(t) + \tau^*(t)[f_k^*(t) + \gamma]$$

   A comparison with the final term on the right-hand side of equation (5.25) suggests that the equation of motion for the Pigouvian emission tax will eliminate the influence of time associated with the stock of pollution in the first best equilibrium.
5. Similar approaches to define second best optimization problems, although in other contexts, can be found in the excellent papers by Chamely (1985, 1986).
6. A nonnegativity constraint may imply that the Hamiltonian is not everywhere differentiable. To be able to focus on public sector aspects of social accounting without adding too much complexity, we assume that this problem is of minor practical importance and proceed as we would have done in the absence of discontinuities.
7. We assume that the terminal condition on x does not bind, in which case we can use $\lim_{t \to \infty} \mu^0(t) = 0$.

6. Green accounting and green taxes in the global economy

The analysis of green accounting may be extended to a global economy where pollution caused by production in one country affects the wellbeing of society in other countries. In particular it is worthwhile to explore the relationship between the circumstances under which the appropriate national and global welfare measures are related to national and/or global policies used to improve the allocation of resources. We also provide a framework for dynamic cost–benefit analysis of environmental tax reform in a global economy, where the pre-reform situation is generated by an imperfect market economy. In so doing, we also introduce sufficient conditions for a tax reform to improve global welfare.

The background is somewhat dichotomous. It is typically argued that the overall – or global – welfare level will increase if countries cooperate instead of forming their environmental policies in isolation. This is trivially true if a tax reform takes the economy to the first best cooperative equilibrium. In practice, however, 'cooperation' does not necessarily mean implementation of the first best; rather, countries agree to make slight changes in their environmental policies. As we intend to show, under these conditions the result is less clear.

The analytical framework for studying global external effects is familiar from research on international pollution control. A well-known example is Mäler (1989). Global external effects are routinely analysed in terms of Nash-non-cooperative differential games in open-loop or feedback-loop form.[1] Work on oligopoly equilibria has provided guidance for solving the implementation problem; see Loury (1986), Polansky (1992), van der Ploeg and de Zeeuw (1992) and Tahvonen and Salo (1996). The idea is to introduce Pigouvian-like taxes in domestic product markets. The taxes are suboptimal, since the externalities are not fully internalized in the non-cooperative Nash equilibrium. Such an equilibrium creates complications for welfare measurement reminiscent of those introduced in Chapter 2.

We consider the evaluation and implementation problem in three cases. The first is where the countries play a non-cooperative Nash game in open-loop form. Here we derive the welfare measures for each country as well as the global welfare measure. The second concerns the first best cooperative solution. This constitutes an important reference case for green accounting at the global level.

The reason is that, in order to measure welfare at the global level by observables related to the sum of the countries' green utility NNPs, the countries have to coordinate their environmental policies before the first best solution can be implemented. This is accomplished by introducing a system of Pigouvian taxes. Such taxes are directly applicable for accounting purposes at the global level because they can be used to solve a missing information problem in market data. Interestingly, however, it is not straightforward to split the global 'green NNP' into national welfare measures: even if the economies were to follow the cooperative solution, welfare measurement at the national level typically requires more information than can be found in each country's market data.

The third case refers to evaluation problems arising in imperfectly controlled market economies, that is, those which are in neither a Nash non-cooperative equilibrium nor a full cooperative equilibrium. Given the highly complicated process of computing Pigouvian-like taxes in a dynamic global economy, we regard this as the most realistic case. But our analysis of the welfare impact of introducing a tax reform in this situation does not take the global economy all the way to the first best equilibrium. The question here is under what conditions such a reform will improve global welfare. An interesting special case is when the imperfect welfare reform starts from the non-cooperative Nash equilibrium.

The cost–benefit rules that measure the impacts of tax reform are derived for marginal projects. The guideline is that countries agree to marginally increase their environmental taxes. We conclude this chapter by studying what we have called 'the almost cooperative solution'. To gain a better understanding of the implementation problem, we use a willingness-to-pay approach to construct a set of environmental taxes, which are approximations of the fully Pigouvian taxes; cf. Chapter 4. We ask whether approximations of the Pigouvian tax structure contribute to increasing the welfare level as compared to the uncontrolled market economy, where the emission tax vector equals zero. We also try to determine whether these taxes are useful for green accounting in a similar way to Pigouvian taxes along a cooperative solution. As in Chapter 4, this is highly relevant from a methodological perspective, since it focuses on the willingness-to-pay technique as a means of gathering policy-relevant information in a global context.

6.1   A TWO-COUNTRY GLOBAL ECONOMY

We introduce a two-country model, where the economy in each country is similar to the Brock (1977) model in Chapter 2. In order to concentrate on dealing with the global external effects arising from pollution, we neglect international trade. The terms-of-trade effects and their complications for welfare measurement are discussed in, for example, Asheim (1996). We also neglect population growth and normalize the population in each country to equal one. Later on, we consider the complications for welfare measurement due to population growth; cf. Chapter 7. We also disregard technological progress.

The instantaneous utility function facing the representative consumer in country i, $i = 1,2$ takes the form

$$u_i(t) = u_i(c_i(t), z_i(t)) \tag{6.1}$$

where $c_i(t)$ is consumption at time t and $z_i(t)$ is an indicator of environmental quality at time t. The instantaneous utility function is increasing in its arguments, strictly concave and twice continuously differentiable. If we denote the part of the stock of pollution generated by production in country i by x_i, the indicator of environmental quality in country i is defined by the concave function

$$z_i(t) = z_i(x_1(t), x_2(t)) \tag{6.2}$$

where $\partial z_i / \partial x_1 < 0$ and $\partial z_i / \partial x_2 < 0$ for all x_1 and x_2. The idea is that pollution is global and deteriorates environmental quality in all countries independently of where it is emitted.

Output is produced by labor (normalized to one), physical capital and emissions (through the use of energy input). Net output is determined by the production function

$$y_i(t) = f_i(k_i(t), g_i(t)) \tag{6.3}$$

where $k_i(t)$ is capital and $g_i(t)$ is energy input. As usual, $y_i(t)$ measures net output, so that depreciation of physical capital is accounted for. We assume that the function $f_i(\cdot)$ is twice continuously differentiable and strictly concave as well as increasing in $g_i(t)$. The stock of physical capital accumulates according to

$$\dot{k}_i(t) = f_i(k_i(t), g_i(t)) - c_i(t) \tag{6.4}$$

The stock of pollution accumulates through the firms' release of emissions. In this model, they originate from the production of energy. Following the analyses in Chapter 2 and 4, we disregard the process of producing energy and assume that emissions in country i at time t are equal to $g_i(t)$. The differential equation for $x_i(t)$ may be written as

$$\dot{x}_i(t) = g_i(t) - \gamma x_i(t) \tag{6.5}$$

where γ is the rate at which the stock of pollution depreciates (assumed to be the same in both countries).

6.2　THE NON-COOPERATIVE NASH OPEN-LOOP SOLUTION

It is well known that differential games are difficult to solve in closed form, and that an equilibrium solution may not exist.[2] However, given that a solution does exist, envelope properties of the value function enable us to derive a set of results relevant for both welfare measurement and cost–benefit analysis. To see this, suppose that the resource allocation in each country is decided by a social planner, who takes as exogenous the path for the part of the stock of pollution generated by the other country. For country i, the planner chooses $c_i(t)$ and $g_i(t)$ to maximize

$$U_i(0) = \int_0^\infty u_i(c_i(t), z_i(t))e^{-\theta t}\,dt \tag{6.6}$$

subject to the equations of motion for $k_i(t)$ and $x_i(t)$, initial conditions $k_i(0) = k_{i0}$ and $x_i(0) = x_{i0}$, and the terminal conditions $\lim_{t\to\infty} k_i(t) \geq 0$ and $\lim_{t\to\infty} x_i(t) \geq 0$. The parameter θ, which represents the rate of time preference, is assumed to be identical across countries.

The present value Hamiltonian is written

$$H_i(t) = u_i(c_i(t), z_i(t))e^{-\theta t} + \lambda_i(t)\dot{k}_i(t) + \mu_i(t)\dot{x}_i(t) \tag{6.7}$$

where $\lambda_i(t)$ and $\mu_i(t)$ are present value shadow prices in terms of utility. The necessary conditions are (neglecting the time indicator)

(i)　$\dfrac{\partial u_i(c_i, z_i)}{\partial c_i}e^{-\theta t} - \lambda_i = 0$

(ii)　$\lambda_i \dfrac{\partial f_i(k_i, g_i)}{\partial g_i} + \mu_i = 0$

(iii)　$\dot{\lambda}_i = -\lambda_i \dfrac{\partial f_i(k_i, g_i)}{\partial k_i}$　　　　　　　　　(6.8)

(iv)　$\dot{\mu}_i = -\dfrac{\partial u_i(c_i, z_i)}{\partial z_i}\dfrac{\partial z_i}{\partial x_i}e^{-\theta t} + \mu_i\gamma$

(v)　$\lim_{t\to\infty} \lambda_i \geq 0\,(= 0 \text{ if } \lim_{t\to\infty} k_i > 0)$

(vi) $\lim_{t \to \infty} \mu_i \geq 0 \, (= 0 \text{ if } \lim_{t \to \infty} x_i > 0)$

$i = 1,2$

Now let

$$\Lambda_i(t) = (c_i(t), g_i(t)), \forall t$$

We define Λ_1^n, Λ_2^n to be a Nash equilibrium iff

(i) $\{\Lambda_1^n(t)\}_0^\infty$ solves the decision problem of country 1 conditional on $\Lambda_2(t) = \Lambda_2^n(t)$ for all t.
(ii) $\{\Lambda_2^n(t)\}_0^\infty$ solves the decision problem of country 2 conditional on $\Lambda_1(t) = \Lambda_1^n(t)$ for all t.

The superindex n denotes the non-cooperative Nash equilibrium in open-loop form. Given the appropriate smoothness and concavity conditions, the simultaneous solution to the equations in (6.8) will represent a non-cooperative equilibrium.

The national welfare level of each country is measured by its (optimal) value function and the global welfare level by the sum of the value functions. If we again use Proposition 2.1, we obtain the following differential equation for the Hamiltonian along the optimal path

$$\frac{dH_i^n(t)}{dt} = -[\theta u_i(c_i^n(t), z_i^n(t)) - \frac{\partial u_i^n(t)}{\partial z_i(t)} \frac{\partial z_i^n(t)}{\partial x_j(t)} \dot{x}_j^n(t)]e^{-\theta t} \tag{6.9}$$

where $j \neq i$, $u_i^n = u_i(c_i^n, z_i^n)$, $z_i^n = z_i(x_1^n, x_2^n)$. The second term on the RHS of (6.9) comes from the direct effect of time on country i's present value Hamiltonian via $x_j(t)$, which is exogenous as long as the countries do not coordinate their decisions. Solving equation (6.9) and transforming the solution into current value gives the following welfare measure for country i:

$$\theta V_i^n(t) = H_i^{cn}(t) + \int_t^\infty \Omega_{ji}^n(s)e^{\theta t} ds \tag{6.10}$$

where $V_i^n(t) = \int_t^\infty u_i(c_i^n(s), z_i^n(s))e^{-\theta(s-t)} ds$ is the value function of country i along the Nash open-loop solution, and $H_i^{cn}(t) = H_i^n(t)e^{\theta t}$ is the current value Hamiltonian. The term $\Omega_{ji}^n(t)$ is a short notation for the last term on the RHS of equation (6.9); it measures the influence of pollution accumulation in country j on welfare in country i. In other words, the non-cooperative open-loop solution only internalizes pollution that is emitted domestically. The external effect from pollution in the other country remains uninternalized, and the last term in equation (6.10) measures the present utility value of the uninternalized part of the marginal external effect. Again, the Hamiltonian at time t does not contain all the relevant information necessary for measuring the national welfare level. Since the second term on the right hand side of equation (6.10) contains forward looking components, knowledge of the future path taken by both economies would also be required. (Note that the marginal externality contains variables related to both economies.)

Measurement of the global welfare level leads to a similar conclusion. Adding up the two national welfare indicators gives

$$\theta \sum_{i=1}^{2} V_i^n(t) = \sum_{i=1}^{2} [H_i^{c^n}(t) + \int_t^{\infty} \Omega_{ji}^n(s)e^{\theta t}ds] \qquad (6.11)$$

The economic relevance of equations (6.10) and (6.11) can be summarized as

Proposition 6.1 *If the economies follow the non-cooperative Nash open-loop solution, each national welfare measure is affected by external effects caused by pollution accumulation in other countries. These external effects remain uninternalized at the global level.*

The implication is that observable market data do not contain all the relevant information required in order to measure national and global welfare. A somewhat unattractive feature of open-loop solutions is that players choose all controls at the outset of the game. Thus the solution will typically be time inconsistent in the sense that if the agents re-optimize, without conditioning on the state of the economies, the new solution will be different from the original outcome. Even when we redo the analysis (cf. Chapter 8) under the feedback solution concept (by conditioning the controls on the state of the economies), the qualitative conclusion about welfare measurement from Proposition 6.1 remains. Essentially, when the countries do not cooperate so as to fully internalize the global external effects, the Hamiltonian at time t will fail to work as a utility-based welfare measure at both the national and global levels. This leads us to consider the cooperative solution.

6.3   THE COOPERATIVE SOLUTION

To derive the conditions for the cooperative solution, where the external effects are fully internalized at the global level, we introduce a global planner who maximizes the sum of the objective functions $U_1(0)$ and $U_2(0)$, subject to the equations of motion for the state variables (k_1, k_2, x_1, x_2) and subject to the initial and terminal conditions. The utility sum is convenient in the sense that the only difference between the non-cooperative and cooperative equilibrium solutions discussed here is how the externality is treated. A more general welfare function would not change anything essential, but will add further complications.

Among the necessary condition are

(i) $\quad \dfrac{\partial u_i(c_i, z_i)}{\partial c_i} e^{-\theta t} - \lambda_i = 0$

(ii) $\quad \lambda_i \dfrac{\partial f_i(k_i, g_i)}{\partial g_i} + \mu_i = 0$

(iii) $\quad \dot{\lambda}_i = -\lambda_i \dfrac{\partial f_i(k_i, g_i)}{\partial k_i}$

(iv) $\quad \dot{\mu}_i = -\left[\dfrac{\partial u_i(c_i, z_i)}{\partial z_i} \dfrac{\partial z_i}{\partial x_i} + \dfrac{\partial u_j(c_j, z_j)}{\partial z_j} \dfrac{\partial z_j}{\partial x_i} \right] e^{-\theta t} + \mu_i \gamma$ $\qquad$ (6.12)

(v) $\quad \lim_{t \to \infty} \lambda_i \geq 0 (= 0 \text{ if } \lim_{t \to \infty} k_i > 0)$

(vi) $\quad \lim_{t \to \infty}, \mu_i \geq 0 (= 0 \text{ if } \lim_{t \to \infty} x_i > 0)$

$\qquad$ for $i = 1, 2$ and $i \neq j$

Let us now assume that

$$\Lambda_i^*(t) = (c_i^*(t), g_i^*(t)), \ \forall t, i = 1, 2$$

solves the social planner's optimization problem, where the superindex* is used to denote the cooperative solution.

Turning to the welfare analysis, let $H^*(t) = \Sigma_{i=1}^{2} H_i^*(t)$ denote the present value Hamiltonian along the cooperative solution, where

$$H_i^*(t) = u_i(c_i^*(t), z_i^*(t)) e^{-\theta t} + \lambda_i^*(t) \dot{k}_i^*(t) + \mu_i^*(t) \dot{x}_i^*(t) \qquad (6.13)$$

From Proposition 2.1 we obtain

$$\frac{dH^*(t)}{dt} = -\theta \sum_{i=1}^{2} u_i(c_i^*(t), z_i^*(t)) e^{-\theta t} \qquad (6.14)$$

since the only non-autonomous time dependence in the global economy stems from the utility discount factor. This is so because the external effects have become fully internalized at the global level.

Solving equation (6.14) and transforming the solution into current value terms gives

$$\theta \sum_{i=1}^{2} V_i^*(t) = H^{c^*}(t) = \sum_{i=1}^{2} H_i^{c^*}(t) \qquad (6.15)$$

This amounts to having proved the following result:

Proposition 6.2 *If the economies follow the cooperative solution, then the current value Hamiltonian for the global economy, which is the sum of the two country-specific contributions to the current value Hamiltonian, is the appropriate global welfare measure.*

This may be further emphasized by linearizing the welfare measure. Applying a standard approximation procedure yields

$$\theta \sum_{i=1}^{2} V_i^*(t) \approx \sum_{i=1}^{2} \lambda_i^*(t)[c_i^*(t) + \dot{k}_i^*(t) + \rho_i^*(t) z_i^*(t) - \tau_i^*(t) \dot{x}_i^*(t)] \qquad (6.16)$$

where $\rho_i^* = (\partial u_i^* / \partial z_i) / \lambda_i^*$ is the marginal willingness to pay for an improvement in environmental quality, and $\tau_i^* = -\mu_i^*/\lambda_i^*$ is the Pigouvian tax that supports the cooperative equilibrium. Clearly, if the economies follow the cooperative equilibrium supported by this environmental tax, all terms in the parentheses on the RHS of equation (6.16) would in principle be recoverable at time t. The marginal willingness to pay for environmental improvements, ρ_i^*, can be estimated by the contingent valuation technique. Moreover, the usefulness of Pigouvian emission taxes for green accounting in a cooperative global economy is obvious from equation (6.16). These taxes measure the social value of marginal improvements in the environment (note the minus sign in front of the last term in parentheses) and provide the same information as market prices in a competitive economy.

Since the countries act as a single decision maker, it is not straightforward to split the global welfare measure into two static national welfare measures. Consider the following proposition.

Proposition 6.3 *If the economies follow the cooperative solution, each national welfare measure contains more information than is provided by its contribution to the (global) current value Hamiltonian. At the country level it holds that*

$$\theta V_i^*(t) = H^{c*}_i(t) + \int_t^\infty \Gamma_i^*(s) e^{\theta t} ds.$$

To see this, we apply Proposition 2.1 to the equation for $H_i^*(t)$ to obtain

$$\frac{dH_i^*(t)}{dt} = -\theta u_i(c_i^*(t), z_i^*(t))e^{-\theta t} + \Gamma_i^*(t) \tag{6.17}$$

where

$$\Gamma_i^*(t) = \Omega_{ji}^*(t) - \Omega_{ij}^*(t), \quad i, j = 1, 2, \ i \neq j \tag{6.18}$$

Obviously $\Gamma_1^* + \Gamma_2^* \equiv 0$. But after using Proposition 2.1 and moving to current value, the national welfare measure will take the form

$$\theta V_i^*(t) = H_i^{c^*}(t) + \int_t^\infty \Gamma_i^*(s)e^{\theta t}ds \tag{6.19}$$

In other words, the national welfare measure will typically contain forward looking components (an exception is a steady state, where the extra term vanishes). Since the marginal benefits and costs of pollution control are balanced at the global level, the sum of the two forward looking components will net out at the global level. From the point of view of an individual country, there is still a discrepancy between what the country pays, in terms of pollution charges, and the benefits it receives from pollution control.

6.4 THE MARKET ECONOMY

Let us now address a number of interrelated issues. We have not yet introduced formal conditions that environmental taxes have to fulfill in order to support the non-cooperative Nash solution and the cooperative solution, respectively. These conditions turn out to be unduly unrealistic to implement, since, among other things, the introduction of these taxes requires that the complete solution paths be known in advance. We therefore formulate the concept of a conditional equilibrium, that is, the equilibrium that the market economies will end up in given a fully specified (although typically suboptimal) dynamic environmental tax. We then consider tax reform in the conditional equilibrium by examining the conditions under which a cooperative project to increase the environmental taxes will be welfare improving at the global level. In particular, we consider the one-country rule in Chapter 4, whereby welfare is increased as long as the conditional environmental tax is systematically lower than the marginal damage. Another concern is to investigate to what extent approximations of Pigouvian taxes can be used for welfare measurement or, more precisely, what determines the magnitude of error if the environmental tax is based on static willingness-to-pay data.

We begin with a brief description of the outcome in the (imperfectly) controlled market economy. Suppose that an emission tax $\tau_i^0(t)$ is levied on the firm in country i, and that the tax revenues $\tau_i^0(t)g_i(t)$ are given to the consumer as a lump-sum transfer. A short cut to the market solution would be to note that the fundamental difference between a first best solution and the decentralized market solution is that the stock of pollution is not a state variable in the latter case; instead it is a side effect of the firms' decisions to pollute, and its path is exogenous to the consumer.

In addition to the initial condition for the stock of physical capital and the transversality condition, the necessary conditions obeyed by the decentralized solution are

(i) $$\frac{\partial u_i(c_i^0, z_i^0)}{\partial c_i} e^{-\theta t} - \lambda_i^0 = 0$$

(ii) $$\frac{\partial f_i^0(k_i^0, g_i^0)}{\partial g_i} - \tau_i^0 = 0$$

(iii) $$\dot{\lambda}_i^0 = -\lambda_i^0 \frac{\partial f_i(k_i^0, g_i^0)}{\partial k_i} \qquad\qquad (6.20)$$

(iv) $$\dot{k}_i^0 = f_i(k_i^0, g_i^0) - c_i^0$$

$$i = 1,2 \text{ and } t \in [0,\infty)$$

The time index has been suppressed and the superindex 0 is used to denote the solution in the controlled global market economy which is conditional on $\tau_i^0(t)$. We refer to this as the conditional equilibrium solution.

6.4.1   A Pigouvian View

We have already hinted that the shadow prices of pollution in a money metrics may be interpreted as Pigouvian-related taxes. With the decentralized solution at our disposal, we are now able to justify this statement.

Proposition 6.4 *(i) If $\tau_i^0(t) = \tau_i^n(t) = -\mu_i^n(t) / \lambda_i^n(t)$ $\forall t, i = 1,2$, the conditional equilibrium replicates the non-cooperative Nash open-loop solution.*
(ii) If $\tau_i^0(t) = \tau_i^*(t) = -\mu_i^*(t) / \lambda_i^*(t)$, $\forall t, i = 1,2$, the conditional equilibrium replicates the cooperative solution.

Proof: To prove (i), replace $\tau_i^0(t)$ in equations (6.20) by $\tau_i^n(t) = -\mu_i^n(t) / \lambda_i^n(t)$. It follows that $(c_i^n(t), g_i^n(t), k_i^n(t), \lambda_i^n(t)), t \in [0,\infty)$ obeys the necessary conditions in equations (6.20). Finally, solving equation (6.5), given the initial condition on $x(0)$, yields $x_i^n(t)$. The proof of (ii) is analogous. ∎

We refer to $\tau_i^n(t)$ as the non-cooperative Pigouvian tax and $\tau_i^*(t)$ as the full Pigouvian tax for country i. To emphasize the difference between the two Pigouvian-related taxes, we solve for the shadow prices for the stock of pollution using the transversality conditions. We obtain (assuming that the terminal condition on x_i does not bind)

$$\mu_i^n(t) = \int_t^\infty \frac{\partial u_i^n(s)}{\partial z_i} \frac{\partial z_i^n(s)}{\partial x_i} e^{-\theta s} e^{-\gamma(s-t)} ds \qquad (6.21)$$

$$\mu_i^*(t) = \int_t^\infty \left[\frac{\partial u_i^*(s)}{\partial z_i} \frac{\partial z_i^*(s)}{\partial x_i} + \frac{\partial u_j^*(s)}{\partial z_j} \frac{\partial z_j^*(s)}{\partial x_i} \right] e^{-\theta s} e^{-\gamma(s-t)} ds \qquad (6.22)$$

$i = 1,2$

Clearly, $\mu_i^n(t)$ and, hence, $\tau_i^n(t)$ only take into account that pollution in country i affects the utility of the consumer in country i (as a consequence of the non-cooperative solution concept). The implication is that non-cooperative Pigouvian taxes only capture part of the social value of additional pollution, which explains the 'missing information problem' in market data. This problem is absent at the global level in the fully cooperative solution, because $\mu_i^*(t)$ and, therefore, $\tau_i^*(t)$ reflect all direct utility effects of pollution caused by country i.

Another aspect of dynamic Pigouvian taxes, under *stock externalities*, is that they are forward looking, and, in practice, impossible to implement. For example, the full cooperative solution cannot be implemented without solving the social planner's problem from today onwards into the entire future. Hence the probability that a global environmental tax reform will bring the global economy to a fully cooperative equilibrium is very close to zero. Policy makers thus have to find conditions under which an environmental tax reform, starting from a conditional equilibrium typically different from the Nash non-cooperative solution, improves not only domestic welfare, but, in particular, global welfare.

6.4.2 Tax Reform in the Conditional Equilibrium

We can now use the properties of the conditional equilibrium introduced above to study which factors determine the welfare consequences that arise if the two countries, starting from a conditional equilibrium, agree to make slight changes in their emission taxes.

The initial tax structure is given by the paths $\{\tau_i^0(t)\}_0^\infty$, $i = 1,2$. We want to measure the welfare consequences of changing these taxes to $\tau_1^0(t) + \alpha$ and $\tau_2^0(t) + \beta$, respectively, for all t, where α and β are positive constants. To focus on efficiency aspects of the tax reform, additional revenues are given back to the consumer in a lump-sum fashion.

The optimal value function is written

$$W^0(0;\xi) = \sum_{i=1}^{2} V_i^0(0;\xi) = \int_0^\infty \left[\sum_{i=1}^{2} u_i(c_i^0(t;\xi), z_i^0(t;\xi)) \right] e^{-\theta t} dt \quad (6.23)$$

where ξ is a parameter vector with α and β as two of its elements, while $V_i^0(0;\xi)$ is the optimal value or maximized utility function of country i, and $W^0(0;\xi)$ is the optimal global value function. Assuming that the optimal value functions are differentiable, we can derive a cost–benefit rule for the suggested tax reform by differentiating the optimal value function with respect to α and β, respectively and evaluating the derivatives at $\alpha = \beta = 0$. Our next step is to evaluate the welfare effect of implementing the agreement to marginally increase emission taxes in both countries:

$$\Delta W^0 = \frac{\partial W^0(0;\xi)}{\partial \alpha} d\alpha + \frac{\partial W^0(0;\xi)}{\partial \beta} d\beta \quad (6.24)$$

It is shown in Appendix D that the cost–benefit rule for α can be written as

$$\frac{\partial W^0(0,\xi)}{\partial \alpha} = \int_0^\infty \left[\sum_{i=1}^{2} \lambda_i^0 \tau_i^0 \frac{\partial g_i^0}{\partial \alpha} + \left(\sum_{i=1}^{2} \sum_{j=1}^{2} \frac{\partial u_i^0}{\partial z_i} \frac{\partial z_i}{\partial x_j} \frac{\partial x_j^0}{\partial \alpha} \right) \right] e^{-\theta t} dt \quad (6.25)$$

where the parameter vector ξ and the time indicator have been suppressed to simplify notation.

In general, a small change in environmental taxation typically affects the welfare level because the tax had not been optimally chosen prior to the reform. The only preexisting distortions here refer to the possibly suboptimal generation of emissions in both countries: the emission tax paths $\{\tau_i^0(t)\}_0^\infty$ do not necessarily reflect the disutility of pollution. Therefore, the global welfare effect of changing country 1's emission tax arises via responses in g_1^0, g_2^0, x_1^0, and x_2^0 whereas the effects from all other behavioral responses will vanish from the welfare measure as a consequence of optimization. The cost–benefit rule for changes in β is, of course, completely symmetric with equation (6.25). We only have to substitute β for α.

It was shown in Chapter 4 that welfare will always increase when an emission tax, which is systematically lower than the marginal damage, is increased. In this spirit, the emission taxes can now be rewritten as if they are 'biased' estimates of the marginal damage. Formally, the emission taxes in the conditional equilibrium are written as

$$\tau_i^0(t) = -\int_t^\infty \left[\frac{\partial u_i^0(s)}{\partial z_i} \frac{\partial z_i^0(s)}{\partial x_i} + \frac{\partial u_j^0(s)}{\partial z_j} \frac{\partial z_j^0(s)}{\partial x_i} + b_i(s) \right] e^{-\theta s} e^{-\gamma(s-t)} ds / \lambda_i^0(t),$$

(6.26)

for all t, where $i = 1.2$ and $i \neq j$. The term $b_i(t)$ is the bias relevant for country i at time t, that is, the magnitude by which the actual emission tax deviates from the correct evaluation of the damage to the environment caused by country i; cf. Chapter 4. Note that a negative bias implies that the tax is set below the marginal damage.

By analogy to Proposition 4.1, we can derive

Proposition 6.5 *If the emission taxes in the conditional equilibrium are written as in equation (6.26), the cost–benefit rules in (6.25) can be rewritten as*

$$\frac{\partial W^0(0,\xi)}{\partial \alpha} = -\int_0^\infty \left[\sum_{i=1}^2 b_i(t) \frac{\partial x_i^0(t)}{\partial \alpha} \right] e^{-\theta t} dt$$

$$\frac{\partial W^0(0,\xi)}{\partial \beta} = -\int_0^\infty \left[\sum_{i=1}^2 b_i(t) \frac{\partial x_i^0(t)}{\partial \beta} \right] e^{-\theta t} dt$$

Proof: See Appendix D.

To evaluate the welfare effects of an agreement to increase or reduce emission taxes permanently at time 0, we have to know of b_1 and b_2 for all t, as well as how α and β affect x_1^0 and x_2^0. Clearly, by increasing the emission tax in one country, the firms in this country would reduce inputs that create emissions. In other words $\partial g_1^0/\partial \alpha < 0$ and $\partial g_2^0/\partial \beta < 0$ for all t. This result follows directly from neoclassical production theory since an increased emission tax works in the same way as an increased factor price. Moreover, since

$$x_i^0(t) = x_i(0)e^{-\gamma t} + \int_0^t g_i^0(s)e^{\gamma(s-t)} ds$$

it follows that $\partial x_1^0/\partial \alpha < 0$ and $\partial x_2^0/\partial \beta < 0$ for all t. However, it remains unclear how increased emission taxes in country 1 (2) affect $x_2^0(x_1^0)$, so the signs of the derivatives $\partial x_1^0/\partial \beta$ and $\partial x_2^0/\partial \alpha$ cannot be determined without additional information. The interpretation is that even if the emission tax chosen by each country underestimates the marginal damage to the environment caused by that country's emissions (that is, even if $b_1 > 0$, and $b_2 > 0$ for all t), it is still not clear that it is optimal to agree on higher emission taxes.[3]

The welfare effect can be related to the biases b_1 and b_2 by imposing restrictions on how the environmental policy pursued in each country affects the production decisions of the other country. The mechanism that complicates the analysis is that an environmental tax in country 1 typically affects the marginal utility of consumption in country 2 directly through a change in the stock of pollution, x_1. The reason is that the environmental quality $z_2(x_1,x_2)$ is a function of pollution in both countries. The changed consumption level induces a change in production, in emissions and in the stock of pollution in country 2. These insights can be used to introduce the following result.

Proposition 6.6 *Suppose that* $u_i(c_i,z_i) = \phi_i(c_i) + \kappa_i z_i$, *and* $\kappa_i > 0$ *is a constant. Then, if* $b_i(t) > 0$, $i = 1,2$ *for all* t, *we have* $\partial W^0(0,\xi) / \partial \alpha > 0$, *and* $\partial W^0(0,\xi)/ \partial \beta > 0$.

The proof rests on the fact that, in the case of additive separability between consumption and environmental quality, a change in α (β) will not affect the marginal utility of consumption in country 2 (1), and $\partial x_2^0/\partial \alpha = 0$ ($\partial x_1^0/\partial \beta = 0$).

In other words, if the environmental taxes in the two market economies are set independently of (not conditioned on) the magnitude of the marginal damage, the separabilty assumption will be sufficient to guarantee that the signs of the bias terms, b_1 and b_2, determine how the emission taxes must be changed in order to improve the welfare level. It is welfare improving to increase (reduce) both emission taxes if the pre-reform emission tax paths systematically underestimate (overestimate) the marginal disutility of pollution. However, we have not in general been able to rule out the possibility that higher emission taxation in say country 1 contributes to increased emissions in country 2.

6.4.3   Some Other Special Cases

Proposition 6.5 may also be regarded as providing a generalization of results derived earlier. Many studies on environmental policy have (at least implicitly) assumed that environmental damage is a 'national problem' by using a *representative agent model*. In the context of our framework, this assumption would imply $\partial z_i / \partial x_j = 0$ for $i = 1,2$, and $j \neq i$. As a consequence, $\partial W^0/\partial \alpha =$

$\partial V_1^0/\partial \alpha$ and $\partial W^0/\partial \beta = \partial V_2^0/\partial \beta$. We can then use Proposition 6.5 to establish the following special case introduced in Chapter 4.

Corollary 6.1 *If* $u_i(c_i,z_i(x_1,x_2)) = \varphi_i(c_i,x_i)$ *for* $i = 1,2$, *the cost–benefit rules for changes in* α *and* β *reduce to read*

$$\frac{\partial W^0(0,\xi)}{\partial \alpha} = -\int_0^\infty b_1(t)\frac{\partial x_1^0(t)}{\partial \alpha}e^{-\theta t}dt$$

$$\frac{\partial W^0(0,\xi)}{\partial \beta} = -\int_0^\infty b_2(t)\frac{\partial x_2^0}{\partial \beta}e^{-\theta t}dt$$

In other words, Proposition 4.1 in Chapter 4 follows as a special case.

A number of studies on international environmental policies are based on the assumption that the alternative to the cooperative outcome is a non-cooperative Nash open-loop game between 'national social planners'. The welfare effect of an agreement between countries to increase their emission taxes, starting from a Nash equilibrium, can be analysed by comparing the shape of the tax that supports the Nash equilibrium and equation (6.26), which defines the conditional tax in terms of the bias.[4] It follows from this comparison that

$$b_i(t) = -\frac{\partial u_j}{\partial z_j}\frac{\partial z_j}{\partial x_i} \quad i = 1,2, i \neq j$$

From Proposition 6.5 we obtain

$$\frac{\partial W^n(0,\xi)}{\partial \alpha} = \int_0^\infty \left[\frac{\partial u_2^n(t)}{\partial z_2}\frac{\partial z_2^n(t)}{\partial x_1}\frac{\partial x_1^n(t)}{\partial \alpha} + \frac{\partial u_1^n(t)}{\partial z_1}\frac{\partial z_1^n(t)}{\partial x_2}\frac{\partial x_2^n(t)}{\partial \alpha}\right]e^{-\theta t}dt \quad (6.27)$$

$$\frac{\partial W^n(0,\xi)}{\partial \beta} = \int_0^\infty \left[\frac{\partial u_1^n(t)}{\partial z_1}\frac{\partial z_1^n(t)}{\partial x_2}\frac{\partial x_2^n(t)}{\partial \beta} + \frac{\partial u_2^n(t)}{\partial z_2}\frac{\partial z_2^n(t)}{\partial x_1}\frac{\partial x_1^n(t)}{\partial \beta}\right]e^{-\theta t}dt \quad (6.28)$$

The Nash non-cooperative equilibrium implies that any externalities which would otherwise arise from the release of emissions by domestic producers become internalized, whereas the externalities which are due to the interaction among countries remain uninternalized. As a consequence, the cost–benefit rule would be expected to reflect interaction effects across countries due to changes in their emission taxes. According to equations (6.27) and (6.28), this is precisely what happens, since α and β affect $u_1(\cdot)$ via x_2 and $u_2(\cdot)$ via x_1. All other behavioral effects of higher emission taxes vanish from the cost–benefit rule as a consequence of optimization on a national basis. Nevertheless, even if the pre-reform equilibrium is the outcome of a non-cooperative Nash game, an agreement to slightly increase emission taxes may change the overall welfare level in either direction.

However, under the conditions in Proposition 6.6 – with the instantaneous utility functions being additive separable – the suggested tax reform will, of course, be welfare improving. Another implication of starting at a non-cooperative equilibrium is that the national effect due to the welfare reform vanishes, that is, $\partial V_1^n/\partial\alpha = \partial V_2^n/\partial\beta = 0$. The positive global welfare effect originates from the influence of α on country 2 via the decrease in x_1^n, and of β on country 1 via the decrease in x_2^n. In other words, if the policy maker in one country does not believe that the other country will adhere to the agreement, she will, under a non-cooperative Nash equilibrium, have no incentive to increase the emission tax.

We have established that global welfare may in fact decrease due to a tax reform where the involved countries agree to slightly increase their environmental taxes, even if the taxes initially are lower than the marginal damage. However, this has not yet been proved formally. A counterexample would suffice. But even under additive separable utility functions (which support the standard result), a formal proof is elusive. Starting from a non-cooperative Nash equilibrium, we can assume that the environmental quality in country 2 does not depend on the stock that has been emitted in country 1, that is, $z_2 = z_2(x_2)$. It then follows that $\partial z_2^n/\partial x_1 = 0$ and $\partial x_2^n/\partial\alpha = 0$. The last derivative is zero because the marginal damage in country 2 does not depend on emissions in country 1. In these circumstances, equation (6.27) tells us that $\partial W^n/\partial\alpha = 0$. As will become clear later on, we have not yet been able to construct a counterexample to the standard result; cf. Chapter 7.

6.5 THE ALMOST COOPERATIVE SOLUTION

The emission tax paths that support the fully cooperative equilibrium clearly play two distinct roles in the context of a market economy: they bring the economy to the social optimum and, according to Proposition 6.2, they are directly useful for accounting purposes at the global level. However, the implementation problems are huge. We therefore investigate the consequences of a more practically feasible approach to welfare measurement. Suppose that, as in Chapter 4, we were to construct static approximations of the fully Pigouvian taxes using currently available (or collectable) willingness-to-pay information. Two questions may then be asked. First, will the approximation of the Pigouvian tax improve the welfare level as compared with the decentralized market solution? Second, is the information provided by such taxes useful from the point of view of social accounting?

A static approximation of the fully Pigouvian taxes refers to a set of emission taxes equal to those that would support the cooperative equilibrium if the marginal disutility of pollution were constant over time. However, since the fully Pigouvian taxes for stock externalities are, in general, forward looking and not constant over time, we assume that the taxes are revised repeatedly as new willingness-to-pay information becomes available. We explored these approximations of Pigouvian taxes in a one-country context in Chapter 4. There, the relevant willingness-to-pay information could be recovered and used by asking questions to the consumer. Here, however, matters become more complicated because the marginal utility of money differs between countries.

To construct a static analogue to the fully Pigouvian tax for country i at time t, we use the effects of a change in x_i on the consumers in countries i and j at time t. More specifically, we would like to measure the sum of the following two terms

$$R_{ii}^0(t)/\lambda_i^{c^0}(t) = \frac{\partial u_i^0(t)}{\partial z_i} \frac{\partial z_i^0(t)}{\partial x_i} / \lambda_i^{c^0}(t) \tag{6.29}$$

$$R_{ji}^0(t)/\lambda_i^{c^0}(t) = \frac{\partial u_j^0(t)}{\partial z_j} \frac{\partial z_j^0(t)}{\partial x_i} / \lambda_i^{c^0}(t) \tag{6.30}$$

where $\lambda_i^{c^0}(t) = \partial u_i^0(t)/\partial c_i(t)$ is the current value utility shadow price of consumption units. If we were to ask the consumer in country i how much he/she is willing to pay to reduce domestic pollution marginally at time t, the answer would be the marginal rate of substitution between x_i^0 and c_i^0, which corresponds to the expression in formula (6.29). It is more difficult to obtain information about the second term (equation (6.30)) by means of the willingness-to-pay technique, since the consumer in country j would be willing to pay $-R_{ji}^0/\lambda_j^{c^0}$ rather than $-R_{ji}^0/\lambda_i^{c^0}$ for a marginal reduction in x_i^0. Therefore, to identify equation (6.30), we need information about the ratio $\lambda_j^{c^0}/\lambda_i^{c^0}$ that is, the relative marginal utility of consumption at equilibrium. In principle, this is recoverable by econometric methods, since estimates of consumer demand parameters provide information about the utility functions.[5] It would be a severe exaggeration to claim that this is routinely done in practice.

Suppose, for the sake of the argument, we are actually able to collect all this information via the willingness-to-pay technique and econometric analysis of consumer demand. This information could then be used to construct a static approximation of the fully Pigouvian taxes. Clearly, collecting all this information is time consuming, which in itself gives rise to complications. Suppose that it takes Δt units of time until new information becomes available, and consider

$$\overline{\tau}_i^0(t) = -\left[\overline{R}_{ii}^0 + \overline{R}_{ji}^0\right]/[(\theta + \gamma)\lambda_i^{c^0}] \tag{6.31}$$

as a possible approximation of the fully Pigouvian tax for country i on the time interval $(t, t + \Delta t)$, where $\overline{R}_{ii}^0$ and $\overline{R}_{ji}^0$ are constants and equal to $R_{ii}^0(t)$ and $R_{ji}^0(t)$, respectively. To design these emission taxes, we have only used information that is recoverable at time t. Hence, $\overline{\tau}_i^0(t)$ may be regarded as a static approximation of the fully Pigouvian tax at time t, where it has been implicitly assumed that the future repercussions of each unit emitted at time t, except for discounting and depreciation, remain constant and equal to the marginal rate of substitution between pollution and consumption at time t. According to this approach the marginal product of energy $\partial f_i(k_i^0, g_i^0)/\partial g_i$ will, under profit maximization, be equal to a static approximation of the future marginal cost of pollution.

Let us now examine to what extent the approximation of the fully Pigouvian tax structure solves the 'missing information problem' which typically invalidates static welfare measurement at the global level. In other words, given an approximation of the fully Pigouvian taxes, under what conditions is it possible to measure global welfare using a static index (interpretable as the sum of green NNPs) similar to the procedure in equation (6.15) above?

We start by substituting $\overline{\tau}_i^0(t)$ into the necessary conditions obeyed by the decentralized economy. It then follows that the necessary conditions in equations (6.20) appear to have been derived from the following pseudo-Hamiltonian.

$$H_p^0(t) = \sum_{i=1}^2 u_i(c_i^0(t), z_i^0(t))e^{-\theta t} + \sum_{i=1}^2 \lambda_i^0(t)\dot{k}_i^0(t) - \sum_{i=1}^2 \lambda_i^0(t)\overline{\tau}_i^0(t)\dot{x}_i^0(t) \tag{6.32}$$

for $i \neq j$, which looks like the sum in utility terms of green NNP measures at time t discounted to present value, given the approximation of the emission tax discussed above. In the appendix, we show that the time derivative of equation (6.32) takes the form

$$\frac{dH_p^0(t)}{dt} = -\theta \sum_{i=1}^2 u_i(c_i^0(t), z_i^0(t))e^{-\theta t} \quad \text{on } (t, t + \Delta t) \tag{6.33}$$

which is analogous to equation (4.17) in Chapter 4. Integrating over each short time interval and summing these integrals up to time T gives

$$H_p^0(T) = H_p^0(t) - \theta \sum_{s=t}^{T-\Delta s} \left[\int_s^{s+\Delta s} \sum_{i=1}^{2} u_i(c_i^0(\varsigma), z_i^0(\varsigma)) e^{-\theta \varsigma} d\varsigma \right] \quad (6.34)$$

To prove the welfare equivalence of the pseudo-Hamiltonian at time t, it would need to be assumed that $H_p^0(T)$ approaches zero when T goes to infinity. This mathematical property of a present value Hamiltonian in 'well-behaved' infinite horizon control problems was derived by Michel (1982). By analogy to the corresponding reasoning in Chapter 4, Michel's result does not apply here, because equation (6.33) holds only on open intervals $(t, t + \Delta t)$. Discrete information collection introduces discontinuities into the problem. The upper limit of integration on $(s, s + \Delta s)$ will, in general, differ from the lower limit of integration on $(s + \Delta s, s + 2\Delta s)$. Every such point of discontinuity may contribute to making the limit of $H_p^0(T)$ different from zero.

As in Chapter 4, only if the prediction errors caused by the discontinuities cancel out, and the pseudo-Hamiltonian approaches zero when time goes to infinity, are we able to derive the welfare measure

$$\theta W^0(t) = H_p^{c^0}(t) \quad (6.35)$$

where $H_p^{c^0}(t) = H_p^0(t)e^{\theta t}$ and $W^0(t)$ is the value function. We summarize this result in the following observation:

Proposition 6.7 *If the fully Pigouvian tax rate by is approximated by $\overline{\tau}_i^0(t)$ and if the contribution to future utility from the discrete estimation procedure for the social damage of pollution becomes small in the sense that $\lim_{T \to \infty} H_p^0(T) \approx 0$, then the global welfare level at time t is closely approximated by the sum of countries' green utility NNP measures.*

Accordingly, approximations of the fully Pigouvian taxes play nearly the same role in social accounting as fully Pigouvian taxes would in the decentralized version of the fully cooperative equilibrium.

Given the conditions in Proposition 6.7, we have reconciled the growth theoretical approach to social accounting with the static willingness-to-pay approach to environmental goods. Under the appropriate linearity and separability assumptions, $\overline{\tau}_i^0(t)$ measures the full Pigouvian tax of country i.

Proposition 6.8 *If willingness-to-pay information can be collected continuously, and if the following two conditions hold: (i) $u_i(c_i(t), z_i(t)) = \phi_i(c_i(t)) + \kappa_i z_i^0(t)$, where κ_i is a constant, and (ii) $z_i = \rho_i^i x_i + \rho_i^j x_j$, where ρ_i^i and ρ_i^j are constants, then $\overline{\tau}_i^0(t) = \tau_i^*(t)$.*

To see this, note that given the assumptions, the marginal damage from pollution is constant over time and the Pigouvian tax for country i equals

$$\tau_i^*(t) = (\kappa_i \rho_i^i + \kappa_j \rho_j^i) / [(\theta + \gamma)\lambda_i^{c^0}(t)] = \bar{\tau}_i^0(t) \text{ for all } t$$

Proposition 6.8 gives a sufficient condition for the tax to be equal to the fully Pigouvian tax and for the economies to follow the socially optimal path. Note that, if the utility function is non-linear in the pollution arguments, not even continuous collection of information would imply that the tax path is Pigouvian, since the instantaneous shadow price of pollution will be forward looking and is not correctly estimated in this case. The fact that the conditions in Proposition 6.8 are not necessary is purely a technicality, because when starting from a steady state, $\tau_i^0(t) = \bar{\tau}_i^0(t) = $ constant for all t. This means that 'the almost cooperative economy' has the same steady state, if it exists, as the cooperative equilibrium.

Continuous measurement of environmental damage is of course also very restrictive. But as shown by Backlund's (2000, 2003) numerical calculations in a one-country context, good approximations of future welfare are obtained even if the distance between measurements is five to ten years; see also Chapter 4.

In the general case, we have not been able to prove that approximations of the Pigouvian tax are welfare improving, compared with the uncontrolled market economy. On the other hand, the cooperative equilibrium and its controlled approximation have the same steady state solution, when the equilibrium is defined conditional on the approximation of the Pigouvian tax paths. Therefore, provided that the tax policy brings the economy to a (unique?) steady state, we will eventually approach the cooperative solution, which can never be approached by the uncontrolled market economy. Hence, sooner or later, the 'almost cooperative solution will be welfare improving. Moreover, the results associated with Proposition 6.5 are of course also valid in this case.

6.6 CONCLUSIONS

Global external effects give rise to fundamental valuation problems relevant to green accounting. Such problems have typically been ignored in previous studies. In this chapter we have explored the conditions under which appropriate national and global welfare measures are related to national and/or global tax policies used in attempts to improve the allocation of resources. We would like to emphasize the following results:

1. If the economies follow the non-cooperative Nash solution path, or any conditional market equilibrium path, neither the national welfare level nor

global welfare can be exactly measured by a static index related to green utility NNP (the Hamiltonian). The reason is that only some of the external effects become internalized along a conditional equilibrium path. The uninternalized part of the external effects, at both the national and global levels, will render the economic system non-autonomous (fundamentally time dependent), which creates valuation problems similar to those in previous chapters.

2. If the economies follow the full cooperative solution path, the global welfare level is appropriately measured by the sum of the individual countries' green utility NNPs. However, since the cooperative solution implies that the countries act as 'a single decision maker', it is not straightforward to split the sum of the utility NNPs into national welfare measures. Even if the external effects have become internalized at the global level, there remains an imbalance between marginal cost and marginal benefits at the national level. Therefore, an interesting implication of welfare analysis in the non-cooperative and cooperative equilibria is that observable static indices do not suffice for measuring national welfare, regardless of whether or not the countries cooperate in order to control for external effects.

3. In the context of a one-country economy – and with no distortions other than environmental damages resulting from production – welfare increases with the magnitude of the emission tax, as long as the tax falls short of the marginal social damage. In general, this does not hold in a multi-country economy, where the environmental policies undertaken by one country are likely to affect the production decisions in other countries. Thus, although the cooperative equilibrium is welfare superior to any other equilibrium, a small step from any conditional equilibrium towards the cooperative equilibrium does not necessarily improve global welfare.

4. If the utility functions in both countries are assumed to be additive separable in consumption and environmental quality, the one country result will go through; that is, global welfare will increase if the conditional equilibrium in which the tax reform is implemented means that initial environmental taxes are systematically lower than the marginal damages in each country.

5. The fully cooperative (and even the non-cooperative Nash) solution cannot be implemented without an enormous amount of information about the future marginal damage along the first best path of the global economy, which is infeasible in the real world. We have shown that it is, in principle, possible to use currently available willingness-to-pay information to implement an 'almost cooperative solution', which has the same steady state as the fully cooperative solution. It remains an open question whether the 'prediction errors' caused by approximation of the Pigouvian tax structure will invalidate the welfare interpretation of the resulting green utility NNP measures (the Hamiltonians).

6. In real world situations, distortionary taxation creates additional complications for welfare measurement, some of which were dealt with in Chapter 5. However, the extent to which it pays to look for approximations of first best Pigouvian taxes remains unclear. Analyzing a (numerical) second best version of the cooperative solution might be a natural next step. In the next chapter, we turn to a numerical version of the model in Chapter 6, augmented with technological progress and population growth. The idea is to check the magnitude of the error that is created in welfare measurement at a conditional equilibrium due to the use of the green NNPs, rather than exact welfare measures.

NOTES

1. Further examples are Barrett (1990, 1994), Carraro and Siniscalco (1993), Cesar (1994), Tahvonen (1994) and Mäler and de Zeuuw (1995), to mention a few.
2. Explicit solutions usually require a set of simplifying assumptions; see for example, Hoel (1978), Clark (1980), Levhari and Mirman (1980), Dockner et al. (1985) and Tahvonen (1984). One of the most comprehensive statements of the theory of differential games has been provided by Basar and Olsder (1982).
3. As in Chapter 4, it is important to distinguish between a small cooperative project – which is the concern here – and the implementation of the full cooperative equilibrium. Our point is simply that the latter trick is virtually impossible in market economies under stock externalities.
4. See also Aronsson and Löfgren (2001).
5. The price index approach outlined in Chapter 3 can also be used; the reader is also referred to Weitzman (2001).

7. Numerical applications: dynamic global economy models

Except for the numerical analysis set out in Chapter 4, where our main concern was to establish whether a static approximation of the Pigouvian tax constitutes a reasonable approximation of the shadow price of pollution, we have so far concentrated on theoretical aspects of social accounting. The theoretical analysis helps us understand how national and global welfare measures depend on the functioning of the economic system. Moreover, it provides a general understanding of how the tool kit developed in earlier chapters can be applied to derive exact welfare measures.

On the other hand, theoretical models do not allow us to assess the empirical importance of different parts of the welfare measures (for example, the relative welfare contributions of technological change, market distortions, and so on). In this chapter, we return to the discussion in Section 4.4, while at the same time shifting our focus to the analysis of global economy models. The main purpose is to address the welfare contributions of external effects and technological change by means of numerical methods. To be more specific, is it necessary to estimate such welfare contributions in order to arrive at an accurate – or at least reasonably accurate – estimate of the correct welfare measure, or is it possible to proceed *as if* the resource allocation is a first best equilibrium with a stationary technology? Given the enormous difficulties involved in practical applications of social accounting, it is helpful to know to what extent different entities are likely to contribute to welfare measures. This is further emphasized by the apparent need for green national accounts: according to Agenda 21, following the 1992 United Nations Conference on Environment and Development (UNCED 1992), the participating countries agreed to develop green national accounts.

In comparison with the numerical analysis in Chapter 4, this chapter offers two extensions. The first is to address the welfare measurement problem in a global economy. This provides a natural complement to Chapter 6, where we compared the equilibrium of an uncontrolled market economy, the non-cooperative Nash equilibrium and a cooperative equilibrium from the perspective of measuring measure welfare at the national and global levels. One idea behind the numerical extension is to provide a better understanding of the complex issues underlying welfare measurement in an economy with several countries.

This is particularly interesting because there are very few studies on welfare measurement in a global economy, despite the fact that spillover effects such as those analyzed in Chapter 6 characterize many environmental problems. Numerical analysis within a similar model framework also enables us to assess the importance of external effects associated with both domestic and transboundary environmental problems.

The second extension is to address the welfare contributions of external effects in production and technological change. The fact that we have (almost) neglected external effects in production so far does not mean that they are unimportant; their absence is a consequence of our choice of reference model, in which external effects arise because a stock of pollution is an argument in the utility function. Moreover, in the context of theoretical studies, it is not particularly important whether external effects are associated with consumption or production. At the same time, we realize that this distinction may be empirically important. The external effects in production analyzed here are due to the stock of greenhouse gases which accumulates from carbon dioxide emissions. The analysis here is carried out in the context of a global economy, where the world is divided into a rich and a poor region. Our basic idea is to assess, in terms of a simplified world economy, how much technological change and external effects in production from greenhouse gases contribute to national and global welfare measures. Since the regions exhibit considerable differences in production possibilities, an additional contribution of this chapter is to compare the two regions from the point of view of the properties of national welfare measures.

7.1   A BASIC ECONOMY WITH TRANSBOUNDARY ENVIRONMENTAL PROBLEMS

We now turn to a straightforward numerical application of the 'global economy problem' in Chapter 6. The basic idea behind the numerical analysis is to be able to illustrate, and discuss in greater detail, some of the issues we addressed in Chapter 6. It also serves as a starting point for the analyses to come in Section 7.2. The model constitutes a two-country economy, where the population in each country is constant and normalized to one. We disregard technological change for the time being; instead, both technological change and population growth will be introduced in Section 7.2.

Our approach focuses on comparing the correct welfare measure – interest on the present value of future utility – with the current value Hamiltonian under three different assumptions about how the resource allocation is determined: (i) the countries are uncontrolled market economies; (ii) the countries act as if they play a non-cooperative Nash game in open-loop form; and (iii) the countries act as if the resource allocation is a cooperative equilibrium. In addition, this comparison is carried out at both the national and global levels. Recall that the model in Chapter 6 did not consider market imperfections other than external effects in consumption associated with environmental quality. Therefore, it is temporarily convenient to neglect technological change and population growth for illustrative purposes, in the sense that any discrepancy between interest on the present value of future utility and the current value Hamiltonian is associated with the welfare contributions of external effects.

7.1.1 The Model

Let us start by introducing the model. Unless indicated otherwise, the notations are the same as in Chapter 6. The instantaneous utility function facing the consumer in each country is of Cobb–Douglas type, that is,

$$u_i(t) = u_i(c_i(t), z_i(t)) = \alpha_{i0} c_i(t)^{\alpha_{i1}} z_i(t)^{(1-\alpha_{i1})} \tag{7.1}$$

for $i = 1,2$ where z_i, the indicator of environmental quality, is defined as

$$z_i(t) = \alpha_{i2} - \alpha_{i3} x_1(t)^{\alpha_{i4}} - \alpha_{i5} x_2(t)^{\alpha_{i6}} \tag{7.2}$$

Turning to the production side of the economy, output is produced using labor, capital and energy. As before, we disregard the possibility that leisure affects utility. Instead, we assume that the consumer supplies one unit of labor inelastically at each point in time. The production function is also assumed to be of Cobb–Douglas type. By suppressing the effect of labor, the net production function can be written

$$f_i(k_i(t), g_i(t)) = \beta_{i0} k_i(t)^{\beta_{i1}} g_i(t)^{\beta_{i2}} - \delta_i k_i(t) \tag{7.3}$$

where δ is the rate of capital depreciation. Net investments in physical capital accumulate according to

$$\dot{k}_i(t) = f_i(k_i(t), g_i(t)) - I_i(g_i(t)) - c_i(t) \tag{7.4}$$

in which $I_i(\cdot)$ is an energy cost function. This function is needed to ensure an interior solution to the choice of energy use in the uncontrolled market economy, since the marginal product of energy does not approach zero for finite k_i and g_i with a Cobb–Douglas production function. The energy cost function, which is assumed to be increasing and strictly convex in its argument, is written

$$I_i(g_i(t)) = \frac{\beta_{i3}}{\beta_{i4}+1} g_i(t)^{\beta_{i4}+1} \tag{7.5}$$

Energy use leads to the release of emissions which, in turn, give rise to the accumulation of a stock of pollution. By assuming a linear emission production function, we have

$$\dot{x}_i(t) = \kappa_i g_i(t) - \gamma_i x_i(t) \tag{7.6}$$

Note that our main objective here is not to construct a realistic model of a global economy; the objective is to provide an intuitive understanding of the factors that determine whether or not external effects have important consequences for welfare measurement. In particular, we would like to find out whether their welfare contributions are sensitive to small changes in the relationship between utility and pollution. As such, the simple structure of the model may be desirable, since it enables us to focus on the external effects without too much distraction from other complexities. At the same time, and irrespective of the structure of the model, the choices of parameter values are important for the resulting economic behavior. Therefore, the sensitivity analyses to be carried out below should enhance our discussion of the factors underlying the welfare consequences of external effects.

In the baseline simulation, the parameter values are[1] $\theta = 0.003$, $\alpha_{10} = \alpha_{20}$ = 0.003, $\alpha_{11} = \alpha_{21} = 0.5$, $\alpha_{12} = \alpha_{22} = 150000$, $\alpha_{13} = \alpha_{23} = 8.33 \times 10^{-8}$, $\alpha_{14} = \alpha_{24} = 1$, $\alpha_{15} = \alpha_{25} = 8.33 \times 10^{-8}$, $\alpha_{16} = \alpha_{26} = 1$, $\beta_{10} = 9900$, $\beta_{20} = 3370$, $\beta_{11} = \beta_{21} = 0.15$, $\beta_{12} = \beta_{22} = 0.6$, $\delta_1 = \delta_2 = 0.001$, $k_1(0) = 12.95$, $k_2(0) = 0.71$, $\beta_{13} = 5500$, $\beta_{23} = 1250$, $\beta_{14} = \beta_{24} = 1.1$, $\kappa_1 = \kappa_2 = 7.2 \times 10^9$, $\gamma_1 = \gamma_2 = 0.01$ and $x_1(0)$ = $x_2(0) = 1$. The simulations were carried out for 50 years using the program package GAMS.

7.1.2   Numerical Results

We now compare the equilibrium in the uncontrolled market economy, the non-cooperative Nash equilibrium in open-loop form and the cooperative equilibrium[2] from the points of view of economic behavior, welfare and welfare measurement. As indicated above, the countries are allowed to differ with respect to production possibilities. Country 1 is able to produce more goods for a given set of production factors and has a greater initial capital stock than country 2. It also has higher energy production costs. These differences between the countries were chosen arbitrarily; we could equally well have assumed that the countries differ in some other way. The purpose is to introduce asymmetries in a simple way. In all other respects, the countries are identical in the baseline simulation. Consider first Figure 7.1, which shows the equilibrium paths for consumption, emissions, the capital stock, the environmental quality and the stock of pollution.

According to Figure 7.1, the equilibrium paths take the same general form in all regimes, although the levels and slopes differ substantially. Consider first country 1, which is better able to produce goods than country 2. Note from Figures 7.1(a)–7.1(e) that the equilibrium in the uncontrolled market economy implies higher consumption as well as gives rise to a higher stock of pollution than the non-cooperative Nash equilibrium and the cooperative equilibrium, respectively. The intuition is, of course, that the marginal cost of energy (for a given amount of energy use) facing the firms is lower in the uncontrolled market economy than in the other two regimes, and lower in the non-cooperative Nash equilibrium than in the cooperative equilibrium. A low marginal cost of energy use will, in turn, stimulate production and serve as an incentive to release emissions. In addition, although the non-cooperative Nash equilibrium and the cooperative equilibrium differ with respect to resource allocation, the most important differences arise between the uncontrolled market economy and the other two regimes. If the uncontrolled market economy were to take the step towards the non-cooperative Nash equilibrium, such a policy change would imply a substantial reduction in energy use, consumption and pollution. This suggests that if environmental policy were imposed on an otherwise uncontrolled market economy, a substantial change in behavior could be accomplished simply because the 'free' assets previously associated with the environment become costly to use for the producers. However, once the non-cooperative Nash equilibrium has been reached, the additional policy changes required to move the economy towards the cooperative equilibrium do not necessarily imply a considerable change in behavior among the agents.[3]

The situation is slightly different for country 2, where output and consumption are relatively low in comparison with country 1. Since consumption and environmental quality are complements by assumption, the results imply that the marginal utility of environmental quality tends to be higher in country 1 than in country 2. As a consequence, the difference in behavior between the equilibrium in the uncontrolled market economy and the non-cooperative Nash equilibrium is not as great in country 2 as in country 1. On the other hand, the behavioral difference between the non-cooperative Nash equilibrium and the cooperative equilibrium is relatively more important in the context of country 2, since the latter regime implies that the environmental policy of country 2 also has to recognize the preferences in country 1.

Given the results derived in Chapter 6, we would expect the contributions of external effects to the welfare measures to be more important in the uncontrolled market economy than in the non-cooperative Nash equilibrium. In addition, since some of the production parameters differ substantially between the two countries, we would also expect the resulting asymmetries to have an influence

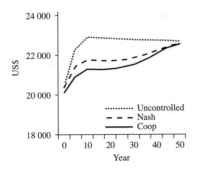

*Figure 7.1(a)   Consumption in
country 1*

*Figure 7.1(b)   Emissions in
country 1*

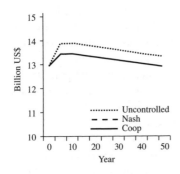

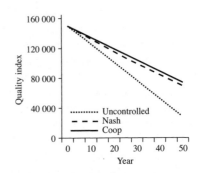

*Figure 7.1(c)   Capital stock in
country 1*

*Figure 7.1(d)   Environmental
quality in country 1*

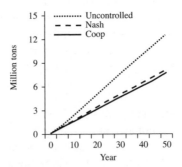

*Figure 7.1(e)   Stock of pollution
in country 1*

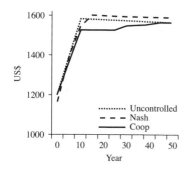

Figure 7.1(f)   Consumption in country 2

Figure 7.1(g)   Emissions in country 2

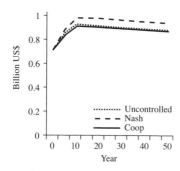

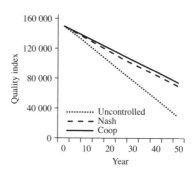

Figure 7.1(h)   Capital stock in country 2

Figure 7.1(i)   Environmental quality in country 2

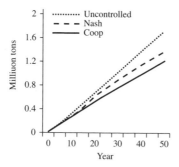

Figure 7.1(j)   Stock of pollution in country 2

on the national welfare measures. Indeed, this is precisely what we find. Consider Table 7.1. Here, we distinguish between national and global welfare measures. The national welfare measure is represented by the utility discount rate times the present value of future utility for country i at time zero, $\theta V_i(0)$, whereas the global welfare measure is the sum of the two national welfare measures, $\theta \sum_{i=1}^{2} V_i(0)$. We analyze these welfare measures in relation to the current value Hamiltonian[4] and the sum of current value Hamiltonians, respectively, which makes it possible to compute the relative contributions of external effects to the national and global welfare measures. The equilibrium values of the Hamiltonian listed in the table refer to each individual economy (first two columns) and to the sum of Hamiltonians in the case of the global economy (third column).

Table 7.1   Welfare measurement in the two-country economy

Type of equilibrium	Country 1	Country 2	Global economy
Uncontrolled economy			
Welfare	110.4	28.5	138.9
Hamiltonian	156.8	40.6	197.4
(Ham./welfare)*100	142.0	142.5	142.1
Non-cooperative Nash			
Welfare	116.6	30.8	147.4
Hamiltonian	120.7	37.0	157.7
(Ham./welfare)*100	103.5	120.1	107.0
Cooperative			
Welfare	116.8	30.9	147.7
Hamiltonian	114.6	33.1	147.7
(Ham./Welfare)*100	98.1	107.1	100.0

To recognize that the model has a finite time horizon, the 'Hamiltonian' referred to in Table 7.1 is measured as $H(0) - H(T)$ where $H(0)$ is the Hamiltonian at time zero, whereas $H(T)$ is the present value Hamiltonian measured at the terminal point; cf. Section 4.4. Since the numerical model has a finite time horizon, $H(T)$ is generally non-zero. This means that $H(0) - H(T)$ is analogous to the first best welfare measure derived in previous chapters. As such, it will be referred to as a Hamiltonian.

Table 7.1 implies that the current value Hamiltonian tends to overestimate welfare in each country, and the sum of current value Hamiltonians tends to overestimate global welfare, in the uncontrolled market economy. The reason is that the welfare contributions of the external effects are negative in this case.

Given the choice of functional forms and parameter values, the results imply that the degree of overestimation is substantial; that is, the relative welfare contribution of the external effect is important in the uncontrolled market economy. In the non-cooperative Nash equilibrium, on the other hand, the degree by which the current value Hamiltonian (sum of current value Hamiltonians) overestimates the national (global) welfare measures is much smaller than in the uncontrolled market economy. This is so for primarily two reasons. First, the domestically generated external effect is internalized in the non-cooperative Nash equilibrium, so that the domestic welfare effects associated with domestic pollution are captured by the Hamiltonian. Second, although the transboundary external effect is not internalized in the non-cooperative Nash equilibrium, it does not contribute as much to the welfare measure as in the uncontrolled market economy. The environmental policy carried out in the non-cooperative equilibrium reduces the transboundary environmental damage in comparison with the uncontrolled market economy.

As we were able to show in Chapter 6, although the sum of current value Hamiltonians constitutes an exact welfare measure at the global level in the cooperative equilibrium, each country-specific Hamiltonian does not provide an exact national welfare measure. Instead, asymmetries will contribute to the national welfare measures, although the welfare effects of these asymmetries cancel out at the global level. For the model and parameter values discussed here, the asymmetries imply that the Hamiltonian underestimates welfare by about 1.8 percent in country 1 and overestimates welfare by approximately 7 percent in country 2. Therefore, despite the fact that the countries in this example differ substantially with respect to production technology, the welfare contributions associated with asymmetries need not necessarily be very large.

7.1.3   Sensitivity Analysis

Are the results presented in Table 7.1 stable in the sense that the general picture remains valid, even if certain key parameters undergo small changes? In particular, what parameters drive the welfare contribution of the external effects in the uncontrolled market economy and the non-cooperative Nash equilibrium? One mechanism is the relationship between the marginal disutility of pollution and the stock of pollution; cf. Chapter 4. This is so because the present value of such marginal disutilities constitutes the present value of the marginal external effect. Since the marginal external effect is a forward looking term in the welfare measure, its influence will also depend on the weight assigned to future utility via the utility discount rate. Two different sensitivity analyses will be carried out: (i) changing the relationship between the instantaneous utility and the stock of pollution generated by each country, and (ii) changing the utility discount rate.

The idea behind the first sensitivity analysis is to make the relationship between environmental quality, z_i, and the two stocks of pollution, x_1 and x_2, slightly non-linear. This is done by increasing the parameters α_{i4} and α_{i6}, for i = 1,2, from 1 to 1.005 and 1.01, respectively. The results are presented in Tables E1 and E2 in Appendix E. By increasing α_{i4} and α_{i6} slightly above 1, the loss of environmental quality associated with increases in x_1 and x_2, respectively, will be higher, the larger the size of each stock. In the reference case, on the other hand, the marginal loss of environmental quality due to higher pollution does not depend on these stocks. The results suggest that this type of non-linearity matters for the welfare contribution of the external effect in the uncontrolled market economy. In the reference case in Table 7.1, the Hamiltonian tends to overestimate welfare by approximately 42 percent at both the national and global levels, whereas the degree of overestimation is 48 percent and 57 percent, respectively, when the four parameters mentioned above take values of 1.005 and 1.01, respectively, instead of 1. In other words, introducing a small non-linearity may have a considerable impact on the welfare contribution of external effects in the uncontrolled market economy. This illustrates why knowledge of preferences is so important in social accounting. In the non-cooperative Nash equilibrium, on the other hand, the same sensitivity analysis has only a minor influence on the welfare contribution of the external effect. Since this welfare contribution was very small to begin with, the relationship between uninternalized external effects and welfare is much weaker in the non-cooperative Nash equilibrium than in the uncontrolled market economy.

The second sensitivity analysis refers to changes in the utility discount rate. The qualitative effects of changes in the utility discount rate are intuitive. If the utility discount rate decreases, the forward looking terms in the welfare measures are assigned a higher weight than before, which means that the relative welfare contribution of the external effect increases. If, on the other hand, the utility discount rate increases, the forward looking terms are assigned a lower weight, and the relative welfare contribution of the external effect decreases. This is illustrated by comparing Table 7.1, where the utility discount rate is 3 percent, with Table E3 in Appendix E, where the utility discount rate is 2.5 percent.

7.2   CARBON DIOXIDE POLLUTION AND EXTERNAL EFFECTS IN PRODUCTION

The analysis carried out in the previous section is interpretable as a numerical application to Chapter 6. As such, it is instructive in the sense of explaining why external effects in consumption may be important in the context of welfare measurement. So far, however, we have not made any attempt to connect the numerical analysis to real-world market data. We have also neglected technological change as well as other external effects associated with environmental damage. Environmental damage may not only affect utility directly; it may also have a direct effect on production possibilities. Although properties of the utility function are estimable by econometric analysis of consumer behavior, the welfare contributions of external effects in production and technological change are presumably easier to measure in practice than external effects in consumption, since production is observable.

Here, we analyze production externalities associated with the release of greenhouse gases to the atmosphere in terms of an aggregate model of the world economy. This analysis is based on Aronsson et al. (2001), where the world economy is divided into rich and poor groups. The rich countries are characterized by large emissions of greenhouse gases per capita, high income per capita, low population growth and relatively low costs in terms of output lost due to an increase in the stock of greenhouse gases in the atmosphere. The poor countries are characterized by small emissions of greenhouse gases per capita, low income per capita, high population growth and relatively high costs in terms of output lost due to an increase in the stock of greenhouse gases. We assume that the stock of greenhouse gases in the atmosphere is associated with a negative external effect in production in each region. The differences between regions described above imply that the external effect is asymmetric.[5] As before, the resource allocation is characterized in three different ways: (i) the regions are uncontrolled market economies, (ii) the regions behave as if they play a Nash game in open-loop form, and (iii) the regions behave as if the resource allocation is a cooperative equilibrium.

7.2.1 The Model

From a theoretical point of view, external effects in production imply complications analogous to those associated with external effects in consumption. Each such external effect gives rise to a forward looking term in the welfare measure. As before, the differences among the three equilibrium concepts refer to whether or not the external effects have become internalized. In the cooperative equilibrium, all external effects are internalized at the global level, whereas all external effects remain uninternalized in the uncontrolled market economy. The non-cooperative Nash equilibrium takes a position in between the two polar cases: the domestically created welfare effects associated with greenhouse gases are internalized, whereas the transboundary external effect remains uninternalized. The implementation process is analogous to that in the case of external effects in consumption. Therefore, although we are considering external effects in production here, we can refer to Chapter 6 instead of repeating the theoretical welfare analysis.

The world is divided into two regions: rich and poor. We assume that consumers share the same preferences, and the instantaneous utility function is of Cobb–Douglas type. The consumers in each region are identical, and the instantaneous utility function facing consumers in region i is written

$$u(c_i(t)) = \alpha_1 c_i(t)^{\alpha_2} \tag{7.7}$$

implying that, in what follows, we disregard direct utility effects of environmental damage. Since the consumers in each region are identical by assumption, the social welfare at the regional level is defined as the sum of individual value functions, which implies assuming a utilitarian social welfare function. The social welfare in region i at time zero is given by

$$U_i(0) = \int_0^T N_i(t) u(c_i(t)) e^{-\theta t} dt \tag{7.8}$$

where $N_i(t)$ is the population size in region i at time t. Since the welfare analysis requires us to simulate the behavior corresponding to each equilibrium regime, the model it is based on a finite time horizon. The population in region i is defined as

$$N_i(t) = N_i(0) \exp\left(\frac{n_{i1}}{n_{i2}} \left(1 - \exp(-n_{i2}t) \right) \right) \tag{7.9}$$

in which n_{i1} and n_{i2} determine the growth rate of the population in region i.

Turning to the production side of the economy, net output per capita is given by the production function

$$f_i(k_i(t), g_i(t), x(t), t) = A_i D_i(t) B_i^t k_i(t)^{\beta_{i1}} g_i(t)^{\beta_{i2}} \tag{7.10}$$

where k_i is the capital stock per capita and g_i the input of fossil fuels per capita. Note that production is influenced by disembodied technological change via B_i^t. The term D_i is defined as

$$D_i(t) = 1 - \beta_{i3} [x(t) / \bar{x}]^{\beta_{i4}} \tag{7.11}$$

in which $x(t)$ is the stock of greenhouse gases in the atmosphere at time t. Equation (7.11) is based on Nordhaus (1993). Following Nordhaus (1993) and Azar and Sterner (1995), we simplify by assuming a linear relationship between the use of fossil fuels in production and the accumulation of greenhouse gases. The stock of greenhouse gases accumulates according to the differential equation

$$\dot{x}(t) = \beta_5 \sum_i N_i(t)g_i(t) - \gamma x(t) \tag{7.12}$$

Note also that since net investments in physical capital are given by

$$\dot{k}_i(t) = f_i(k_i(t), g_i(t), x(t), t) - I_i(g_i(t)) - c_i(t) \tag{7.13}$$

we have to specify the costs associated with using fossil fuels as an input, $I_i(\cdot)$. This cost is assumed to take the form

$$I_i(g_i(t)) = \frac{\beta_{i6}}{1 + \beta_{i7}} g_i(t)^{(1+\beta_{i7})} \tag{7.14}$$

Below, we use this model to compare the equilibrium in the uncontrolled market economy, the non-cooperative Nash equilibrium in open-loop form and the cooperative equilibrium in the context of welfare measurement at the national and global levels. Nordhaus and Yang (1996) compare these three equilibrium concepts from the point of view of strategies in climate change policy. Their study is based on the so-called Regional Integrated Model of Climate and the Economy (RICE) model, which is a multi-region numerical general equilibrium model. Although the RICE model is much more disaggregated than our model here, we are, nevertheless, able to provide a complement to the study by Nordhaus and Yang in the sense of comparing the three equilibria from the point of view of social accounting.

7.2.2 Data and Parameters

We estimate the parameters of the production function by applying ordinary least squares to data for the time period 1950–90. In an attempt to avoid some of the endogeneity problems inherent in such estimations, the explanatory variables are lagged one year. The parameter estimates for the production function in the rich and poor regions, respectively, are given in Table E4 in Appendix E. The stock of physical capital per capita for the rich region is approximated by using estimates of the capital stock for France.[6] As regards the poor region, data on capital stocks are only available for a few years. The capital stock in the poor region is, therefore, assumed to grow at the same rate as in the rich region. Although this may seem to be a restrictive assumption, it is not important for the results reported below. Emissions of carbon dioxide per capita as well as output per capita for the rich region were measured using data for Western Europe, and for the poor region using data for Africa.[7]

In the reference case, the parameters of the utility function are chosen as $\alpha_1 = 0.0067$, $\alpha_2 = 0.8$, $T = 70$ and $\theta = 0.03$. The parameters of the population equations are $N_r(0) = 800\,000\,000$, $N_p(0) = 5200\,000\,000$, $n_{r1} = 0.06$, $n_{p1} = 0.015$, $n_{r2} = 0.05$ and $n_{p2} = 0.025$. The subindices r and p refer to rich and poor, respectively. The parameters of the equations for D_r and D_p are chosen such that $\beta_{r3} = 0.005$, $\beta_{p3} = 0.05$, $\beta_{r4} = 1$ and $\beta_{p4} = 1$. Continuing with the accumulation equation for greenhouse gases, we have $\beta_5 = 0.4$ and $\gamma = 0.001$. The parameters of the cost equation for fossil fuel use are $\beta_{r6} = 1250$, $\beta_{p6} = 5500$, $\beta_{r7} = 1.1$ and $\beta_{p7} = 1.1$. Finally, the initial stocks of physical capital and greenhouse gases are $k_r(0) = 12.95$, $k_p(0) = 0.71$ and $x(0) = 160\,000\,000\,000$, whereas $\bar{x} = 600\,000\,000\,000$. The simulation period is 1991–2060. The basis for choosing parameter values is to be able to reproduce, as closely as possible, the observed consumption, production and emission structure during the first years of the simulation period.

Some additional comments are called for. The rate of technological change, which is estimated as the separate effect of time in the production function, is approximately 1.5 percent per year in the rich region and –1 percent in the poor region. In the reference case, the effect of doubling the stock of greenhouse gases in the atmosphere is to reduce the annual production of final goods by approximately 5 percent in the poor region and 0.5 percent in the rich region.[8] By comparison, Nordhaus (1993) assumes the damage to be 1.33 percent for the global economy. Fankhauser (1992) finds that the most likely cost of doubling the stock of carbon dioxide is to reduce the gross world product by between 1 and 2 percent. However, Frankhauser also points out that the expected cost is higher in developing countries.[9] The rate of time preference is 3 percent, and the rate of population growth is approximately 0.5 percent in the rich region and 1.5 percent in the poor region. It is worth emphasizing that a utility discount rate of 3 percent is relatively low, considering that the economy in the rich region grows by approximately 1.5 percent per year. If the discount rate is lower than the growth rate, the Hamiltonian does not converge to zero when T approaches infinity.

7.2.3   Decomposition of the Welfare Measures

The basic idea here is to decompose the welfare measures in each regime into (i) the Hamiltonian (green NNP in utility terms), (ii) technological change, (iii) population growth and (iv) external effects in production associated with the stock of greenhouse gases in the atmosphere. As before, let the superindices $*$, n and 0 denote the cooperative equilibrium, the non-cooperative Nash equilibrium and the equilibrium in the uncontrolled market economy, respectively. Consider first the present value Hamiltonians corresponding to each regime:

The cooperative equilibrium:

$$H^*(t) = \sum_{i=1}^{2}[N_i(t)u(c_i^*(t))e^{-\theta t} + \lambda_i^*(t)\dot{k}_i^*(t)] + \mu^*(t)\dot{x}^*(t)$$

The non-cooperative Nash equilibrium:

$$H_i^n(t) = N_i(t)u(c_i^n(t))e^{-\theta t} + \lambda_i^n(t)\dot{k}_i^n(t) + \mu_i^n(t)\dot{x}^n(t)$$

$$H^n(t) = \sum_{i=1}^{2}H_i^n(t)$$

The uncontrolled market economy:

$$H_i^0(t) = N_i(t)u(c_i^0(t))e^{-\theta t} + \lambda_i^0(t)\dot{k}_i^0(t)$$

$$H^0(t) = \sum_{i=1}^{2}H_i^0(t)$$

Since there is only one stock of greenhouse gases for the economy as a whole, there is no natural way of splitting the global present value Hamiltonian between the regions in the cooperative equilibrium. In order to make the analysis equivalent to that carried out in Chapter 6 (where each individual economy generates its own stock of pollution), we use the following artificial split in the simulations;

$$\tilde{H}_i^*(t) = N_i(t)u(c_i^*(t))e^{-\theta t} + \lambda_i^*(t)\dot{k}_i^*(t) + \mu^*(t)\dot{x}_i^*(t)$$

where $\dot{x}_i = \beta_5 N_i g_i - \gamma x_i$ and $x = \Sigma_i x_i$, implying that $H^*(t) = \Sigma_i \tilde{H}_i^*$.

For expositional ease, let T approach infinity and apply the following short notations;

$$P_i(0) = \int_0^{\infty} \frac{\partial H_i(t)}{\partial N_i(t)}\dot{N}_i(t)dt \qquad \text{(value of population growth)}$$

$$\Lambda_i(0) = \int_0^{\infty} N_i(t)\lambda_i(t)\frac{\partial f_i(\cdot)}{\partial t}dt \qquad \text{(value of technological change)}$$

$$E_{ij}(0) = \int_0^\infty N_i(t)\lambda_i(t)\frac{\partial f_i(\cdot)}{\partial x(t)}\dot{x}_j(t)dt \quad \text{(value of externality imposed on } i \text{ by } j)$$

in which we have used $x = \Sigma_i x_i$.

Since the present value Hamiltonian and the current value Hamiltonian are identical at time zero, the following national and global welfare measures can be defined for the three regimes:

The cooperative equilibrium:

$$\theta V_i^*(0) = \tilde{H}_i^*(0) + P_i^*(0) + \Lambda_i^*(0) + E_{ij}^*(0) - E_{ji}^*(0) \qquad (7.15a)$$

$$\theta \sum_{i=1}^2 V_i^*(0) = H^*(0) + \sum_{i=1}^2 [P_i^*(0) + \Lambda_i^*(0)] \qquad (7.15b)$$

The non-cooperative Nash equilibrium:

$$\theta V_i^n(0) = H_i^n(0) + P_i^n(0) + \Lambda_i^n(0) + E_{ij}^n(0) \qquad (7.16a)$$

$$\theta \sum_{i=1}^2 V_i^n(0) = H^n(0) + \sum_{i=1}^2 [P_i^n(0) + \Lambda_i^n(0) + E_{ij}^n(0)] \qquad (7.16b)$$

The uncontrolled market equilibrium:

$$\theta V_i^0(0) = H_i^0(0) + P_i^0(0) + \Lambda_i^0(0) + E_{ii}^0(0) + E_{ij}^0(0) \qquad (7.17a)$$

$$\theta \sum_{i=1}^2 V_i^0(0) = H^0(0) + \sum_{i=1}^2 [P_i^0(0) + \Lambda_i^0(0) + E_{ii}^0(0) + E_{ij}^0(0)] \quad (7.17b)$$

7.2.4 Results

Let us now compare the equilibrium in the uncontrolled market economy, the non-cooperative Nash equilibrium and the cooperative equilibrium from the point of view of welfare measurement. In the simulations, the uncontrolled market economy[10] constitutes the reference case. Consider Table 7.2. The term *HI* is interpretable as an indicator of how accurately the Hamiltonian measures welfare at time zero; cf. Section 4.4. Its construction is based on the observation that, without the influence of technological change and population growth, the

Hamiltonian facing the global planner in the cooperative equilibrium will be an exact global welfare measure. In this situation, the index is equal to 100.[11]

Table 7.2   Welfare measurement in the stylized world economy

Type of equilibrium	Rich	Poor	Global economy
Uncontrolled economy			
HI	34.0	105.0	55.7
Tech	44.0	−29.0	21.0
E_{ii}	−0.1	−1.2	−0.5
E_{ij}	−0.1	−1.0	−0.4
Pop	22.2	26.2	24.2
Non-cooperative Nash			
HI	33.7	102.8	55.6
Tech	44.4	−28.8	21.1
E_{ij}	−0.1	−1.2	−0.5
Pop	22.0	27.2	23.8
Cooperative			
HI	33.7	102.8	55.6
Tech	44.4	−28.8	21.0
$E_{ij} - E_{ji}$	0.4	−1.0	–
Pop	21.7	27.0	23.4

Note: The numbers in the table measure the percentage contribution of each term.

For each of the three regimes, *HI* greatly underestimates the welfare in the rich region. According to Table 7.2, the Hamiltonian only contributes to about 34 percent of welfare, measured as the utility discount rate times the present value of future utility. The reason is that the Hamiltonian does not reflect the influence of technological change, and the results imply that the relative welfare contribution of technological change is considerable.[12] The estimated welfare contribution of technological change is close to the results of Weitzman (1997) and Weitzman and Löfgren (1997). Their results suggest that given the contribution of technological progress in the US economy, NNP has to be increased by 40–50 percent in order to be a welfare indicator. However, since these two studies did not control for the influence of market imperfections, their estimates of the influence of technological change may also reflect non-autonomous time dependencies of the economic system arising for reasons other than technological change.

In addition, it seems as if population growth may have a considerable effect on future welfare. The influence of population growth is due to the assumption that the social welfare function is a utility sum, which is relatively common in welfare economics. An alternative would be to carry out the welfare analysis in per capita terms. If the welfare analysis is performed on a per capita basis, the influence of population growth vanishes, whereas most of the other qualitative results remain. As a consequence, the Hamiltonian would be a better welfare indicator if the welfare analysis were performed on a per capita basis, since the prediction error that is otherwise due to population growth would vanish in that case. In the poor region, the Hamiltonian slightly overestimates welfare, since the welfare contribution of technological change is negative. The external effects that remain uninternalized in the non-cooperative Nash equilibrium and the uncontrolled market economy have more important impacts on the poor region than on the rich region, although they are still very small in comparison with the other sources of welfare.

After having controlled for the influence of technological change, and possibly also the welfare effect of population growth (depending on the form of the social welfare function), these results play down the importance of incorporating external effects in production from greenhouse gases into the welfare measures of the uncontrolled market economy. This is observed by recognizing that the welfare contributions of these external effects are very small. In other words, the biases of the welfare measures for the uncontrolled market economy, due to neglecting the welfare contribution of this type of external effects, are negligible. The main reason is, of course, that the effect of greenhouse gases on output is relatively small (at least in the rich region). Meanwhile, it is necessary to exercise caution when interpreting these results. The simulations are based on real-world market data reflecting the actual policies undertaken to control the environment. This means that existing emission taxes (or part of them) are most likely hidden in the estimate of the marginal cost of emissions facing firms (see note 10). As a consequence, energy use and emissions in our simulated uncontrolled market equilibrium may actually be closer to their first best counterparts than they would have been had the data reflected an uncontrolled market economy in the true sense. In other words, although the shadow price of greenhouse gases is set to zero in the uncontrolled market economy, we are likely to underestimate emissions and, therefore, the stock of greenhouse gases in an uncontrolled market economy.

Two sensitivity analyses have been carried out. The first involved increasing the relative damage from greenhouse gases by a factor of ten in the rich region, and doubling the damage in the poor region. The idea is to control for the possibility that the impact of greenhouse gases on output has been underestimated. Our concern is to study whether these changes have an influence on the welfare contribution of the external effects in production in the uncontrolled market economy and non-cooperative Nash equilibrium. As it turns out, these changed assumptions have a relatively small impact on the results. Although the welfare contributions of the external effects increase, they still represent a very small share of the welfare measure. In the uncontrolled market economy, where the influence of the external effects is relatively more important than in the other regimes, the external effects, measured as the sum of E_{ii} and E_{ij} when the changed assumptions have been implemented, represent 2.6 percent of the welfare measure in the rich region, 4.8 percent in the poor region and 3.3 percent for the global economy. The relative contributions of the other sources of welfare are also similar to those in Table 7.2.

The second sensitivity analysis involves increasing the growth rate in the poor region from approximately –1 percent per year to 0.5 percent per year. The main difference in comparison with our earlier results is that the Hamiltonian underestimates welfare in the poor region. The reason is that the poor region is now growing instead of shrinking, so that the welfare contribution of technological change becomes positive. The welfare contributions of the external effects are of a magnitude similar to that in Table 7.2.

7.3   MORE ON EXTERNAL EFFECTS IN PRODUCTION

The analysis above suggests that the welfare contribution of external effects in production, which are associated with the stock of greenhouse gases in the atmosphere, is negligible. This result is also robust in the sense that the changed assumptions implicit in the sensitivity analyses have only a small impact on the welfare contributions of the external effects.

The small, or even negligible, welfare contribution of external effects may seem surprising. Does this result carry over to other types of external effects in production? Based on the results of previous numerical studies, the answer is no. Although the external effects in production that are associated with greenhouse gases seem to be of minor importance in terms of their welfare contribution, there may be other kinds of market imperfections hidden in the model used here. As mentioned above, the impact of technological change may be overestimated, simply because it is not possible to distinguish the influence of technological change from that of omitted variables. In addition, we have disregarded the driving forces behind technological change. One such driving force emphasized in the literature on economic growth is human capital formation, and some of its welfare contribution is likely to be associated with a positive external effect in production. Therefore, although the external effects in production due to the stock of greenhouse gases in the atmosphere give rise to relatively small welfare contributions, when controlling for the direct effect of time on output, other external effects on the production side of the economy (possibly hidden in the model) should, nevertheless, be important to consider in social accounting.

7.5   SUMMARY AND DISCUSSION

It is important to distinguish between numerical simulations and empirical research. Some of the parameters in the models set out above were chosen on a more or less *ad hoc* basis, implying that neither the equilibrium trajectories nor the estimated contributions of different parts of the welfare measures, in themselves, have to be reliable. On the other hand, the numerical analysis enables us to understand the relative welfare contribution of different factors on a qualitative basis, if the sensitivity analysis is carried out in a sensible way, as well as helps us isolate the driving forces behind the results. The latter aspect should be emphasized here, since one of our objectives has been to clarify the conditions under which external effects are empirically important in the context of social accounting.

We conclude with two broad observations. The first is analogous to an observation made in Chapter 4 and deserves to be pointed out once again. If the marginal disutility of pollution rises rapidly when the stock of pollution increases, the relative welfare contribution of the associated external effects in consumption is likely to have a greater influence than otherwise. Although this observation is trivial in itself, it suggests that knowledge of preferences is fundamental in social accounting, which is one reason why the information we require for welfare measurement is difficult to capture empirically. In addition, the magnitude by which the relative welfare contribution of the external effect increases, as a consequence of introducing a very modest non-linearity in the relationship between environmental quality and pollution, may be considerable. From this point of view, the basic message is certainly not trivial. The second observation is that, after having controlled for technological change, part of which may be associated with human capital formation, external effects in production due to greenhouse gases may not be of great importance to consider for purposes of welfare measurement. This result, obtained by estimation of a production function, is also in line with the estimates of the influence of greenhouse gases on production in previous studies.

NOTES

1. From a technical point of view, the model set out here is a highly simplified version of the model to be described and used in Section 7.2, where the world is divided between a rich and poor region. The basis for choosing parameter values in the baseline simulation is, first, to

allow the countries to differ with respect to production possibilities and, second, to be able to calculate the general equilibrium in each regime.

2. As in Chapter 6, the social welfare function underlying the cooperative equilibrium is the sum of the two country-specific optimal value functions. This makes it easy to focus on the welfare contributions of external effects, since the only difference between the three equilibrium concepts refers to how the external effects are treated.

3. Similar results were found by Nordhaus and Yang (1996). See also Aronsson et al. (1998), who show that the introduction of a small energy tax (energy related to nuclear power) in an otherwise uncontrolled market economy may bring the resource allocation surprisingly close to the first best equilibrium.

4. The concept of the Hamiltonian is the same as in Chapter 6. In the context of an uncontrolled market economy, this means that we use the Hamiltonian implicit in the consumer's optimization problem evaluated in the general equilibrium.

5. Caplan et al. (1999) also recognize that the external effect of global warming may be asymmetric and analyze the effects of global warming on production and welfare under different assumptions about corrective policies.

6. See Maddison (1995a, 1995b) and Ark and Crafts (1996).

7. The data were provided by Carbon Dioxide Information Center, Oak Ridge National Laboratory.

8. By using a numerical model based on a similar relationship between the stock of greenhouse gases and output, Bovenberg and Goulder (2001) show that it is possible to implement carbon abatement policies in the USA without substantial costs to the economy.

9. See also Mirza (2002) for an application to Bangladesh.

10. The concept of 'uncontrolled market economy' suggests that the government does not try to control emissions. In reality, taxes are levied on the use of fossil fuels in most countries, whereby emission taxes can be interpreted as shadow prices for greenhouse gases in real terms. However, these taxes are not easily recovered for a composite of countries, which we deal with here. We simplify the analysis by treating existing taxes as part of the firms' marginal costs.

11. Recall the problem of approximation errors discussed in Section 4.4.

12. Note that technological change is measured by the separate effect of time on output (that is, the effect of time that does not arise via the production factors). Therefore, the influence of technological change may be overestimated, since the separate effect of time in the production function may also reflect the influence of omitted variables.

8. Three emerging issues in social accounting

This chapter concerns three issues which are highly relevant for social accounting, although they have been neglected (or at least not dealt with thoroughly) in previous chapters. In Section 8.1, we consider some additional aspects of welfare measurement in a differential game framework, thereby extending the analyses in Chapters 5 and 6. Section 8.2 addresses the implications of unemployment for social accounting as well as the related issue of union wage formation. Finally, in Section 8.3, we examine a situation where the social planner has objectives for the distribution of utility or consumption across consumers at each point in time and consider the implications of distributional objectives for social accounting.

8.1 WELFARE MEASUREMENT IN NASH FEEDBACK-LOOP GAMES AND STACKELBERG GAMES

In this section, we consider two aspects of welfare measurement related to differential games. The first is welfare measurement in the case where the resource allocation is governed by a Nash game in feedback-loop form. This complements our analysis of the welfare measurement problem associated with a Nash game in open-loop form in Chapter 6. The second aspect concerns deriving welfare measures for the leader and follower, respectively, in a Stackelberg game. Welfare measurement in a Stackelberg game situation was discussed in Chapter 5, where the government acts as leader and the private sector as follower in the context of an optimal tax problem. Here, we provide a more formal treatment of players and strategies. We keep the analysis simple by introducing a model where two agents compete in harvesting a common renewable resource. A possible interpretation is to view the differential game as being played between two different fishing fleets. The analysis is based on Löfgren (1999).

8.1.1 The Model

There are two agents, $i = 0,1$, each of whom tries to maximize a functional equation, which depends on the agent's own actions and the actions of the competitor. Each agent knows the actions of the competitor and treats them as given in both the feedback-loop Nash game and the Stackelberg game. In the latter case, however, the leader (agent zero) conditions his/her actions on the fact that the competitor acts as if he/she plays a non-cooperative open-loop Nash game.

The objective functions are written in the following manner:

$$\underset{c_i(t)}{\text{Max}} \int_0^\infty f_i(x(t), c_0(t), c_1(t)) e^{-\theta t} dt \quad i = 0, 1 \tag{8.1}$$

subject to

$$\dot{x}(t) = f(x(t)) - c_0(t) - c_1(t) \tag{8.2}$$

$$x(0) = x^0 \tag{8.3}$$

The control variables, $c = (c_0, c_1)$, can be interpreted as harvests of the fish (natural resource) stock, x. The objective functions, $f_i(\cdot)$ for $i = 0, 1$, are twice continuously differentiable and strictly concave in x, c, and the growth function, $f(\cdot)$, is twice continuously differentiable and strictly concave in x. The differential game may have a solution under weaker conditions; inevitably, however, there is some kind of Lipschitz-continuity condition on the differential equation (8.2). This implies that the solution of the game is restricted to smooth strategies.[1] The utility discount rate, θ, is for simplicity assumed to be the same for both players.

8.1.2 Welfare Measurement under Feedback Control

Under an open-loop strategy each player chooses all the values of his/her controls at the outset of the game. Thus the value of the control at each point in time is only a function of time. Each player is committed to his/her entire course of action at the beginning of the game and will not revise it at any subsequent point in time. This is a strong assumption, which is unlikely to be satisfied in many real-world situations. Given that an optimal open-loop solution is possibly time inconsistent, that is if the optimal path is recalculated after some time has elapsed, the original path will no longer be optimal, there are incentives for the players to change their minds. Thus a more appropriate way of modeling the players' strategies may be to suppose that they condition on the state of the system at each point in time. That is, the control at each point in time is characterized by the requirement that $c_0 = c_0(x, t)$, and similarly for c_1. In such circumstances, the optimal solution is called a feedback control, and it will be time consistent, or subgame perfect.

Given that c_1 is conditioned on x as well, we can write the Hamiltonian of the feedback control problem of player zero as (suppressing the time indicator)

$$H_0(x, c_0, c_1, \lambda_0) = f_0(x, c(x,t))e^{-\theta t} + \lambda_0(f(x) - c_0(x,t) - c_1(x,t)) \quad (8.4)$$

where $c(x,t) = (c_0(x,t), c_1(x,t))$. The first order conditions can be written

$$\frac{\partial H_0}{\partial c_0} = 0 \quad (8.5a)$$

$$\dot{\lambda}_0 = -\frac{\partial H_0}{\partial x} - \frac{\partial H_0}{\partial c_1}\frac{\partial c_1}{\partial x} \quad (8.5b)$$

It is worth noting that the dependence of c_0 on x does not enter equation (8.5b), since c_0 is optimally chosen in (8.5a). We can now make use of Proposition 2.1 to derive the welfare measure. Differentiating the Hamiltonian totally with respect to time yields

$$\frac{dH_0^n}{dt} = -\theta f_0^n(\cdot)e^{-\theta t} + \frac{\partial f_0^n}{\partial c_1}\frac{\partial c_1^n}{\partial t}e^{-\theta t} - \lambda_0\frac{\partial c_1^n}{\partial t} \quad (8.6)$$

where the derivatives are taken along the optimal path $\{x^n(s), c_0^n(s), c_1^n(s)\}_t^T$, and the superindex n refers to Nash equilibrium. For $T \to \infty$ we can integrate equation (8.6) forwards to obtain

$$H_0^n(t) = \theta V_0^n(t) - \int_t^\infty \left\{ \frac{\partial f_0^n}{\partial c_1}\frac{\partial c_1^n}{\partial s}e^{-\theta s} - \lambda_0\frac{\partial c_1^n}{\partial s} \right\}ds$$

in which $V_0^n(t) = \int_t^\infty f_0^n(s)\exp(-\theta(s-t))ds$ is player zero's value function evaluated in the feedback-loop equilibrium. Again, in a steady state, there is direct proportionality between the Hamiltonian at time t and the value function. Outside the steady state, the discounted value of the future marginal damage done to player zero by player one has to be deducted. This term takes the same general form as it would have taken in a Nash game of open-loop form. Therefore, although the open-loop strategy, in itself, may appear to be unrealistic, its general welfare properties are not necessarily different from those corresponding to a more general framework.

8.1.3 Welfare Measurement in a Stackelberg Differential Game[2]

In a Stackelberg game, one player acts as leader and the other as follower. The follower behaves as a Nash competitor, that is, treats the harvest of the leader as an exogenous variable. This generates a reaction function, which the leader exploits by choosing his/her strategy conditional on the follower's reaction function as well as on the follower's future valuations of changes in today's fish stock. The latter variable is treated as an additional state variable. Here, player one is the follower and, consequently, player zero the leader. In the open-loop version of the Stackelberg game, we start by solving the follower's problem, treating the control of the leader as an exogenous function of time, $c_0(t)$. The follower solves the following optimal control problem:

$$\text{Max}_{c_1} \int_0^\infty f_1(x(t), c_0(t), c_1(t)) e^{-\theta t} dt \tag{8.7}$$

subject to

$$\dot{x}(t) = f(x(t)) - c_0(t) - c_1(t) \tag{8.8}$$
$$x(0) = x^0$$

The current value Hamiltonian of the follower can be written (suppressing the time indicator)

$$H_1^c(x, c, \lambda_1^c, t) = f_1(x, c) + \lambda_1^c(f(x) - c_0 - c_1) \tag{8.9}$$

in which $c = (c_0, c_1)$. The first order conditions are

$$\dot{\lambda}_1^c - \theta \lambda_1^c = -\frac{\partial H_1^c}{\partial x} \qquad \lim_{t \to \infty} e^{-\theta t} \lambda_1^c = 0 \tag{8.10}$$

$$\frac{\partial H_1^c}{\partial c_1} = \frac{\partial f_1(x, c_0, c_1)}{\partial c_1} - \lambda_1^c = 0 \tag{8.11}$$

Equation (8.11) defines the optimal control of the follower as a function

$$c_1^* = c_1^*(x, c_0, \lambda_1^c) \tag{8.12}$$

Substituting equation (8.12) into equations (8.8) and (8.10) yields the following two-point boundary problem:

$$\dot{\lambda}_1^c - \theta \lambda_1^c = -\frac{\partial H_1^c(x, c_0, \lambda_1^c)}{\partial x} \qquad \lim_{t \to \infty} e^{-\theta t} \lambda_1^c = 0 \tag{8.13}$$

$$\dot{x} = f(x) - c_0 - c_1^*(x, c_0, \lambda_1^c) \qquad x(0) = x^0$$

which can, in principle, be solved for $x(t)$ and $\lambda_1^c(t)$.

Let us now turn to the behavior of the leader. In order to determine the optimal control, the leader takes $y = (x, \lambda_1^c)$ as a vector of state variables, which is governed by the dynamic equations

$$\dot{x} = f(x) - c_0 - c_1^{\bullet} \qquad x(0) = x^0 \qquad (8.14)$$

$$\dot{\lambda}_1^c - \theta\lambda_1^c = -\frac{\partial H_1^c}{\partial x} \qquad \lim_{t \to \infty} e^{-\theta t} \lambda_1^c = 0$$

Substituting for $c_1^{\bullet}$ from equation (8.12) gives, in vector notation

$$\dot{y} = g(y, c_0) \qquad (8.15)$$

With the same substitution into the leader's objective function, his/her payoff can be written

$$\int_0^{\infty} f_0(x, c_0, c_1^{\bullet}) e^{-\theta s} ds = \int_0^{\infty} \hat{f}_0(y, c_0) e^{-\theta s} ds \qquad (8.16)$$

The leader's present value Hamiltonian along the optimal path can be written in the following manner:

$$H_0^{\circ}(y^{\circ}, c_0^{\circ}, \mu^{\circ}, t) = \hat{f}_0(y^{\circ}, c_0^{\circ}) e^{-\theta t} + \mu^{\circ} g(y^{\circ}, c_0^{\circ})$$

where the superindex denotes that the leader has made an optimal choice. The co-state vector $\mu^{\circ} = (\mu_0^{\circ}, \mu_1^{\circ})$ fulfills

$$\dot{\mu}_0 = -\frac{\partial H_0}{\partial x} \qquad \lim_{t \to \infty} \mu_0 = 0 \qquad (8.17)$$

$$\dot{\mu}_1 = -\frac{\partial H_0}{\partial \lambda_1^c} \qquad \lim_{t \to \infty} \mu_1 = 0$$

In addition, the Hamiltonian is maximized for each t by choosing

$$\frac{\partial H_0}{\partial c_0} = 0 \qquad (8.18)$$

The control obtained from equation (8.18), $c_0^{\circ} = c_0^{\circ}(y^{\circ}, \mu^{\circ})$, is used in equation (8.17) to solve the boundary problem defined by equations (8.17) and (8.14).

Applying Proposition 2.1 to the present value Hamiltonian of the leader yields

$$\frac{dH_0^{\circ}}{dt} = -\theta \, \hat{f}_0(y^{\circ}, c_0^{\circ}) e^{-\theta t}$$

If $\lim_{T \to \infty} H_0^0(T) = 0$, the leader's present (current) value Hamiltonian at time t is directly proportional to the present (current) value of future profit at time t. The factor of proportionality is the utility discount rate. A similar analysis of the follower's Hamiltonian, along the optimal path, shows that the value function will not be directly proportional to the Hamiltonian.[3] The reason is that the leader's control enters the optimization problem as an exogenous variable, which creates non-autonomous time dependence in addition to the dependency created by the discount factor.

8.2 IMPERFECT COMPETITION IN THE LABOR MARKET

The second issue addressed in this chapter is the consequences of unemployment in the context of social accounting. Such an extension is clearly motivated by high unemployment rates in many countries. It is also relevant from a more technical point of view: the appropriate way to measure welfare contributions associated with the labor market depends to a large extent on the functioning of this market. If the economy is a first best equilibrium, then, as shown in Chapter 5, the real wage rate constitutes the social marginal value of leisure in real terms. In addition, future changes in employment are not part of the welfare measure in a first best setting, because the utility value of the marginal product of labor equals the marginal utility of leisure at each point in time.

The consequences of unemployment for social accounting have been addressed by Aronsson (1998b). Our analysis is based on his study. We show that unemployment has two important implications for social accounting as compared with the valuation principles that apply in a first best setting. First, the present value of future changes in employment becomes part of the national welfare measure and, second, the wage rate does not necessarily measure the marginal value of leisure time. We also find that careful examination of the causes of unemployment may simplify the valuation procedures considerably.

So as to concentrate on the labor market, we disregard emissions and environmental damage throughout this section. To begin with, let us simply assume that the wage rate is set above the market clearing wage rate at each point in time, in which case employment is determined by the labor demand. Starting with the consumption side of the economy, we follow the convention used in most of the previous chapters whereby population growth is disregarded and population is normalized to equal one. The instantaneous utility function facing the consumer is written as $u(t) = u(c(t), h(t))$, where c is consumption and

h leisure. Leisure is, in turn, defined as a time endowment, T, less the time spent in market work, l. We assume that the instantaneous utility function is increasing in each argument and strictly concave. Since the consumer is rationed in the labor market in the sense that employment is determined by the labor demand, his/her problem is to choose the time path for consumption so as to maximize the present value of future utility:

$$U(0) = \int_0^\infty u(c(t), h(t))e^{-\theta t} dt \qquad (8.19)$$

subject to an asset accumulation equation. The consumer holds one asset; physical capital, k, and the asset accumulation equation is written

$$\dot{k}(t) = \pi(t) + r(t)k(t) + w(t)l(t) - c(t) \qquad (8.20)$$

As before, π is profit income, r the interest rate and w the wage rate. In a way similar to previous chapters, we also impose a No Ponzi Game (NPG) condition.

The production side of the economy is competitive. To simplify the analysis, we model the production side by a single competitive firm. The firm chooses l and k to maximize the profit

$$\pi(t) = f(l(t), k(t)) - w(t)l(t) - r(t)k(t) \qquad (8.21)$$

where the wage rate and the interest rate are exogenous to the firm. The production function is assumed to be increasing in each argument and strictly concave.

Let us, for the time being, disregard the wage formation process and simply assume that the wage path, $\{w^0(t)\}_0^\infty$, exceeds the market clearing wage path at each point in time. This means excess supply of labor at each point in time, implying that employment is determined by the labor demand. Conditional on this wage path, we obtain the general equilibrium paths for the other variables, $\{c^0(t), l^0(t), k^0(t), \lambda^0(t)\}_0^\infty$, by combining the necessary conditions for the consumer and the firm. The superindex 0 is used to denote that the equilibrium is the outcome of an imperfect market economy.

Substituting this solution into the present value Hamiltonian implicit in the consumer's problem gives

$$H^0(t) = u(c^0(t), h^0(t))e^{-\theta t} + \lambda^0(t)\dot{k}^0(t) \qquad (8.22)$$

where we have used the fact that the equation of motion for the capital stock in the general equilibrium is given by

$$\dot{k}^0(t) = f(l^0(t), k^0(t)) - c^0(t)$$

By applying Proposition 2.1, the time derivative of the present value Hamiltonian becomes

$$\frac{dH^0(t)}{dt} = -\theta u(c^0(t), h^0(t))e^{-\theta t} + [\lambda^0(t)f_l^0(t) - u_h^0(t)e^{-\theta t}]\dot{l}^0(t) \quad (8.23)$$

where $f_l^0(\cdot) = f_l(l^0, k^0)$ and $u_h^0(\cdot) = u_h(c^0, h^0)$ The second term on the right-hand side of equation (8.23) arises because the wage rate is such that $\lambda^0 f_l^0(\cdot) - u_h^0(\cdot)e^{-\theta t} > 0$ at each point in time. In other words, the marginal product of labor in utility terms exceeds the marginal utility of leisure, and the difference between them reflects the value of an instantaneous increase in employment. At the same time, since the change in employment at time t can be either positive or negative, the sign of the second term on the right-hand side of equation (8.23) is ambiguous. In the first best, on the other hand, the change in employment does not influence the time derivative of the present value Hamiltonian, because the marginal product of labor in utility terms equals the marginal utility of leisure at each point in time.

By assuming that the present value Hamiltonian approaches zero as time goes to infinity, the welfare measure is given by

$$\theta V^0(t) = H^{c^0}(t) + \int_t^\infty [\lambda^{c^0}(s)f_l^0(s) - u_h^0(s)]\dot{l}^0(s)e^{-\theta(s-t)}ds \quad (8.24)$$

where $V^0(t) = \int_t^\infty u(c^0(s), h^0(s))e^{-\theta(s-t)}ds$ is the value function, $H^{c^0}(t) = H^0(t)e^{\theta t}$ the current value Hamiltonian and $\lambda^{c^0}(t) = \lambda^0(t)e^{\theta t}$ the current value shadow price of capital.

We have derived the following result:

Proposition 8.1 *If the equilibrium is characterized by unemployment, welfare is appropriately measured by the sum of the current value Hamiltonian and the present value of future changes in employment. Future increases (decreases) in employment contribute to a rise (a decline) in welfare.*

Equation (8.24) is based on the assumption that the excess supply in the labor market is permanent. However, there is a possible distinction between permanent and temporary unemployment in the sense that a future change in employment will contribute to the welfare measure only if the labor market is characterized by disequilibrium when this change in employment occurs. To see this, consider a temporary disequilibrium in the labor market such that

$$\lambda^0(t)f_l^0(t) - u_h^0(t)e^{-\theta t} > 0 \text{ for } t \in (t_1, t_2) \text{ and}$$

$$\lambda^0(t)f_l^0(t) - u_h^0(t)e^{-\theta t} = 0 \text{ otherwise}$$

This situation indicates that the welfare measure at time $t < t_1$ is directly affected by the changes in employment that occur during the time interval (t_1, t_2), while the changes in employment that occur outside this time interval have no direct effect on the welfare measure. It is easy to show that, if unemployment is temporary in the sense described above, equation (8.24) changes to read (for $t < t_1$)

$$\theta V^0(t) = H^{c^0}(t) + \int_{t_1}^{t_2} [\lambda^{c^0}(s)f_l^0(s) - u_h^0(s)]\dot{l}^0(s)e^{-\theta(s-t)}ds \qquad (8.24a)$$

since $-u_h(c,h)e^{-\theta t} + \lambda f_l(l,k) = 0$ is fulfilled outside (t_1, t_2).

As shown in Chapter 5, the marginal value of leisure in real terms is appropriately measured by the real wage rate under perfect competition. This result no longer applies here. To see this, consider once again a linear approximation of the instantaneous utility function. For the model set out above we have $u(c^0, h^0) \approx \lambda^{c^0}c^0 + u_h^0 h^0$, which means that u_h^0/λ^{c^0} measures the marginal value of leisure in real terms in the linearized welfare measure. Since u_h^0/λ^{c^0} falls short of the marginal product of labor under unemployment, the marginal value of leisure cannot be measured by using the wage rate.

So far, we have not made any assumption about the cause of imperfect competition in the labor market. In other words, we just assume (without any explanation) that the wage rate exceeds the market clearing wage rate at each point in time. There are, of course, many possible causes of unemployment in real-world economies. As one among several alternatives, let us briefly consider union wage setting.[4] Given that union wage setting is the cause of unemployment, this may also provide a clue for handling the complications due to unemployment in practical applications to social accounting. In other words, the 'additional information' that union wage setting is the cause of unemployment will simplify the forward looking part of equation (8.24).

Our analysis of social accounting under union wage setting is based on Aronsson and Löfgren (1998). Suppose that a monopoly union chooses the wage rate at each point in time to maximize the consumer's objective function subject to the asset accumulation equation, the NPG condition and the additional restriction that employment is determined by the labor demand, $l(w(t), r(t))$. We also assume that the wage formation system is decentralized in the sense that the union treats profit income and the interest rate as exogenously given. The union may be regarded as part of a 'wage setting household', which chooses

consumption and the real wage rate (instead of the labor supply) simultaneously.[5]
In addition to the necessary condition for consumption and the equation of
motion for the shadow price of physical capital (which are both well known
and, therefore, suppressed above), we have to derive a necessary condition for
an optimal choice of wage rate. By substituting the labor demand function into
the instantaneous utility function and asset accumulation equation, respectively,
the first order condition for the wage rate can be written

$$\lambda^0(t)f_l^0(t) - u_h^0(t)e^{-\theta t} = -\lambda^0(t)f_l^0(t)\frac{1}{\varepsilon(t)} > 0 \qquad (8.25)$$

where $\varepsilon(t) < 0$ is the wage elasticity of the labor demand at time t. The right-
hand side of equation (8.25) measures the mark-up over the reservation wage
rate chosen by the union and provides the expression we are looking for: an
exact measure of the difference between the marginal product of labor in utility
terms and the marginal utility of leisure. Using equation (8.25), equation (8.24)
can be rewritten as

$$\theta V^0(t) = H^{c^0}(t) - \int_t^\infty \lambda^{c^0}(s)f_l^0(s)\frac{1}{\varepsilon(s)}l^0(s)e^{-\theta(s-t)}ds \qquad (8.26)$$

Equation (8.26) may be interpreted as:

Proposition 8.2 *Under monopoly union wage setting, future changes in
employment will affect the welfare level via the mark-up over the reservation
wage rate chosen by the union. The greater (smaller) future wage elasticities
of the labor demand in absolute value, the less (more) will future changes in
employment contribute to welfare.*

Proposition 8.2 is useful from a practical point of view. If we were able to
estimate the wage elasticity of the labor demand, preferably using an iso-
elastic function, we could calculate a money-metric utility corresponding to the
second term on the right-hand side of equation (8.26) using predictions of future
productivity and future changes in employment. In addition, Proposition 8.2
gives guidelines for a qualitative test of the importance of the forward looking
term. Given that union wage setting is a reasonable description of the labor
market, it is clear that the smaller the wage elasticity of the labor demand in
absolute value, the more biased the welfare measure if we neglect union wage
formation and treat the labor market as if it were competitive.

8.3 DISTRIBUTIONAL OBJECTIVES

A possible criticism of most previous studies on social accounting is that they neglect objectives for distribution of consumption (or utility) across individuals. It may be argued that, since green NNP in utility terms contains no information about the distribution across consumers, it is likely to fail as a welfare measure. Here, we address the role of distributional objectives in social accounting. The main purpose is to show that the argument above is not, in general, correct: distributional objectives themselves do not invalidate the welfare interpretation of the current value Hamiltonian. Instead, what matters is that the distributional objectives are fully implemented in a socially optimal setting. Otherwise, if the distribution is not optimal from society's point of view, welfare cannot be measured solely by using the current value Hamiltonian. This suggests that a suboptimal distribution may influence the welfare measure in the same general way as other imperfections in the market economy.

The subsequent analysis is based on Aronsson and Löfgren (1999a). As in the preceding section, we disregard emissions and environmental damage. We also disregard the possibility that leisure is an argument in the utility function, by assuming that each consumer supplies one unit of labor inelastically at each point in time. In addition, to simplify notation, we consider a model economy with only two consumers. Each consumer has an instantaneous utility function of the form

$$u_i(t) = u_i(c_i(t)) \tag{8.27}$$

for $i = 1,2$, where c_i is the consumption of individual i. Net output is produced by labor (which is constant and, therefore, suppressed) and physical capital. The net investments are given by

$$\dot{k}(t) = f(k(t)) - c_1(t) - c_2(t) \tag{8.28}$$

with $k(0) = k_0$ and $\lim_{t \to \infty} k(t) \geq 0$. We assume that the utility function and production function are increasing in their respective arguments and strictly concave.

Most previous studies on social accounting are based on representative agent models. Although such models are often useful, they do not provide a framework suitable for analyzing the implications of objectives for the distribution across individuals. We extend the analysis by allowing for objectives related to the distribution across agents at each point in time. Suppose that society's preferences for the distribution of consumption/utility across individuals at a given point in time can be represented by an instantaneous social welfare function, $\Gamma(u_1, u_2)$, which is increasing in each argument. Assume further that the instantaneous social welfare function is concave. Then, consider a situation where the resource allocation is optimal from society's point of view. To derive the socially optimal resource allocation, we follow the analytical approach used earlier by assuming that the resource allocation is decided on by a social planner. The social planner chooses the control variables $c_1(t)$ and $c_2(t)$ at each point in time to maximize

$$\int_0^\infty \Gamma(u_1(c_1(t)), u_2(c_2(t)))e^{-\theta t}\,dt$$

subject to equation (8.28) as well as to initial and terminal conditions for the physical capital stock. The present value Hamiltonian can be written as

$$H(t) = \Gamma(u_1(c_1(t)), u_2(c_2(t)))e^{-\theta t} + \lambda(t)\dot{k}(t) \tag{8.29}$$

Since the problem facing the social planner has a very simple structure, we will not go into the necessary conditions. Let $\{c_1^*(t), c_2^*(t)\}_0^\infty$ be the path for the control variables that solves the social planner's optimization problem. By substituting the optimal solution into the present value Hamiltonian, differentiating with respect to time and using Proposition 2.1, we obtain

$$\frac{dH^*(t)}{dt} = -\theta\Gamma(u_1(c_1^*(t)), u_2(c_2^*(t)))e^{-\theta t} \tag{8.30}$$

According to equation (8.30), the only non-autonomous time dependence of the economic system originates from the utility discount factor. The reason is that we have assumed a stationary technology, and the control variables are optimally chosen subject to the resource constraint. Since the present value Hamiltonian will approach zero as time goes to infinity, we can solve equation (8.30) and derive the welfare measure

$$\theta\int_t^\infty \Gamma(u_1(c_1^*(s)), u_2(c_2^*(s)))e^{-\theta(s-t)}\,ds = H^c(t) \tag{8.31}$$

The left-hand side of equation (8.31) is the welfare indicator – measured as the present value of future social welfare – times the utility discount rate, whereas the right-hand side is the current value Hamiltonian evaluated at the optimum, $H^{c*}(t) = H^*(t)e^{\theta t}$. The interpretation of equation (8.31) is given in Proposition 8.3:

Proposition 8.3 *If the distribution across agents is part of a socially optimal policy, the present value of future social welfare is proportional to the current value Hamiltonian implicit in the social planner's optimization problem.*

The intuition behind Proposition 8.3 is straightforward: since the resource allocation is optimally chosen from society's point of view, the shadow price contains all relevant information about future utility. In other words, the optimal distribution is already part of the current value Hamiltonian, so that no additional information about the distribution is necessary in order to measure welfare. The main implication of equation (8.31) is that distributional objectives themselves do not invalidate the welfare interpretation of the current value Hamiltonian underlying the social optimization problem.

In order to gain a better understanding of the information required to calculate green NNP in real terms in this case, let us linearize the current value Hamiltonian:

$$\lambda^{c^*}(t)[c_1^*(t) + c_2^*(t) + \dot{k}^*(t)]$$

As before, the linearized current value Hamiltonian is defined as the shadow price of capital times green NNP in real terms. Note that the conventional NNP and green NNP coincide in this simple model, since the only consumption concept refers to goods and services, and net investments refer solely to physical, man-made, capital.

It should be kept in mind that equation (8.31) is based on the assumption of a socially optimal resource allocation. If the actual distribution does not fully reflect the distributional objectives at each point in time, we can no longer measure welfare solely by using the current value Hamiltonian. Note that our intention is not to explain why a suboptimal distribution may arise. Our (more modest) objective is to show what the exact welfare measure looks like, when the distribution of consumption and/or utility is suboptimal over a time interval. Let us relax the assumption that the distribution across agents is socially optimal at each instant and define a new set of consumption paths, $\{c_1^0(t), c_2^0(t)\}_0^\infty$, which are given by

$$c_1^0(t) = c_1^*(t) + \delta \text{ and } c_2^0(t) = c_2^*(t) - \delta \text{ for } t \in (t_1, t_2)$$

$$c_1^0(t) = c_1^*(t) \text{ and } c_2^0(t) = c_2^*(t) \text{ otherwise}$$

where $0 < \delta < c_1^*(t), c_2^*(t)$. That is, the distribution of consumption is suboptimal for $t \in (t_1, t_2)$, while it is optimal for $t \le t_1$ and $t \ge t_2$. However, output, the capital stock and aggregate consumption, $c_1 + c_2$, remain as they were in the first best optimum. The latter is particularly appealing, since it enables us to concentrate the analysis on the implications of a suboptimal distribution. By using the short notation

$$a_i = \frac{\partial \Gamma(\cdot)}{\partial u_i} \frac{\partial u_i(\cdot)}{\partial c_i} e^{-\theta t} - \lambda,$$

the welfare measure at time t $(< t_1)$ becomes

$$\theta \int_t^\infty \Gamma(u_1(c_1^0(s)), u_2(c_2^0(s))) e^{-\theta(s-t)} ds = H^{c^0}(t) + \int_{t_1}^{t_2} \sum_{i=1}^{2} a_i^0(s) \dot{c}_i^0(s) e^{\theta t} ds \qquad (8.32)$$

since $a_i^0(t) \neq 0$ during the time interval of suboptimal distribution. We have derived the following result:

Proposition 8.4 *If the distribution is not socially optimal at each point in time, the present value of future social welfare is proportional to the sum of the current value Hamiltonian and the present value of future changes in consumption, which occur during the time interval of suboptimal distribution.*

In general, even if aggregate consumption has the desired level, green NNP in utility terms will fail as a welfare measure when the distribution of consumption is suboptimal. Therefore, a suboptimal distribution across agents affects the welfare measure in the same way as other market imperfections.

NOTES

1. For more details, see Basar and Olsder (1982).
2. A more general treatment of Stackelberg differential games may be found in Basar and Olsder (1982) and the references therein. Stackelberg differential games with non-smooth solutions are considered in Wishart and Olsder (1979). A seminal paper in this context is Cruz (1978).
3. Recall that a similar result was derived in Chapter 5, where the current value Hamiltonian of the government (the leader) constitutes a welfare measure, whereas the current value pseudo-Hamiltonian of the private sector (the follower) does not.
4. An overview of models of unionized labor markets is given by Oswald (1985).
5. The idea of capturing the behavior of a monopoly union in the context of a wage setting household originates from Löfgren (1994).

9.   Welfare measurement under uncertainty

It has been established in Chapter 2 that a static equivalent of welfare is embedded in a deterministic autonomous Ramsey problem. It has also been shown that technological progress and imperfect market conditions will complicate welfare measurement, as well as add terms that contain forward looking components. In this chapter we show that the results derived under an assumption of perfect certainty are special cases of more general results which form part of the toolkit of stochastic dynamic optimization. More precisely, such results follow as special cases of the first order conditions of a stochastic Ramsey problem. Here, as in Chapter 7, we introduce population growth explicitly into the analysis. We also provide intuition for some of the technicalities created by introducing growth as a continuous-time stochastic process known as Brownian motion (often called a Wiener process).

The chapter[1] is organized as follows. After briefly reviewing some of the mathematical tools of stochastic control theory in Section 9.1, we use these tools in Section 9.2 to analyze a stochastic Ramsey problem originally introduced by Merton (1975). In Section 9.3 we derive stochastic versions of previous welfare measures. Section 9.4 contains a paralleled analysis for a stochastic version of our workhorse model. The derivation of a cost–benefit rule is dealt with in Section 9.5, and a general principle for obtaining a closed form solution is examined in Section 9.6. We illustrate these principles and the cost–benefit rule by a numerical example. Section 9.7 sums up the results and offers suggestions for further reading.

9.1   CONTINUOUS-TIME STOCHASTIC PROCESSES

In this section we introduce the mathematical tools that are necessary for the preceding welfare analysis, which means that it will be rather abstract. A reader familiar with Ito calculus can jump directly to Section 9.2.

A stochastic process is a variable, $X(t)$, that evolves over time in a way that is – at least – to some extent random. In economic modeling, continuous-time stochastic processes are typically introduced in capital theory and financial economics. The most widely studied continuous-time process is a Brownian motion. The name originates from the English botanist Robert Brown, who in 1827 observed that small particles immersed in a liquid exhibit ceaseless irregular motions. Einstein (1905) is generally given credit for the precise mathematical formulation of the Brownian motion process, but an even earlier equivalent formulation was set down by Louis Bachelier (1900) in his theory of stock option pricing.

A stochastic process $X(t)$ is characterized by its distribution function $G(x, t)$:

$$\text{Prob}\{X(t) \leq x\} = G(x, t) \tag{9.1}$$

According to equation (9.1) the probability of finding that the process is not above some level x at time t is given by the value of the (possibly time dependent) distribution function evaluated at x. If the derivative $\partial G(x,t) / \partial x = g(x,t)$ exists, it can be used to characterize $X(t)$ as follows:

$$\text{Prob}\{x \leq X(t) \leq x + dx\} = G(x + dx, t) - G(x, t) = \tag{9.2}$$
$$= \left\{ G(x,t) + \frac{\partial G}{\partial x}(x,t)dx + O(dx) \right\} - G(x,t) = g(x,t)dx + O(dx)$$

The second equality in equation (9.2) follows from a first order Taylor expansion of $G(\cdot)$ around the point x. Here $O(dx)$ denotes terms that are of higher order than dx and, therefore, can be ignored when dx is small. More specifically, a term is of order $O(dx)$ if $\lim_{dx \to 0} O(dx)/dx = 0$. The function $g(x, t) = \partial G(x, t)/\partial x$ is the density function evaluated at $X = x$.

A Brownian motion, $B(t)$, or a Wiener process, is a stochastic process with the following properties:

(i)   the sample paths of $B(t)$ are continuous
(ii) $B(0) = 0$
(iii) the increment $B(t+\tau) - B(\tau)$ is normally distributed with mean zero and variance $\sigma^2 t$.
(iv) if (t, τ) and (t^1, τ^1) are disjoint intervals, then the increments $B(\tau) - B(t)$, and $B(\tau^1) - B(t^1)$ are independent random variables.

Let $dB = B(t + dt) - B(t)$. Then, if we denote the standard normal density function by $\phi(\cdot)$, the normality of the increments implies that

$$\text{Prob}[\beta \leq dB \leq \beta + d\beta] = \frac{1}{\sqrt{\sigma^2 dt}} \phi(\beta)d\beta = \left(\frac{1}{\sqrt{2\pi\sigma^2 dt}} \right) \exp\left(\frac{-\beta^2}{2\sigma^2 dt} \right) d\beta$$

$$\tag{9.3}$$

for a sufficiently small $d\beta$. Moreover, the first two moments of the distribution are

$$E\{dB\} = 0 \qquad\qquad E\{(dB)^2\} = \sigma^2 dt \qquad\qquad (9.4)$$

The variance of the increment dB is of order dt (proportional to the small interval dt). This gives rise to many mathematical complications. To see this, dividing both sides of the expression for the variance by $(dt)^2$ we obtain

$$E\left\{\left(\frac{dB}{dt}\right)^2\right\} = \frac{\sigma^2}{dt} \to \infty \qquad \text{as } dt \to 0 \qquad\qquad (9.5)$$

In other words, $B(t)$ is not differentiable, but nevertheless everywhere continuous.

The fourth condition of the increments of a Brownian motion process is frequently referred to as the Markov property. This reflects a kind of lack of memory, in the sense that the past history of a process does not influence its future position. The requirement of independent increments, however, is more restrictive than to require that the 'future' state only depends on the present state, which is the true Markov property.

There are other special features of a Brownian process. To exemplify, let the capital stock $K(t)$ follow a Brownian motion, that is, $E[dK] = 0$ and $E[(dK)^2] = \sigma_k^2 dt$, where $\sigma_k^2 dt$ is the variance of the increments in the capital stock. Let the production function be $Y = F[t,K(t)]$. Estimating dY at (t, K) for changes dt and dK by a second order Taylor expansion yields

$$dY = \frac{\partial F}{\partial t} dt + \frac{\partial F}{\partial K} dK + \frac{1}{2}\left[\frac{\partial^2 F}{\partial t^2}(dt)^2 + 2\frac{\partial^2 F}{\partial t \partial K} dt dK + \frac{\partial^2 F}{\partial K^2}(dK)^2\right] \qquad (9.6)$$

Since $K(t)$ is stochastic, so is Y, and the differential dY therefore makes sense in terms of moments or distributions. Taking expectations of (9.6) conditional on $K(t) = k$ gives

$$E\{dY|K(t) = k\} = \frac{\partial F(t,k)}{\partial t} dt + \frac{1}{2}\frac{\partial^2 F(t,k)}{\partial K^2}\sigma_k^2 dt + O(dt) \qquad (9.7)$$

The first second order derivative within brackets in (9.6) is merged in the term $O(dt)$, while the second vanishes because $E(dK) = 0$. The third term within brackets, which contains the second derivative of the production function times the variance of dK, is introduced since it can be shown that $E[dK^2]$ is of order dt rather than $(dt)^2$. Therefore, the expected change in production over the short interval dt consists of two terms. The first can be interpreted as technological progress, and the second measures the effect of an additional unit of capital on the marginal product of capital, which is scaled by $E[dK^2]$ $= \sigma_K^2 dt$. This term is presumably non-positive since production functions are usually assumed to be strictly concave. The interpretation is that the uncertainty of K is greater, the longer the time horizon. The expected value of a change in a strictly concave function is thus reduced by an amount that increases with time – a consequence of Jensen's inequality $E[f(x)] < (>) f(E(x))$ for a strictly concave (convex) function.

The Brownian motion induces a new calculus known as the Ito calculus after its inventor; see Ito (1944, 1946).[2] This is expressed as:

$$dY = \frac{\partial F}{\partial t} dt + \frac{\partial F}{\partial K} dK + \frac{1}{2} \frac{\partial^2 F}{\partial K^2} \sigma_K^2 dt + O(dt) \qquad (9.8)$$

where $\lim_{dt \to 0} O(dt) / dt = 0$.

Equation (9.8), which measures the first order differential of a function containing a stochastic variable that follows a Brownian motion process, is frequently referred to as Ito's lemma (or Ito's rule).

We can be more precise about the stochastic process by specifying the following general Brownian motion process:[3]

$$dK = a(K,t)dt + b(K,t)dz \qquad (9.9)$$

Here $a(K, t)$ and $b(K, t)$ are known non-random functions, which are usually referred to as the drift and variance components of the process; dz is the increment of the process, and it holds that $E[dz] = 0$ and $E[dz^2] = dt$. This means that dz can be represented by $dz = \varepsilon\sqrt{dt}$ where $\varepsilon \sim N(0, 1)$. Substitution of (9.9) into (9.8) now gives

$$dY = \left[\frac{\partial F}{\partial t} + a(K,t)\frac{\partial F}{\partial K} + \frac{1}{2} b^2(K,t)\frac{\partial^2 F}{\partial K^2} \right] dt + b(K,t)\frac{\partial F}{\partial K} dz + O(dt) \qquad (9.10)$$

Note that

$$dK^2 = a^2 dt^2 + 2abdtdz + b^2 dz^2$$

$$= b^2 dz^2 + O(dt) = b^2 dt + O(dt) \qquad (9.11)$$

since $dtdz = \varepsilon \, dt^{3/2} \propto dt^{3/2}$, and $dz^2 = \varepsilon^2 \, dt \propto dt$ (the sign $\propto$ means 'proportional to').

To introduce a more specific example, let $Y = \ln K$, and let dK follow a Brownian motion of the following shape:[4]

$$dK = \alpha K dt + \sigma K dz \qquad (9.12)$$

We now have

$$\frac{\partial F}{\partial t} = 0, \quad \frac{\partial F}{\partial K} = \frac{1}{K} \quad \text{and} \quad \frac{\partial^2 F}{\partial K^2} = -\frac{1}{K^2}$$

Moreover, $a(K, t) = \alpha K$ and $b(K, t) = \sigma K$, which substituted into (9.10) yields[5]

$$dY = \left(\alpha - \frac{\sigma^2}{2} \right) dt + \sigma dz \qquad (9.13)$$

However, over any finite interval ΔT, the change in $\ln K$ is normally distributed with mean $(\alpha - \sigma^2/2)\Delta T$ and variance $\sigma^2 \Delta T$. Again, the reason why the expected value of the change in production grows more slowly than the drift in the capital accumulation equation is the strict concavity of the production function.

9.2   A CONTINUOUS-TIME STOCHASTIC RAMSEY MODEL

We are now ready to proceed towards a continuous-time optimal growth problem under uncertainty. Early contributions in this area confined themselves to linear technologies. Phelps (1962), Leland (1968), Levhari and Srinivasan (1969) and Hahn (1970), for example, examined an optimal consumption-saving decision under uncertainty with a given linear production technology. In two seminal papers, Mirrlees (1965, 1971) treated the stochastic Ramsey problem in a continuous-time neoclassical one-sector model, subject to uncertainty about technological progress. Brock and Mirman (1972) and Mirman (1973) worked with the corresponding problem in a discrete-time context. They proved, among other things, the existence, uniqueness and stability of a steady state (asymptotic) distribution.

The analysis below relies heavily on Merton (1975), who treats the asymptotic properties of both the neoclassical growth model developed by Solow (1956) and the Ramsey (1928) optimal growth model, when the growth of the labor force follows a geometric Brownian motion process. We concentrate on welfare measurement and in particular examine the relationship between the welfare measures following from stochastic and deterministic optimal growth problems.

Let $F(K, L)$ be a linear homogeneous net production function (that is, depreciation has been accounted for), where K denotes units of capital input and L denotes units of labor input. The capital stock evolves according to

$$\dot{K}(t) = F(K(t), L(t)) - C(t) \tag{9.14}$$

Let $k = K/L$ and differentiate totally with respect to time. Using the linear homogeneity of the production function, it follows that

$$\dot{k}(t) = f(k(t)) - c(t) - nk(t) \tag{9.15}$$

where $f(k)$ is net output per capita and n is the growth rate of the population. It is assumed that $L(t) = L(0)e^{nt}$, $L(0) > 0$, $0 < n < 1$. Equation (9.15) is a variation of the Solow neoclassical differential equation of capital stock growth under certainty. Note that $dL / dt = nL$ or $dL = nLdt$.

Throughout the book, except in Chapter 7, we have neglected the possibility of population growth, since it was not essential to our analyses under perfect certainty. Now, suppose that the growth of the labor force is described by the stochastic differential equation

$$dL = nLdt + \sigma Ldz \tag{9.16}$$

The stochastic part is dz, where $z = z(t)$ is a Brownian motion process defined on some probability space. Hence the increments of the process, dz, are independent random variables with mean zero and variance $(t-s)$, $t \geq s$. In particular, we have seen already that $z(t)$, $t \geq 0$ (the sample path) is nowhere differentiable, which generates a well-known problem of integration of the differential equation (9.16).[6,7] The drift of the process is governed by the expected rate of labor growth per unit of time, n. In other words, over a short interval of time, dt, the proportionate change of the labor force (dL/L) is normally distributed with mean ndt and variance $\sigma^2 dt$.

We are now ready to transform the uncertainty about the growth in the labor force into uncertainty about growth of the capital labor ratio $k = K/L$. We use Ito's lemma or, more particularly, equation (9.8) above. To this end define

$$k(t) = \frac{K(t)}{L} = Z(L, t) \tag{9.17}$$

From equation (9.8) we know that

$$dk = \frac{\partial Z}{\partial t} dt + \frac{\partial Z}{\partial L} dL + \frac{1}{2} \frac{\partial^2 Z}{\partial L^2} dL^2 \tag{9.18}$$

Next, note that

$$\frac{\partial Z}{\partial t} = f(k) - c \qquad\qquad dL = nLdt + \sigma Ldz$$

$$\frac{\partial Z}{\partial L} = -\frac{K(t)}{L^2} = -\frac{k}{L} \qquad (dL)^2 = \sigma^2 L^2 dt \qquad (9.19)$$

$$\frac{\partial^2 Z}{\partial L^2} = 2\frac{K(t)}{L^3} = \frac{2k}{L^2}$$

In the derivation of the expression for $(dL)^2$ we have used that $dzdt$ is $O(dt)$ and that $(dz)^2 = dt$. After substitution into (9.18), we obtain

$$dk = \left[f(k) - c - (n - \sigma^2)k \right]dt - k\sigma dz \qquad (9.20)$$

In other words, we have translated uncertainty with respect to the growth rate of the labor force into uncertainty with respect to capital per unit of labor and, indirectly, to uncertainty with respect to output per unit of labor.

We are now ready to formulate a minor variation of Merton's (1975) version of the stochastic Ramsey problem. The main difference lies in Merton's assumption that saving is a fixed proportion of production, and the control problem consists of choosing an optimal saving function. Here we choose an optimal consumption function.

Let $u(c(t))$ be a twice continuously differentiable and strictly concave utility function, where $c(t)$ denotes per capita consumption. The optimization problem is to find an optimal consumption policy. The stochastic Ramsey problem can be written

$$\underset{c(t)}{Max}\ E_0\left\{ \int_0^\infty u\big(c(t)\big)e^{-\theta t}dt \right\} \qquad (9.21)$$

subject to

$$dk = \left[f(k(t)) - c(t) - (n - \sigma^2)k(t) \right]dt - \sigma k(t)dz \quad k(0) = k_0 \qquad (9.22)$$

$$c(t) \geq 0 \quad \forall t$$

E_0 denotes that mathematical expectations are taken conditional on the information available at time zero. The only non-autonomous time dependence in the above problem is introduced through the discount factor. As will become clear below, the absence of such time dependence will simplify the analysis. However, as has already been established in previous chapters, a more fundamental time dependence generated by, for example, technological progress or externalities, adds extra complications to welfare measurements. For this reason, we need a general formulation of the first order conditions for a maximum. Readers who wish to skip the mathematical technicalities below can move directly to Section 9.3, where we discuss welfare measurement, as well as compare the deterministic and the stochastic first order conditions.

The formulation of the optimization problem in equations (9.21) and (9.22) is incomplete in at least two respects. First of all, we have to specify the information on which the choice of the control function is based (this is not required in the deterministic Ramsey problem). In most contexts it is realistic to assume that the control process $c(t)$ is allowed to be conditioned solely on past observed values of the state process $k(t)$. In such a case, mathematicians would say that the control process is adapted to the state process. One special case is a control function of the form $c(t) = c(t,k(t))$, where $c(t)$ is a deterministic function. In the context of our discussion of feedback controls in connection with non-cooperative Nash games, we recognize that this is a feedback control law. More specifically, we condition the control on the state of the system at time t.

Given that we have chosen a control law, we can substitute it into the stochastic differential equation to obtain

$$dk = [f(k(t)) - c(t, k(t)) - (n - \sigma^2)k(t)]dt - \sigma k(t)dz$$

$$(9.22')$$

$$k(0) = k_0$$

An admissible control is also required to imply that the above stochastic differential equation has a unique solution.

A second problem with the above formulation is that there are restrictions on the control process but not on the capital stock (the state variable). In such circumstances the problem is likely to be nonsensical. If the utility function is unbounded in $c(t)$, the consumer can increase his utility to any given level by consuming an appropriately large amount at every t. However, this would mean that the capital stock, or wealth, goes below zero, and when it does, goods would not be produced, only consumed. This problem can be handled in different ways, but one of the most elegant is the following. Define $T = \inf[t > 0 \mid k(t) = 0] \wedge \infty$ [$x \wedge y$ means $\min(x,y)$], and rewrite the objective function as

$$E_0 \left\{ \int_0^T u(c(t))e^{-\theta t} dt \right\}$$

This formulation ensures that when the consumer holds no wealth, all activity is terminated. Before introducing the necessary condition for an optimal consumption path (control process), we define the value function and the optimal value function. The former is defined by

$$J(0, k_0^c, c) = E_0 \left\{ \int_0^T u(c(t, k(t))) e^{-\theta t} dt \right\}$$

given the dynamics in (9.22'). Here the bottom and top indexes $0,c$ denote that the path starts at zero and is driven by the control function $c(t,k(t))$. The optimal value function is defined by (skipping the top index c)

$$V(0, k_0) = \sup_c J(0, k_0, c)$$

In other words, $J(0,k_0,c)$ is the expected utility of using the control function $c(t,k(t))$ over the time interval $[0,T]$, given the starting point k_0 at time zero. The optimal value function gives the expected maximum utility over the same interval, starting at the initial condition. If we start at t with initial condition k_t, the optimal value function is $V(t,k_t)$.

We can know use the following theorem:

Theorem 9.1 (*The Hamilton–Jacobi–Bellman or HJB equation*) Assume that (a) *the optimal value function* V *is in* C^{12} *and* (b) *an optimal control* c* *exists. The following will then hold*:

(i) *V* satisfies the equation

$$\frac{\partial V(t,k)}{\partial t} + \sup_c \{u(c(t))e^{-\theta t} + h\frac{\partial V(t,k)}{\partial k} + \frac{1}{2}\frac{\partial^2 V(t,k)}{\partial k^2}\sigma^2 k^2\} = 0$$

$$\forall(t,k) \in D, \text{ where } h(k,c,n,\sigma^2) = f(k) - c - (n - \sigma^2)k;$$

(ii) the transversality condition is $V(T,k(T)) = 0$;
(iii) for each $(t,k) \in D$ the supremum in the HJB is attained by $c^* = c^*(t,k)$ where $D = [0, T] \times R_+$

A proof is outlined in an Appendix F.[8]

9.3 WELFARE MEASUREMENT

After many preliminaries we are now ready to perform the welfare analysis. The only non-autonomous time dependence in the above problem is introduced through the discount factor. This implies that the model to be discussed here is a stochastic analogue to the model in Chapter 2, where welfare was appropriately measured by the utility value of the net national product. Following Aronsson and Löfgren (1995), similar results can be derived using the present model, which contains uncertainty from the point of view of the social planner. Our starting point is the optimal value function

$$V\left(t,k_t\right) = \underset{c}{\text{Max}}\ E_t\left\{\int_t^T u\left[c(\tau)\right]e^{-\theta\tau}d\tau\right\} \tag{9.23}$$

subject to equation (9.22'), which is the Brownian motion equation for the capital stock, and $k(t) = k_t$. We now have

$$e^{\theta t}V\left(t,k_t\right) = \underset{c}{\text{Max}}\ E_t\left\{\int_t^T u[c(\tau,k(\tau))]e^{-\theta(\tau-t)}d\tau\right\} = W(t,k_t) \tag{9.24}$$

$$k(t) = k_t$$

where $W(t,k_t)$ is the optimal current value function. For the case when $T = \infty$ it is straightforward to prove that[9]

Observation 1: $V(t,k_t) = V(0,k_t)e^{-\theta t}$

which means that the current value function, $W(k_t) = V(0,k_t)$, does not depend on the starting point. This implies that

$$V_t = \frac{d}{dt}\left[e^{-\theta t}W\right] = -\theta e^{-\theta t}W$$

and the HJB equation can be rewritten in the following manner:

$$\theta W = \underset{c \in A}{\text{Max}}\left[u(c(t)) + W_k h(k,c;\sigma,n) + \frac{1}{2}\sigma^2 k^2 W_{kk}\right] \tag{9.25}$$

where $W_k = \partial W(\cdot)/\partial k$ and $W_{kk} = \partial^2 W(\cdot)/\partial k^2$. We can now define a co-state variable $p(t)$ as

$$p(t) = W_k(k(t)) \tag{9.26}$$

and its derivative

$$\frac{\partial p}{\partial k}(t) = W_{kk}(k(t)) \tag{9.27}$$

Given the optimal consumption policy, (9.25) can be written (neglecting the top index on $k(t)$, and the time index to save notational clutter) as

$$\theta W\left(k_t\right) = u\left(c^*\right) + ph(k,c^*;n,\sigma) + \frac{1}{2}\frac{\partial p}{\partial k}\sigma^2 k^2 = H^{c^*}\left(k,p,\frac{\partial p}{\partial k}\right) \quad (9.28)$$

The function $H^{c^*}(\cdot)$ can be interpreted as a 'generalized' Hamiltonian in current value terms (see below). This generalized Hamiltonian plays a key role in the welfare measure. However, prior to carrying out the welfare analysis, and in order to relate the results here to those in Chapter 2, we derive the conditions describing how the variables k and p develop over time. Using (9.22') and the definition of H^{c^*}, we obtain

$$dk = h(k,c^*;n,\sigma)dt - \sigma k dz = \left[H^{c^*}_p\left(k,p,\frac{\partial p}{\partial k}\right)\right]dt - \sigma k dz = H^{c^*}_p dt - \sigma k dz \quad (9.29)$$

where $H^{c^*}_p = \partial H^{c^*}/\partial p$. Equation (9.29) describes how k develops over time under the optimal consumption policy. To find the corresponding condition for p, we use Ito's lemma and derive

$$d\tilde{p} = \left[V_{kt} + V_{kk}h + \frac{1}{2}V_{kkk}\sigma^2 k^2\right]dt - V_{kk}\sigma k dz \quad (9.30)$$

where $\tilde{p}(t) = p(t)e^{-\theta t}$. As in the case of perfect certainty, it is often convenient to relate $d\tilde{p}$ to derivatives of 'the Hamiltonian'. Using the expression $-V_t = H^{c^*}e^{-\theta t} = \theta We^{-\theta t}$ to compute V_{kt}, we can, after substitutions, rewrite (9.30) to read

$$d\tilde{p} = -H^*_k e^{-\theta t}dt - \sigma k e^{-\theta t}W_{kk}dz \quad (9.31)$$

where $H^{c^*}_k = \partial H^{c^*}/\partial k$. Next, since $d\tilde{p} = (dp - \theta p dt)e^{-\theta t}$, (9.31) is easily transformed into current value terms, that is,

$$dp - \theta p dt = -H^{c^*}_k dt - \sigma k W_{kk}dz \quad (9.32)$$

Let us now interpret equations (9.28), (9.29) and (9.32). In so doing, we relate them to their counterparts under certainty. Equation (9.28) clearly implies that the generalized Hamiltonian in current value terms equals interest on the expected future utility. This means that (9.28) is the welfare measure we are looking for. Using the definition of $W(\cdot)$, the analogue of the welfare measure in Chapter 2 becomes

$$\theta E_t \left\{ \int_t^T u(c^*)e^{-\theta(\tau-t)}d\tau \right\} = H^{c^*}\left(k,p,\frac{\partial p}{\partial k}\right) = u(\cdot) + ph + \frac{1}{2}\frac{\partial p}{\partial k}\sigma^2 k^2 \qquad (9.28')$$

The interpretation of the generalized current value Hamiltonian is that it is the sum of the instantaneous utility, the expected infinitesimal increment of capital valued at its marginal expected current value, plus the valuation of the risk associated with a given investment. If an individual is risk averse (loving), $\partial p/\partial k = W_{kk}$ is negative (positive), and, loosely speaking, welfare is lower (higher) under uncertainty than under certainty.

The stochastic differential equation (9.29) reveals how capital evolves over time along the optimal path, while equation (9.32) is the corresponding stochastic differential equation for the development of the co-state variable over time which, by definition, is interpreted as the derivative of the optimal value function with respect to the state variable.

In the deterministic case $\sigma = 0$ and

$$H^{c^*} = u\left(c^*\right) + ph\left(k,c^*;0,n\right) = \theta \int_t^\infty u\left(c^*\right)e^{-\theta(s-t)}ds \qquad (9.33)$$

which is the welfare measure corresponding to the deterministic Ramsey problem in Chapter 2. Moreover, since the wiener process is eliminated from the equations for dk and dp, the time derivates dk/dt and dp/dt are well defined. Hence we have

$$\frac{dk}{dt} = h(k,c^*;0,n) = f(k) - nk - c^*$$

$$\frac{dp}{dt} - \theta p = -\frac{\partial H^{c^*}}{\partial k}$$

which are current value dynamic equations for the deterministic Ramsey problem in Chapter 2.

As a final phase of the analysis, consider the case of non-attributable technological progress, such that time becomes a separate argument in the production function. Following the analysis in Chapter 2, the per capita production function can be written $f(k, t)$, where $\partial f(\cdot)/\partial t$ measures the effect of non-attributable technological progress on output. Using this production function, the optimal value function in present value terms is written

$$V\left(t,k(t)\right) = \underset{c}{\text{Max }} E_t \left[\int_t^T u(c(s))e^{-\theta s}ds \right] \qquad (9.34)$$

subject to

$$dk = [f(k,t) - c - (n - \sigma^2)k]dt - \sigma k dz, \quad k(0) = k_0 \qquad (9.35)$$

and $k(t) \geq 0$. Now, define the current value function

$$W(k(t),t) = e^{\theta t}V(k(t),t) \qquad (9.36)$$

Observation 1 is no longer valid, since the production function depends explicitly on time, and $V_t = [-\theta W + W_t]e^{-\theta t}$, where $W_t = \partial W/\partial t$. The Hamilton–Jacobi–Bellman equation then becomes

$$\theta W - W_t = \max_c \left[u(c) + W_k h(k,c,t;\sigma,n) + \frac{1}{2}W_{kk}\sigma^2 k^2 \right] \qquad (9.37)$$

Let $c^*(t,k)$ be the optimal consumption policy. Substituting this into (9.37) gives the welfare measure

$$H^{c^*}\left(k, p, \frac{\partial p}{\partial k}, t\right) + W_t = \theta W \qquad (9.38)$$

where $H^{c^*} = u(\cdot) + ph + \frac{1}{2}\frac{\partial p}{\partial k}\sigma^2 k^2$ evaluated along the optimal path and p has the same interpretation as previously. Equation (9.38) implies that the expected future utility, W, is proportional to the sum of the generalized Hamiltonian, H^{c^*}, and the expected present value of marginal technological progress, W_t. The corresponding result derived in Chapter 2 follows as a special case when $\sigma \to 0$.

9.4   THE STOCHASTIC WORKHORSE

We now augment the stochastic version of the Ramsey model with a stochastic pollution equation and a pollution externality. In other words, we introduce a stochastic version of the Brock model. Hence the stochastic population growth which generated the stochastic Ramsey problem is retained.

We modify the objective function to read

$$U(0) = \int_0^\infty u(c(t), x(t))e^{-\theta t}dt \qquad (9.39)$$

In other words, we insert the stock of pollution, $x(t)$, as an additional argument in the utility function. The evolution of the capital stock per capita obeys the stochastic differential equation

$$dk(t) = [f(k(t), g(t)) - c(t) - (n - \sigma_1^2)k(t)]dt - \sigma_1 k(t)dw_1 \qquad (9.40)$$

$$k(0) = k_0$$

where $g(t)$ is again interpreted as the input of energy per capita. The stock of pollution evolves according to

$$dx(t) = g(t)x(t)dt - \sigma_2 \gamma x(t)dw_2 \qquad (9.41)$$

$$x(0) = x_0$$

i.e. $dx(t)$ follows a geometric Brownian motion process with drift. The stochastic increments dw_1 and dw_2 are independent. The form of the process is chosen to keep $x(t)$ positive. To see how the process works, we introduce the following heuristic argument. Let us guess an exponential form of the solution to equation (9.41) by trying $X = \ln x$ to derive

$$dX = \left(g(t) - \frac{\sigma_2^2 \gamma^2}{2} \right) dt - \sigma_2 \gamma dw_2 \qquad (9.42)$$

$$X(0) = \ln x_0 = X_0$$

This equation does not have X on the RHS, so that we can integrate directly to get

$$X(t) = \ln x_0 + \int_0^t g(s)ds - \frac{\sigma_2^2 \gamma^2}{2} t + \sigma_2 \gamma w_2 \qquad (9.43)$$

and taking antilogarithms we obtain

$$x(t) = x_0 e^{\left(\int_0^t g(s)ds - \frac{\sigma_2^2 \gamma^2 t}{2} + \sigma_2 \gamma w_2 \right)} \qquad (9.44)$$

as a candidate for the solution of (9.41). More formally, define the process of $x(t)$ by (9.44). It is then straightforward to show that $x(t)$ so defined solves the stochastic differential equation (9.41).

As in Section 9.3 we assume that the control process is adapted to the state process and we choose to allow a feedback control. If we define

$$y(t) = \begin{bmatrix} c(t) \\ g(t) \end{bmatrix} \quad s(t) = \begin{bmatrix} k(t) \\ x(t) \end{bmatrix} \qquad (9.45)$$

the control process can be written in the following manner: $y(t) = y(t,s(t))$, where $y(t)$ is a deterministic control function. By substituting the control functions into the stochastic differential equations (9.40) and (9.41) we obtain

$$ds(t) = \begin{bmatrix} dk(t) \\ dx(t) \end{bmatrix} = \begin{bmatrix} h(c(t,k,x)g(t,k,x),k;\sigma_1,n) \\ e(t,k,x) \end{bmatrix} dt - \begin{bmatrix} \sigma_1 k \\ \sigma_2 \gamma \end{bmatrix} dw(t) \quad (9.46)$$

$$s(0) = \begin{bmatrix} k_0 \\ x_0 \end{bmatrix}$$

where $e = g(t)x(t)$.

As in the preceding section an admissible control is required to imply that the above system of stochastic differential equations has a unique solution. We also require that $y(t) \geq 0$. Moreover, to avoid a nonsensical solution, we introduce the rule that $T = \inf[t > 0 | k(t) = 0] \wedge \infty$.

Hence, we can write the optimal value function as

$$J(0, s_0) = \sup_y \int_0^T u(c(t), x(t)) e^{-\theta t} dt \quad (9.47)$$

subject to equations (9.46). Again, the value function will satisfy a HJB equation similar to that in Theorem 9.1 above. The generalized HJB equation can be written

$$\frac{\partial V(t,s)}{\partial t} + \sup_y \left\{ u(c(t), x(t)) e^{-\theta t} + \Delta^y V(t,s) \right\} = 0 \quad \forall (t,s) \in D \quad (9.48)$$

Here Δ^y is a differential operator. Next, start from equation (9.46) and write compactly in vector notation

$$ds_t^y = a^y(t,s)dt - \sigma^y(t,s)dw(t) \quad (9.46')$$

where the top index denotes that the process is driven by the control function $y(t)$ or a fixed vector y. To clarify $\sigma^y(t,s) = \sigma^y(t,s,y(t,s))$, if the process is driven by a control function, and if the control vector is fixed, y is substituted for $y(t,s)$.

We now define a matrix[10]

$$M^y = \sigma^y(t,s,y)\sigma^y(t,s,y)' \quad (9.49)$$

where the prime denotes the transpose of a vector. The partial differential operator can now be defined as

$$\Delta^y = \sum_{i=1}^{2} a^y(t,s)\frac{\partial}{\partial s_i} + \frac{1}{2}\sum_{i=1}^{2}\sum_{j=1}^{2} M_{ij}^y \frac{\partial^2}{\partial s_i \partial s_j} \qquad (9.50)$$

with an obvious modification for a case with n stochastic differential equations. For the present case with two SDEs, after applying the operator, we have

$$-\frac{\partial V(t,s)}{\partial t} = \sup_y \left\{ u(c(t),x(t))e^{-\theta t} + \frac{\partial V(t,s)}{\partial k}h(t,s) + \frac{\partial V(t,s)}{\partial x}e(t,s) \right.$$
$$\left. + \frac{1}{2}\left[\frac{\partial^2 V(t,s)}{\partial k^2}\sigma_1^2 k^2 + \frac{\partial^2 V}{\partial x^2}\sigma_2^2\gamma^2 x^2 \right] \right\} \qquad (9.48')$$

After applying the same technicalities as in the one dimensional case in Section 9.3 we obtain an expression corresponding to equation (9.28), that is,

$$-\frac{\partial V(t,s)}{\partial t} = \sup_y H\left(t,s,y,\tilde{p},\frac{\partial \tilde{p}}{\partial s}\right) = H^*\left(t,s,\tilde{p},\frac{\partial \tilde{p}}{\partial s}\right) \qquad (9.51)$$

Here H^* is the generalized present value 'Hamiltonian', and $\tilde{p}(t) = (\tilde{p}_k,\tilde{p}_x) = (\partial V/\partial k, \partial V/\partial x)$ defines the stochastic co-state variables in present value. Since the increments dw_1 and dw_2 are uncorrelated, a multidimensional analogue of the co-state stochastic differential equations has the following shape:

$$d\tilde{p}_k = -H_k^* dt - \frac{\partial^2 V}{\partial k^2}\sigma_1 k dw_1 - \frac{\partial^2 V}{\partial k \partial x}\sigma_2 \gamma x dw_2 \qquad (9.52)$$

$$d\tilde{p}_x = -H_x^* dt - \frac{\partial^2 V}{\partial x^2}\sigma_2 \gamma x dw_2 - \frac{\partial^2 V}{\partial x \partial k}\sigma_1 k dw_1$$

The derivation of the general form of the stochastic co-state equations follows the reasoning in Section 9.3, where there is only one state variable. Thus, we can begin by defining the co-state variable as the derivative of the optimal value function with respect to the state variables and take the first differential using Ito's Lemma. The resulting expression contains a term which is the cross-derivative of the optimal value function with respect to time and the state variable. The shape of this derivative can be obtained by taking the first derivative of the HJB equation with respect to the state variable, again using Ito calculus. Substituting the resulting expression for the cross-derivative into the original co-state differential equation and canceling terms gives the result in (9.52). For details, see Appendix F. The calculations in the *n*-state variable case are straightforward, although somewhat messy.[11] They are therefore omitted.

Again, we have shown that buried in the HJB partial differential equation is our first best welfare measure.

9.5　COST–BENEFIT RULES[12]

The form of the co-state equation 9.52 contains the key to the shape of a cost–benefit rule under Brownian motion. Since the co-state variable measures the marginal contribution to the value function due to an increase in the state variable, they can be used to derive a cost–benefit rule. The trick is to introduce an artificial or, rather, an unnecessary state variable in terms of a parameter that describes a project. In the model above, the parameter γ could represent a project that improves the assimilative capacity of the environment. Since it is a constant, we can write its differential equation as $d\gamma = 0, \gamma(0) = \gamma$. This gives us three stochastic differential equations, one of which is highly deterministic. We can nevertheless elicit a co-state variable by defining it as the partial derivative of the optimal value function, that is, $\tilde{p}_\gamma = \partial V / \partial \gamma$. We can then use the general form of the co-state equation in (9.52) to write

$$d\tilde{p}_\gamma = -H_\gamma^*(\cdot)dt + \frac{\partial^2 V}{\partial \gamma^2}\sigma_3 dw_3 - \frac{\partial^2 V}{\partial \gamma \partial k}\sigma_1 kdw_1 - \frac{\partial^2 V}{\partial \gamma \partial x}\sigma_2 \gamma x dw_2 \quad (9.53)$$

However, $\sigma_3 \equiv 0$ by assumption and we can integrate (9.53) over the interval (t,T) to get

$$\tilde{p}_\gamma(T) = \tilde{p}_\gamma(t) - \int_t^T H_\gamma^*(\cdot)ds - \int_t^T \frac{\partial^2 V}{\partial \gamma \partial k}\sigma_1 kdw_1 - \int_t^T \frac{\partial^2 V}{\partial \gamma \partial x}\sigma_2 \gamma x dw_2 \quad (9.54)$$

If $\tilde{p}_\gamma(T) = 0$, according to the tranversality condition, we obtain the cost–benefit rule as

$$\tilde{p}_\gamma(t) = \int_t^T H_\gamma^*(\tau)d\tau + \int_t^T \frac{\partial^2 V}{\partial \gamma \partial k}\sigma_1 kdw_1 + \int_t^T \frac{\partial^2 V}{\partial \gamma \partial x}\sigma_2 \gamma x dw_2 \quad (9.55)$$

Taking mathematical expectations of both sides and using the fact that the last two integrals are Ito integrals, we have[13]

$$E(\tilde{p}_\gamma) = E\left\{\int_t^T H_\gamma^*(\tau)d\tau\right\} \qquad (9.56)$$

which is a close analogue to the corresponding cost–benefit rule in the deterministic case in Chapter 2.

Project uncertainty can be introduced in this context by specifying the differential equation for the project state variable as

$$d\gamma = \sigma_3 dw_3, \quad \gamma(0) = \gamma_0 \qquad (9.57)$$

Now all terms in equation (9.53) are relevant, and equation (9.55) will contain one more Ito integral. In mathematical expectations the answer will look the same as in equation (9.56).

9.6   ADDITIONAL COMMENTS ON THE SOLUTION OF THE HJB EQUATION

Theorem 9.1 and its multidimensional analogue comprise a necessary condition, since the theorem states that if $\hat{y}$ is an optimal control, then the value function fulfills the HJB equation, and $\hat{y}$ realizes the supremum in the equation. The formal proof of this theorem is rather involved and omitted here; an intuitive informal sketch can been found in, for example, Björk (1998) and in Appendix F. The formal proof of a slightly sharper theorem, where the *ad hoc* assumption that a solution exists is relaxed, may be found in Öksendahl (2000, Chapter 11).

A surprising aspect is that the HJB equation also acts as a sufficient condition. The so-called 'verification theorem' states that if there are two functions $V(t,x)$ and $y(t,x)$, where $V(t,x)$ solves the HJB equation and the admissible control function $y(t,x)$ implies that the supremum is attained in equation (9.48), then the former function is identical to the optimal value function, while the latter is the optimal control function. The proof is accessible, and can be studied in both Björk (1998) and Öksendahl (2000).

Surprisingly, the fact that we have restricted the control function to be a feedback (or Markov) control is not so restrictive. One can show that it typically coincides with the optimal control conditioned on the whole history of the state process.[14]

Technically and schematically, we handle the solution of a stochastic control problem in the following manner. We consider the HJB as a partial differential equation for an unknown function V. Fix an arbitrary point (t,s) and solve the static optimization problem

$$\underset{y}{\text{Max}}\left[u(t,s,y)e^{-\theta t}+\Delta^{y}V(t,s)\right]$$

The optimal solution will depend on the arbitrary point and the function V. We can write

$$\hat{y}=\hat{y}(t,s,V)$$

substitute this into the HJB equation and solve for V. The last step entails the hardest problems. However, it is sometimes helpful to borrow the form of the instantaneous utility function as a blueprint for the form of V.

The following exercise illustrates the solution process as well as the derivation of the cost–benefit rule. We consider the following stochastic control problem

$$V(t,x)=\underset{c}{\text{Min}}\, E_{t}\left[\int_{t}^{\infty}(x^{2}(s)+c^{2}(s))e^{-\rho s}ds\right]$$

where the underlying process is given by

$$dx(s)=c(x(s))ds+\sigma\gamma dw(s)$$
$$x(t)=x_{t}$$

Defining $\tilde{p}_{\gamma}=V_{\gamma}$, we want to calculate $E_{t}(\tilde{p}_{\gamma})$, where the subindex t indicates that the process starts at time t. The problem can be approached in two ways: either explicitly solve the stochastic optimal control problem and develop all expressions explicitly before carrying out the calculation or, more simply, use the cost–benefit rule in equation (9.56). The second approach means less work.

We start with the first approach. The HJB equation becomes

$$-\frac{\partial V}{\partial t}=\underset{c}{\text{Min}}\left[e^{-\rho t}(x^{2}+c^{2})+c\frac{\partial V(t,x)}{\partial x}+\frac{1}{2}\sigma^{2}\gamma^{2}\frac{\partial^{2}V(t,x)}{\partial x^{2}}\right]$$

Minimizing with respect to the control variable gives

$$c=-\frac{1}{2}e^{\rho t}\frac{\partial V(t,x)}{\partial x}$$

Inserting the expression for the control variable into the HJB equation, we obtain

$$0=e^{-\rho t}x^{2}-\frac{1}{4}e^{\rho t}\left(\frac{\partial V(t,x)}{\partial x}\right)^{2}+\frac{\partial V(t,x)}{\partial t}+\frac{1}{2}\sigma^{2}\gamma^{2}\frac{\partial^{2}V(t,x)}{\partial x^{2}}$$

By using separation of variables as a blueprint for the value function, write $V(t,x) = e^{-\rho t}\phi(x)$, and $\phi(x) = ax^2 + b$. We may then solve for the parameters. If the control is only allowed to assume negative values we may conclude, by referring to Theorem 11.2.2. in Öksendahl (2000), that we have found the unique solution to the stochastic optimal control problem under consideration. In fact, the parameter a does not depend on γ. The optimal value function is given by

$$V(t,x) = e^{-\rho t}\left(x^2 + \frac{\sigma^2\gamma^2}{\rho}\right)a$$

and the minimized present value Hamiltonian becomes

$$H^* = e^{-\rho t}[x^2(1-a^2)+\sigma^2\gamma^2 a]$$

Therefore,

$$\tilde{p}_\gamma = 2e^{-\rho t}\frac{\sigma^2}{\rho}\gamma a = \int_t^\infty H_\gamma^*(s)ds$$

In this particular case, taking expectations makes no difference.

Now moving to the second approach, by definition

$$-\frac{\partial V(t,x)}{\partial t} = H^*(t,x,\gamma,V_x,V_{xx})$$

Differentiation of H^* with respect to γ gives

$$H_\gamma^* = \sigma^2\gamma V_{xx} = 2e^{-\rho t}\sigma^2\gamma a$$

where we have used the explicit solution. Therefore according to our cost–benefit result

$$E_t(\tilde{p}_\gamma) = E_t\left[\int_t^\infty H_\gamma^*(s)ds\right] = 2e^{-\rho t}\frac{\sigma^2}{\rho}\gamma a$$

9.7   SUMMARY AND CONCLUDING COMMENTS

We have shown how the Hamilton–Jacobi–Bellman equation from stochastic control theory can be used to derive the appropriate welfare measure under uncertainty, which turns out to be analogous to its deterministic counterpart. A generalized Hamiltonian is directly proportional to the expected future utility along the optimal path. Not surprisingly, but neatly, the stochastic welfare measure collapses to the corresponding deterministic measure, when $\sigma \to 0$.

The main part of the analysis was based on the assumption that non-autonomous time dependence enters only through the discount factor. In the more general case with non-attributable technological progress or externalities, the situation is only slightly more complex; cf. Löfgren (1992) regarding deterministic technological progress, and Aronsson and Löfgren (1993, 1995) for the general deterministic case. The generalized Hamiltonian will be augmented with an extra component measuring the expected present value of marginal technological progress.

Weitzman (1998) shows that similar results continue to hold in expectations, when the rate of time preference follows a geometric Brownian motion. In Weitzman (2003), he demonstrates how the relationship between a Stratonovich integral and an Ito integral can be used to get rid of the variance component in the generalized Hamiltonian. This way of introducing the result corresponds, except for mathematical expectations, exactly to the original result in Weitzman (1976).

We have, of course, only offered a narrow, but hopefully self-contained, presentation of modern stochastic methods in economics and finance. Many interesting topics remain to be covered. For instance, a statistician or even an economist might be interested in answering a question of the following type. If the capital stock $k(t)$ follows a particular stochastic process, say a Brownian motion, and its current value is k_0, what is the probability that the capital stock would be in a certain range at some later time t? The answer requires a description of how the probability distribution of the capital stock evolves over time. In particular, we might be interested in deriving a steady state or equilibrium distribution of the capital stock, which would, in turn, through utility, production and saving functions enable us to calculate the moments of essentially all relevant entities of the growth problem. But this turns out to be a rather difficult task. The existence problem of a stationary distribution for a stochastic differential equation has been solved in the mathematical literature for special cases. The particular model used in this chapter was analyzed in this respect by Merton (1975). He showed that the stationary distribution for the capital stock is, in general, not unique, but in the case of a Cobb–Douglas production function, the uniqueness problem can be solved by asking which constant saving function is optimal.

Today, there are many textbook presentations of Ito calculus and stochastic control theory which are accessible to non-mathematicians. We would like to recommend the book by Dixit and Pindyck (1994) as a starter. Essentially the same material from a finance perspective is available in Björk (1998) and, at a more advanced level, in Duffie (1992). Malliaris and Brock (1991) is a good survey of the entire field, starting with measure theory, through Ito calculus and stochastic control, and ending with applications to economics and finance. One of the best textbooks dealing with stochastic differential equations is Öksendahl (2000). A true professional could consult Krylov (1980).

NOTES

1. The first three sections of this chapter are partly based on Aronsson and Löfgren (1995) and Aronsson et al. (1997), while Sections 9.4–9.6 contain new material.
2. An alternative way of defining a stochastic integral under Brownian motion was introduced by Stratonovich (1966). It results in a more conventional, but perhaps less practical, calculus.
3. A process whose trend and volatility are functions of the state is often referred to as a diffusion process.
4. Samuelson (1965) called this specific process geometric Brownian motion with drift.
5. Terms of magnitude $O(dt)$ are ignored in equation (9.13).
6. Since $dz = \varepsilon\sqrt{dt}$, we have $\dfrac{dz}{dt} = \dfrac{\varepsilon}{2} dt^{-1/2}$ and $\lim_{dt \to 0} \dfrac{\varepsilon}{2} dt^{-1/2} = +\infty$ for $\varepsilon > 0$.

   Hence, (9.16) cannot be written as a derivative.
7. For more details see Malliaris and Brock (1991) and/or Åström (1970).
8. A formal proof is found in Öksendahl (2000), Chapter 11. The notation C^{12} denotes the class of differentiable functions, where a member is differentiable once with respect to the first argument and twice with respect to the second.
9. Proof: $V(t, k_t) = e^{-\theta t} \operatorname*{Max}_{c} \int_{t}^{\infty} u(c(\tau))e^{-\theta(\tau - t)}d\tau = e^{-\theta t} \operatorname*{Max}_{c} \int_{0}^{\infty} u(c(\tilde{\tau}))e^{-\theta\tilde{\tau}}d\tilde{\tau} = e^{-\theta t}V(0, k_t)$
10. Here σ^y is a 2×2 matrix with σ_1 and σ_2 along the main diagonal.
11. The n-dimensional case is not difficult to guess, however.
12. See also Aronsson et al. (2002).
13. See, for example, Björk (1998, pp. 31–2). The reasons are that the process is adapted and that the increments are independent.
14. See Theorem 11.2.3 in Öksendahl (2000).

Appendices

APPENDIX A

Derivation of Equation (4.5)

By applying the approach to the dynamic envelope theorem suggested by Léonard (1987), let us define the present value Hamiltonian:

$$\bar{H}(t,\xi) = u(c^0(t,\xi), x^0(t,\xi))e^{-\theta t} + \lambda(t)\dot{k}^0(t,\xi) \tag{A1}$$

for an arbitrary and differentiable function $\lambda(t)$ In equation (A1), we have used that $\dot{k}^0 = f(k^0, g^0) - c^0$ in the general equilibrium. With the exception that the function $\lambda(t)$ is arbitrary and does not depend on the parameter vector ξ, equation (A1) is equivalent to the maximized present value Hamiltonian of the consumer evaluated in the general equilibrium for the imperfectly controlled market economy.

Since $u(c^0, x^0)e^{-\theta t} = \bar{H} - \lambda \dot{k}^0$, and by applying the rules of partial integration, the optimal value function can be written as

$$V^0(0;\xi) = \int_0^\infty [\bar{H}(t;\xi) + \dot{\lambda}(t)k^0(t;\xi)]dt - \lambda(t)k^0(t;\xi)\Big|_0^\infty \tag{A2}$$

The cost–benefit rule we are looking for is derived by differentiating equation (A2) with respect to α and evaluating the resulting derivative at the initial equilibrium, where $\lambda(t) = \lambda^0(t;\xi)$ and $\alpha = 0$. We can write the cost–benefit rule as

$$\frac{\partial V^0(0;\xi)}{\partial \alpha} = \int_0^\infty \left[\frac{\partial \bar{H}^0(t;\xi)}{\partial \alpha} + \dot{\lambda}^0(t;\xi)\frac{\partial k^0(t;\xi)}{\partial \alpha} \right]dt \tag{A3}$$

since $k(0)$ is fixed and $\lim_{t\to\infty}\lambda^0(t;\xi) = 0$. Note that (if time argument and the vector ξ are suppressed for notational convenience)

$$\frac{\partial \bar{H}^0}{\partial \alpha} = u_x^0 e^{-\theta t}\frac{\partial x^0}{\partial \alpha} + \lambda^0\left(f_k^0 \frac{\partial k^0}{\partial \alpha} + f_g^0 \frac{\partial g^0}{\partial \alpha} \right) \tag{A4}$$

where $u_x^0 = u_x(c^0, x^0)$, $f_k^0 = f_k(k^0, g^0)$ and $f_g^0 = f_g(k^0, g^0)$. Equation (A4) is derived by using equation (4.1), which implies $\partial \bar{H}^0/\partial c = 0$. By substituting equation (A4) into equation (A3), while using equations (4.2) and (4.3), we obtain equation (4.5).

APPENDIX B

Derivation of Equation (4.17)

Differentiate the pseudo-Hamiltonian totally with respect to time to obtain

$$\frac{dH_p^0(t)}{dt} = \frac{\partial H_p^0(t)}{\partial c(t)} \dot{c}^0(t) + \frac{\partial H_p^0(t)}{\partial g(t)} \dot{g}^0(t) + \frac{\partial H_p^0(t)}{\partial k(t)} \dot{k}^0(t) + \frac{\partial H_p^0(t)}{\partial \lambda(t)} \dot{\lambda}^0(t) \qquad (B1)$$

$$+ \frac{\partial H_p^0(t)}{\partial x(t)} \dot{x}^0(t) + \frac{\partial H_p^0(t)}{\partial t}$$

Now, $\partial H_p^0(t)/\partial c(t) = \partial H_p^0(t)/\partial g(t) = 0$ and

$$\frac{\partial H_p^0(t)}{\partial \lambda(t)} \dot{\lambda}^0(t) = - \frac{\partial H_p^0(t)}{\partial k(t)} \dot{k}^0(t)$$

What then remains is

$$\frac{dH_p^0(t)}{dt} = \frac{\partial H_p^0(t)}{\partial x(t)} \dot{x}^0(t) + \frac{\partial H_p^0(t)}{\partial t} \qquad (B2)$$

$$= [u_x^0(t)e^{-\theta t} - \gamma \frac{\bar{u}_x^0(t)}{\theta + \gamma} e^{-\theta t}] \dot{x}^0(t) - \theta u(c^0(t), x^0(t))e^{-\theta t}$$

$$- \theta \frac{\bar{u}_x^0(t)}{\theta + \gamma} \dot{x}^0(t)$$

$$= -\theta u(c^0(t), x^0(t))e^{-\theta t}$$

since $\bar{u}_x^0(t)$ is constant and equal to $u_x(c^0(t), x^0(t))$.

APPENDIX C

Proof of Proposition 5.4

Differentiating equation (5.2) with respect to α, and evaluating the derivative at the decentralized equilibrium, gives

$$\frac{\partial^2 x^0(t;\xi)}{\partial t \partial \alpha} = \frac{\partial g^0(t;\xi)}{\partial \alpha} - \gamma \frac{\partial x^0(t;\xi)}{\partial \alpha} = \frac{\partial^2 x^0(t;\xi)}{\partial \alpha \partial t} \tag{C1}$$

By solving equation (C1) for $\partial g^0/\partial \alpha$, substituting into equation (5.50) and integrating by parts, we obtain (neglecting the time indicator and the vector ξ)

$$\frac{\partial V^0(0;\xi)}{\partial \alpha} = \int_0^\infty \left[\phi^0 \left(\tau_l^0 f_l^0(\cdot) \frac{\partial l^0}{\partial \alpha} + \tau_k^0 f_k^0(\cdot) \frac{\partial k^0}{\partial \alpha} \right) \right.$$
$$\left. + \{ u_x^0(\cdot) e^{-\theta t} + \phi^0 \tau^0 \gamma - \dot{\phi}^0 \tau^0 - \phi^0 \dot{\tau}^0 \} \frac{\partial x^0}{\partial \alpha} \right] dt \tag{C2}$$

Then, by substituting equations (5.19) and (5.52) for $\dot{\phi}^0$ and $\dot{\tau}^0$, respectively, into equation (C2), we can derive equation (5.53). ∎

APPENDIX D

Proofs of some Mathematical Results in Chapter 6

Straightforward differentiation of the optimal value function in equation (6.23) with respect to α gives

$$\frac{\partial W(0,\alpha)}{\partial \alpha} = \int_0^\infty \left[\sum_{i=1}^2 \frac{\partial u_i^0}{\partial c_i} \frac{\partial c_i^0}{\partial \alpha} + \sum_{i=1}^2 \sum_{j=1}^2 \frac{\partial u_i^0}{\partial z_i} \frac{\partial z_i^0}{\partial x_j} \frac{\partial x_j^0}{\partial \alpha} \right] e^{-\theta t} dt \tag{D1}$$

where the time indicator has been suppressed and the derivatives are evaluated at $\alpha = 0$.

The first sum can be rewritten as $\Delta C = \sum_{i=1}^2 \lambda_i^0 (\partial c_i^0 / \partial \alpha)$, since $\lambda_i^0 = (\partial u_i^0/\partial c_i) e^{-\theta t}$. From assumed differentiability and Young's Theorem we use the equation for the accumulation of capital to get

$$\frac{\partial^2 k_i^0}{\partial t \partial \alpha} = \frac{\partial f_i^0}{\partial k_i} \frac{\partial k_i^0}{\partial \alpha} + \frac{\partial f_i^0}{\partial g_i} \frac{\partial g_i^0}{\partial \alpha} - \frac{\partial c_i^0}{\partial \alpha} = \frac{\partial^2 k_i^0}{\partial \alpha \partial t} \tag{D2}$$

The next step is to solve (D2) for $\partial c_i^0/\partial \alpha$ and substitute the result into $\int_0^\infty \Delta C dt$. Note that

$$\int_0^\infty \lambda_i^0(t) \frac{\partial^2 k_i^0(t)}{\partial \alpha \partial t} dt = \lambda_i^0(t) \frac{\partial k_i^0(t)}{\partial \alpha} \Big|_0^\infty - \int_0^\infty \dot{\lambda}_i^0(t) \frac{\partial k_i^0(t)}{\partial \alpha} dt = -\int_0^\infty \dot{\lambda}_i^0(t) \frac{\partial k_i^0(t)}{\partial \alpha} dt$$

since $k_i^0(0)$ is fixed and $\lim_{t\to\infty}\lambda_i^0(t) = 0$. In addition, since $\dot{\lambda}_i^0(t) = -\lambda_i^0(t)(\partial f_i^0(t)/\partial k_i(t))$ and $\partial f_i^0(t)/\partial g_i(t) = \tau_i^0(t)$ the resulting expression reduces to

$$\int_0^\infty \Delta C dt = \int_0^\infty \left[\sum_{i=1}^2 \lambda_i^0 \tau_i^0 \frac{\partial g_i^0}{\partial \alpha}\right] dt \tag{D3}$$

which after substitution in equation (D1), proves the claim in (6.25).

We now turn to the proof of Proposition 6.5. With equation (6.25) at our disposal, we start by differentiating the equation for the accumulation of emissions (6.5) with respect to α to obtain

$$\frac{\partial^2 x_i^0}{\partial t \partial \alpha} = \frac{\partial g_i^0}{\partial \alpha} - \gamma \frac{\partial x_i^0}{\partial \alpha} = \frac{\partial^2 x_i^0}{\partial \alpha \partial t} \tag{D4}$$

By assuming that the tax function $\tau_i^0(t)$ is differentiable with respect to time, and bounded from above, we can make use of the following result:

$$\int_0^\infty \lambda_i^0(t)\tau_i^0(t)\frac{\partial^2 x_i^0(t)}{\partial \alpha \partial t} dt = \left[\lambda_i^0(t)\tau_i^0(t)\frac{\partial x_i^0(t)}{\partial \alpha}\right]_0^\infty - \int_0^\infty \left[\dot{\lambda}_i^0(t)\tau_i^0(t) + \lambda_i^0(t)\dot{\tau}_i^0(t)\right]\frac{\partial x_i^0(t)}{\partial \alpha} dt =$$

$$-\int_0^\infty [\dot{\lambda}_i^0(t)\tau_i^0(t) + \lambda_i^0(t)\dot{\tau}_i^0(t)]\frac{\partial x_i^0(t)}{\partial \alpha} dt \tag{D5}$$

This follows since $x_i^0(0)$ is fixed and the transversality condition implies that the shadow price of capital vanishes at infinity. By solving equation (D4) for $\partial g_i^0/\partial \alpha$, substituting into equation (6.23), and then using $\dot{\lambda}_i^0 = -\lambda_i^0(\partial f_i^0/\partial k_i)$ and (D5), equation (6.25) becomes (suppressing the time indicator)

$$\frac{\partial W(0,\alpha)}{\partial \alpha} = \int_0^\infty \left\{\sum_{i=1}^2\left[\lambda_i^0(\frac{\partial f_i^0}{\partial k_i} + \gamma) - \lambda_i^0\dot{\tau}_i^0\right] + \left[\sum_{i=1}^2\sum_{j=1}^2 \frac{\partial u_i^0}{\partial z_i}\frac{\partial z_i^0}{\partial x_j}\frac{\partial x_j^0}{\partial \alpha}\right]e^{-\theta t}\right\} dt \tag{D6}$$

The final step in the proof is to show that the form of the environmental tax in equation (6.26) implies that

$$\dot{\tau}_i^0 = \left[\sum_{j=1}^2 \frac{\partial u_j^0}{\partial z_j}\frac{\partial z_j^0}{\partial x_i} + b_i\right]e^{-\theta t} / \lambda_i^0 + \tau_i^0\left(\frac{\partial f_i^0}{\partial k_i} + \gamma\right) \tag{D7}$$

for $i = 1,2$ and $i \neq j$. Substitution of (D7) into (D6) proves the first claim in the theorem. The cost–benefit rule for changes in β can, of course, be derived in a similar manner.

Finally, we show that equation (6.33) results from differentiation of (6.32) on the open interval $(t, t + \Delta t)$. By differentiating equation (6.33) totally with respect to time, using the first order conditions for an optimal path results in the following equation

$$\frac{dH_p^0}{dt} = \sum_{i=1}^{2} \frac{\partial H_p^0}{\partial x_i} \frac{dx_i^0}{dt} + \frac{\partial H_p^0}{\partial t} \tag{D8}$$

Using $\bar{R}_i^0 = \bar{R}_{ii}^0 + \bar{R}_{ji}^0$, we have for $i \neq j$ that

$$\frac{dH_p^0}{dt} = \sum_{i=1}^{2} \left[\left(\frac{\partial u_1^0}{\partial z_1} \frac{\partial z_1^0}{\partial x_i} + \frac{\partial u_2^0}{\partial z_2} \frac{\partial z_2^0}{\partial x_i} \right) - \frac{\bar{R}_i^0}{\theta + \gamma} \gamma \right] \frac{dx_i^0}{dt} e^{-\theta t}$$

$$- \theta \sum_{i=1}^{2} u_i(c_i^0, z_i^0) e^{-\theta t} - \sum_{i=1}^{2} \frac{\bar{R}_i^0 \theta}{\theta + \gamma} \frac{dx_i^0}{dt} e^{-\theta t}$$

$$= -\theta \sum_{i=1}^{2} u_i(c_i^0, z_i^0) e^{-\theta t} \quad \text{on } (t, t + \Delta t) \tag{D9}$$

which proves the claim.

Note here the property of the pseudo-Hamiltonian; it is constructed such that the non-autonomous time dependence from the external effect, via the stock of pollution, is offset by the time dependence of the approximation of the present value shadow price of pollution, which gives the desired differential equation for $H_p^0(t)$.

APPENDIX E

Table E1   Sensitivity analysis: $\alpha_{i4} = 1.005$ *and* $\alpha_{i6} = 1.005$ *for* i = 1,2

Type of equilibrium	Country 1	Country 2	Global economy
Uncontrolled economy			
Welfare	108.0	27.9	135.9
Hamiltonian	159.9	41.4	201.3
(Ham./welfare) × 100	148.1	148.4	148.1
Non-cooperative Nash			
Welfare	115.3	30.6	145.9
Hamiltonian	119.7	37.1	156.8
(Ham./welfare) × 100	103.8	121.2	107.5
Cooperative			
Welfare	115.6	30.6	146.2
Hamiltonian	113.3	32.9	146.2
(Ham./welfare) × 100	98.0	107.5	100.0

Table E2   Sensitivity analysis: $\alpha_{i4} = 1.01$ *and* $\alpha_{i6} = 1.01$ *for* i = 1,2

Type of equilibrium	Country 1	Country 2	Global economy
Uncontrolled economy			
Welfare	105.1	27.2	132.3
Hamiltonian	164.6	42.6	207.2
(Ham./welfare) × 100	156.6	156.6	156.6
Non-cooperative Nash			
Welfare	114.0	30.3	144.3
Hamiltonian	118.7	37.2	155.9
(Ham./welfare) × 100	104.1	122.8	108.0
Cooperative			
Welfare	114.3	30.4	144.7
Hamiltonian	112.0	32.7	144.7
(Ham./welfare) × 100	98.0	107.6	100.0

Table E3 Sensitivity analysis: $\theta = 0.025$

Type of equilibrium	Country 1	Country 2	Global economy
Uncontrolled economy			
Welfare	100.2	25.9	126.1
Hamiltonian	152.9	39.7	192.6
(Ham./welfare) × 100	152.6	153.3	152.7
Non-cooperative Nash			
Welfare	106.7	28.3	135.0
Hamiltonian	111.2	35.1	146.3
(Ham./welfare) × 100	104.2	124.0	108.4
Cooperative			
Welfare	106.9	28.4	135.3
Hamiltonian	104.5	30.8	135.3
(Ham./welfare) × 100	97.8	108.4	100.0

Table E4 The estimated parameters in the production functions

	Rich	Poor
A_i	5223.96	3372.87
	(580.808)	(63.138)
B_i^t	1.0149	0.9899
	(4.512)	(4.567)
β_{i1}	0.152	0.227
	(2.294)	(4.792)
β_{i2}	0.297	0.348
	(3.494)	(4.084)

Note: *t*-values in parentheses.

APPENDIX F

The following is an 'engineer's' derivation of the key (the HJB) equation in Theorem 9.1.

$$V\left(k(t),t\right) = \sup_c E_t \left\{ \int_t^\infty u\left[(c(\tau)\right]e^{-\theta\tau}d\tau \right\} \tag{F1}$$

$$= \sup_c E_t \left\{ \int_t^{t+\Delta t} u(c(\tau))e^{-\theta\tau}d\tau \right\} + \sup_c E_{t+\Delta t} \left\{ \int_{t+\Delta t}^\infty u(c(\tau))e^{-\theta\tau}d\tau \right\}$$

$$= \sup_c E_t \left[\int_t^{t+\Delta t} u(c(\tau))e^{-\theta\tau}d\tau + V\left(k(t+\Delta t), t+\Delta t\right) \right]$$

$$= \sup_c E_t \left[u\left(c(t)\right)e^{-\theta t}\Delta t + V\left(k(t),t\right) + \right.$$

$$V_k\left(k(t),t\right)\Delta k + V_t\left(k(t),t\right)\Delta t + \frac{1}{2}V_{kk}\left(k(t),t\right)(\Delta k)^2$$

$$\left. +V_{kt}\left(k(t),t\right)\Delta k\Delta t + \frac{1}{2}V_{tt}\left(k(t),t\right)\Delta t^2 + O(\Delta t) \right]$$

The first equality follows by definition. The second equality in (F1) follows from Bellman's principle of optimality – 'every part of the optimal path must be optimal'. The third equality is a consequence of the definition of a value function, while the fourth equality follows from the Taylor expansion of the value function, which implies assuming that $V(\cdot)$ has continuous partial derivatives of all orders less than three. If the stochastic differential equation for capital is approximated by

$$\Delta k = \left[f(k) - (n - \sigma^2)k - c \right]\Delta t - \sigma k\Delta z + O(\Delta t) \tag{F2}$$

$$= h(k, c; \sigma, n)\Delta t - \sigma k\Delta z + O(\Delta t)$$

we can substitute for Δk in (9.23), and use the multiplication rules for Ito calculus – in particular $(\Delta z)^2 = \Delta t$ – to obtain the first order differential as

$$\sup_c E_t \left\{ \left[u(c)e^{-\theta t} + V_k h + V_t + \frac{1}{2}V_{kk}\sigma^2 k^2 \right] \Delta t - V_k \sigma \Delta z + O(\Delta t) \right\} = 0 \qquad \text{(F3)}$$

Note that the value function at time t appears on both sides of equation (F1), so netting out creates the zero in the RHS of equation (F3). Passing through the expectation parameter, dividing both sides by Δt, and taking the limit as $\Delta t \to 0$, we obtain

$$0 = \sup_c \left[u(c)e^{-\theta t} + V_t + V_k h + \frac{1}{2}V_{kk}\sigma^2 k^2 \right] \qquad \text{(F4)}$$

This equation is known as the Hamilton–Jacobi–Bellman equation of stochastic control theory, and it is typically written as

$$-V_t = \sup_c \left[u(c)e^{-\theta t} + V_K h + \frac{1}{2}V_{kk}\sigma^2 k^2 \right] \qquad \text{(F4')}$$

Turning to the shape of the stochastic co-state variables in Section 9.4, recall that we have written the vector of co-state variables in present value terms as follows:

$$\tilde{p} = (\tilde{p}_k, \tilde{p}_x) = (V_k, V_x) \qquad \text{(F5)}$$

Using Ito's formula on $\tilde{p}_k$ implies

$$d\tilde{p}_k = \left\{ V_{kt} + V_{kk}h + V_{kx}e + \frac{1}{2} \left[V_{kkk}\sigma_1^2 k^2 + V_{xxx}\sigma_2^2 \gamma^2 x^2 \right] \right\} dt \qquad \text{(F6)}$$
$$- V_{kk}\sigma_1 k dw_1 - V_{kx}\sigma_2 \gamma x dw_2$$

Since $V_{kt} = V_{tk}$, it follows from equation (9.48') that[1]

$$-V_{tk} = H_k^* + V_{kk}h + V_{kx}e + \frac{1}{2} \left[V_{kkk}\sigma_1^2 k^2 + V_{xxx}\sigma_2^2 \gamma^2 x^2 \right] \qquad \text{(F7)}$$

which, if inserted into the SDE equation for the co-state, yields the first part of equation system (9.52). The co-state equation for x follows analogously.

The same procedure as above can be used in the $N+1$ state variable case, where the project is the first state variable, to show that

$$\tilde{p}_1(t) = \int_t^T H_1^*(s)ds + \sum_{i=2}^{N+1} \int_t^T V_{1i}(x,s)\sigma_i(x,s)dw_i \qquad \text{(F8)}$$

where x is the vector of state variables, and dw_i the Wiener increment of the ith stochastic process. In expectations taken at time t, this reduces to equation (9.56).

NOTE

1. We have omitted the top index $*$ on k and x.

References

Aghion, P. and Howitt, P. (1998), Capital Accumulation and Innovation as Complementary Factors in Long-Run Growth. *Journal of Economic Growth* **3**(2), 111–30.

Ahlroth, S. (2001), Green Accounts for Sulphur and Nitrogen Deposition in Sweden. Implementation of a Theoretical Model in Practice. Department of Forest Economics, SLU No. 25. (Ph.Lic. dissertation).

Ahlroth, S., Björklund, A. and Forslund, A. (1997), The Output of the Swedish Education Sector. *Review of Income and Wealth* **43**, 89–104.

Allen, R.G.D. (1986), *Index Numbers in Theory and Practice*. London: Macmillan.

Ark, B. and Crafts, N. (1996), *Quantitative Aspects of Post-War European Economic Growth*. Cambridge: Cambridge University Press.

Aronsson, T. (1998a), Welfare Measurement, Green Accounting and Distortionary Taxes. *The Journal of Public Economics* **70**, 273–95.

Aronsson, T. (1998b), A Note on Social Accounting and Unemployment. *Economics Letters* **59**, 381–84.

Aronsson, T. (1999), On Cost Benefit Rules for Green Taxes. *Environmental and Resource Economics* **13**, 31–43.

Aronsson, T. (2001), Green Taxes and Uncertain Timing of Technological Change. *Resource and Energy Economics* **23**, 41–62.

Aronsson, T. and Löfgren, K.G. (1993), Welfare Consequences of Technological and Environmental Externalities in the Ramsey Growth Model. *Natural Resource Modeling* **7**(1), 1–14.

Aronsson, T. and Löfgren, K.G. (1995), National Product Related Welfare Measure in the Presence of Technological Change, Externalities and Uncertainty. *Environmental and Resource Economics* **5**, 321–32.

Aronsson, T. and Löfgren, K.G. (1996), Social Accounting and Welfare Measurement in a Growth Model with Human Capital. *The Scandinavian Journal of Economics* **98**, 185–201.

Aronsson, T. and Löfgren, K.G. (1998), Green Accounting in Imperfect Market Economies – A Summary of Recent Research. *Environmental and Resource Economics* **11**, 273–87.

Aronsson, T. and Löfgren, K.G. (1999a), Welfare Equivalent NNP under Distributional Objectives. *Economics Letters* **63**, 239–43.

Aronsson, T. and Löfgren, K.G. (1999b), Pollution Tax Design and Green National Accounting. *The European Economic Review* **43**, 1457–74.

Aronsson, T. and Löfgren, K.G. (2001), Green Accounting and Green Taxes in the Global Economy. In Folmer, H. Gabel, L., Gerking, S. and Rose, A. (eds) *Frontiers of Environmental Economics*. Cheltenham, UK and Northampton, USA: Edward Edgar.

Aronsson, T., Backlund, K. and Löfgren, K.G. (1998), Nuclear Power, Externalities and Non-Standard Pigouvian Taxes: A Dynamic Analysis under Uncertainty. *Environmental and Resource Economics* **11**, 177–95.

Aronsson, T., Backlund, K. and Löfgren, K.G. (2001), Welfare Measurement in an Imperfect Global Economy: Rich versus Poor Regions, *Umeå Economic Studies* no. 574.

Aronsson, T., Johansson, P.O. and Löfgren, K.G. (1997), *Welfare Measurement, Sustainability and Green National Accounting*, Cheltenham, UK and Lyme, USA: Edward Elgar.

Aronsson, T. Löfgren, K.G. and Marklund, P.O (1999), On the Output of the Swedish Education Sector – Additional Comments. *The Review of Income and Health* **45**, 533–42.

Aronsson, T. Löfgren, K.G. and Nyström, K. (2002), Stochastic Cost Benefit Rules: A Back of a Lottery Ticket Calculation Method. Umeå University (mimeographed).

Asheim, G.B. (1994a), Net National Product as an Indicator of Sustainability. *The Scandinavian Journal of Economics* **96**, 257–65.

Asheim, G.B. (1994b), Capital Gains and 'Net National Product' in Open Economies. Department of Economics, University of Oslo (mimeographed).

Asheim, G.B. (1996), Capital Gains and 'net national product' in Open Economies. *Journal of Public Economics* **59**, 419–34.

Asheim, G.B. and Weitzman, M.L. (2001), Does NNP Growth Indicate Welfare Improvement? *Economic Letters* **73**, 233–9.

Åström, K. (1970), *Introduction to Stochastic Control Theory*. New York: Academic Press.

Azar, C. and Sterner, T. (1995), Discounting and Distributional Considerations in the Context of Global Warming. Working Paper: Institute Report 1995:03. Chalmers University of Technology.

Bachelier, L. (1900), Théorie de la Speculation. Annales de l'École Normale Superieure **17**, 21–86. Translated in P.H. Cootner (ed.) (1964), *The Random Character of Stock Market Prices*. Cambridge, MA.: MIT Press.

Backlund, K. (2000), Welfare Measurement, Externalities and Pigouvian Taxation in Dynamic Economies. Umeå Economic Studies No. 527 (Ph.D. dissertation).

Backlund, K. (2003), On the Role of Green Taxes in Social Accounting. *Environmental and Resource Economics* **25**, 33–50.

Barrett, S. (1990), The Problem of Global Environmental Protection. *Oxford Review of Economic Policy* **6**, 68–79.

Barrett, S. (1994), Self-Enforcing International Environmental Agreements. *Oxford Economic Papers* **46**, 878–94.

Barro, R.J. and X. Sala-i-Martin (1995), *Economic Growth*. New York: McGraw-Hill.

Basar, T. and Olsder, G.J. (1982), *Dynamic Noncooperative Game Theory*. London: Academic Press.

Björk, T. (1994), *Stokastisk Kalkyl och Kapitalmarknadsteori, Del 1: Grunderna*, Matematiska Institutionen, KTH, Stockholm.

Björk, T. (1998), *Arbitrage Theory in Continuous Time*. Oxford: Oxford University Press.

Boulding, K. (1966), The Economics of the Coming Spaceship Earth. In *Environmental Quality in a Growing Economy*. Baltimore: John Hopkins Press for Resources for the Future.

Bovenberg, A.L. and Goulder, L.H. (2001), Addressing Industry-Distributional Concerns in U.S. Climate-Change Policy, Draft–December 2001, Stanford University, NBER and Resources for the Future.

Bovenberg, A.L. and de Mooij, R. (1994), Environmental Levies and Distortionary Taxation. *American Economic Review* **84**, 1085–9.

Brock, W.A. (1977), A Polluted Golden Age, in V.L. Smith (ed.), *Economics of Natural and Environmental Resources*, New York: Gordon & Breach.

Brock, W.A. and Mirman, L. (1972), Optimal Economic Growth under Uncertainty: The Discounted Case. *Journal of Economic Theory* **4**, 479–513.

Caplan, A.J., Ellis, C.J. and Silva, E.C.D. (1999), Winners and Losers in a World with Global Warming: Noncooperation, Altruism, and Social Welfare. *Journal of Environmental Economics and Management* **37**, 256–71.

Carraro, C. and Siniscalco, D. (1993), Strategies for the International Protection of the Environment. *Journal of Public Economics* **52**, 309–28.

Cesar, H.S.J. (1994), *Control and Game Models of Greenhouse Effects*. Lecture Notes in Economic and Mathematical Systems 146. Springer Verlag.

Chamley, C. (1985), Efficient Taxation in a Stylized Model of Intertemporal General Equilibrium. *International Economic Review* **26**, 451–68.

Chamley, C. (1986), Optimal Taxation of Capital Income in General Equilibrium with Infinite Lives. *Econometrica* **54**, 607–22.

Chiang, A.C. (2000), *Fundamental Methods of Mathematical Economics*. McGraw-Hill Book Company.

Clark, C.M. (1980), Restricted Access to Common Property Fishing Resources: A Game Theoretic Analysis. In Liu, P.T. (ed.), *Dynamic Optimization and Mathematical Economics*. New York: Plenum Press.

Crocker, T. (1966), Structuring of Atmospheric Pollution Control Systems. In Wolozin, H. (ed.). *The Economics of Air Pollution*. New York: W.W. Norton and Co.

Crus, J.B. (1978), Leader–Follower Strategies for Multilevel Systems. *IIEE Transactions and Automatic Control*. AC-23 No. 2, 244–54.

Dasgupta, P. and Mäler, K.G. (1991), The Environment and Emerging Development Issues. *Beijer Reprint Series* No. 1. The Royal Swedish Academy of Sciences.

Dixit, A. and Pindyck, R.S. (1994), *Investment under Uncertainty*. Princeton, NJ: Princeton University Press.

Dockner, E., Feightinger, G. and Jörgensen, S. (1985), Tractable Classes of Nonzero-sum Open Loop Nash Differential Games: Theory and Examples. *Journal of Optimization Theory and Applications* **14**, 179–97.

Duffie, D. (1992), *Dynamic Asset Pricing Theory*. Princeton, NJ: Princeton University Press.

Eatwell, J., Milgate, M. and Newman, P. (eds) (1987). *The New Palgrave: A Dictionary of Economics*. London: Macmillan.

Einstein, A. (1956), *Investigations on the Theory of Brownian Motion*. New York: Dover. (Contains Einstein's 1905 paper on Brownian motion.)

Fankhauser, S. (1992), Global Warming: Damage Costs: Some Monetary Estimates. Centre for Social and Economic Research on the Global Economy. Working Paper 92–29 (revised version). University College London and East Anglia University, UK.

Frisch, R. (1932), *New Methods of Measuring Marginal Utility*. Tübingen: S.C.B. Mohr.

Goulder, L.H. (1995), Effects of Carbon Taxes in an Economy with Prior Tax Distortions: An Intertemporal General Equilibrium Analysis. *Journal of Environmental Economics and Management* **29**, 271–97.

Hahn, F.H. (1970), Savings under Uncertainty. *Review of Economic Studies* **37**, 21–31.

Hamilton, K. (1994), Green Adjustments to GDP. *Resource Policy* **20**, 155–68.

Hamilton, K. and Clemens, M. (1999), Genuine Saving in Developing Countries. *World Bank Economic Review* **13**(2), 333–56.

Hamilton, K. and Lutz, F. (1996), Green National Accounts: Policy Uses and Empirical Experience. Paper No. 039. Environmental Economic Series. Environmental Department, World Bank, Washington, DC.

Hanemann, M. (1994), Valuing the Environment Through Contingent Valuation. *The Journal of Economic Perspectives* **8**, 19–43.

Hartwick, J. (1990), Natural Resources, National Accounting and Economic Depreciation. *Journal of Public Economics* **43**, 291–304.

Hartwick, J. (1992), Deforestation and National Accounting. *Environmental and Resource Economics* **2**, 513–21.

Heal, G. and Kriström, B. (2001), National Income and the Environment. Working Paper Series. SSRN Electronic Paper Collection.

Hoel, M. (1978), Distribution and Growth as a Differential Game Between Workers and Capitalists. *International Economic Review* **19**, 335–50.

Hultkrantz, L. (1992), National Account of Timber and Forest Environmental Resources in Sweden. *Environmental and Resource Economics* **2**, 283–305.

Ito, K. (1944), *Stochastic Integral*. Proceedings of the Imperial Academy. Tokyo **20**, 519–24.

Ito, K. (1946), *On a Stochastic Integral Equation*. Proceedings of the Imperial Academy. Tokyo **22**, 32–5.

Jorgenson, D.W. and Fraumeni, B.M. (1992), Investment in Education and U.S. Economic Growth. *The Scandinavian Journal of Economics* **94** (suppl.), 51–70.

Kemp, M.C. and van Long, N. (1982), On the Evolution of Social Income in a Dynamic Economy: Variations of the Samuelsonian Theme, in G.R. Feiwel (ed.), *Samuelson and Neoclassical Economics*. Boston, MA.: Kluwer–Nijhoff.

Krylov, R. (1980), *Controlled Diffusion Processes*. New York: Springer-Verlag.

Leland, H.E. (1968), *Dynamic Portfolio Theory*. Ph.D. dissertation. Department of Economics, Harvard University.

Léonard, D. (1987), Costate Variables Correctly Value Stocks at Each Instant. *Journal of Economic Dynamics and Control* **11**, 117–22.

Levhari, D.R. and Mirman, L.J. (1980), The Great Fish War: An Example Using a Dynamic Nash–Cournot Solution. *Bell Journal of Economics* **11**, 322–44.

Levhari, D. and Srinivasin, T.N. (1969), Optimal Savings under Uncertainty. *Review of Economic Studies* **36**, 153–63.

Li, C.H. and Löfgren, K.G. (2002), On the Choice of Money Metrics in Dynamic Welfare Analysis: Utility versus Money Measures. Umeå Economic Studies No. 590.

Löfgren, K.G. (1992), Comments on C.R. Hulten, Accounting for the Wealth of Nations: The Net versus Gross Output Controversy and its Ramifications. *The Scandinavian Journal of Economics* **94** (suppl.), 25–8.

Löfgren, K.G. (1992a), A Note on the Welfare Gains from Genetic Progress in Forestry: What can the Market Tell Us? *Forest Science* **38**, 479–83.

Löfgren, K.G. (1994), Monopoly Union Wage Setting and Evaluation of Public Projects: An Intertemporal General Equilibrium Approach. *Labour* **8**, 55–77.

Löfgren, K.G. (1999), Welfare Measurement and Cost Benefit Analysis in Nash and Stackelberg Differential Fish Games. *Natural Resource Modeling* **12**, 291–305.

Loury, G. (1996), A Theory of Oligopoly: Cournot–Nash Equilibrium in Exhaustible Resource Markets with Fixed Supplies. *International Economic Review* **27**, 3–42.

Lucas, Jr, R.E. (1988), On the Mechanics of Economic Development. *Journal of Monetary Economics* **22**, 3–42.

Maddison, A. (1995a), *Monitoring the World Economy*. Paris: OECD.

Maddison, A. (1995b), *Explaining the Economic Performance of Nations*. Aldershot, UK and Brookfield, USA: Edward Elgar.

Mäler, K.G. (1989), The Acid Rain Game. In H. Folmer and E. Van Ireland (eds), *Valuation Methods and Policy Making in Environmental Economics*, Amsterdam: Elsevier.

Mäler, K.G. (1991), National Accounts and Environmental Resources. *Environmental and Resource Economics* **1**, 1–15.

Mäler, K.G. and de Zeeuw, A.J. (1995), Critical Loads in Games of Transboundary Pollution Control, *Nota di Lavora 7.95*, Fondazione Eni Enrico Mattei, Milano.

Malliaris, A.G. and Brock, W.A. (1991), *Stochastic Methods in Economic and Finance*. Amsterdam: North Holland.

Merton, R. (1975), An Asymptotic Theory of Growth under Uncertainty. *Review of Economic Studies* **42**, 375–93.

Michel, P. (1982), On the Transversality Condition in Infinite Horizon Optimal Control Problems. *Econometica* **50**, 975–85.

Mirman, L. (1973), Steady State Behavior of One Class of One Sector Growth Models with Uncertain Technology. *Journal of Economic Theory* **6**, 219–42.

Mirrlees, J.A. (1965), *Optimum Accumulation under Uncertainty* (mimeographed).

Mirrlees, J.A. (1971), *Optimum Growth and Uncertainty*. IEA Workshop in Economic Theory. Bergen.

Mirza, M.M.Q. (2002), Global Warming and Changes in the Probability of Occurrence of Floods in Bangladesh and Implications. *Global Environmental Change* **12**, 127–38.

Nordhaus, W.D. (1993), Rolling the Dice: An Optimal Transition Path for Controlling Greenhouse Gases. *Resource and Energy Economics* **15**, 27–50.

Nordhaus, W.D. and Kokkelenberg, E.C. (1999), *Nature's Numbers: Expanding the National Economic Accounts to Include the Environment*. National Academy Press: Washington, DC.

Nordhaus, W. and Yang, Z. (1996), A Regional Dynamic General Equilibrium Model of Alternative Climate Change Strategies. *American Economic Review* **84**, 742-65.

Öksendahl, B. (2000), *Stochastic Differential Equations: An Introduction with Applications*. Berlin/Heidelberg/New York: Springer-Verlag.

Oswald, A.J. (1985), The Economic Theory of Trade Unions: An Introductory Survey. *The Scandinavian Journal of Economics* **87**, 160–93.

Peskin, H.M. and Peskin, J. (1978), The Valuation of Nonmarket Goods in Income Accounting. *The Review of Income and Wealth* **24**, 71–91.

Pezzey, J. (1995), Non-declining Wealth is not Equivalent to Sustainability. Dept. of Economics, University College, London (mimeographed).

Phelps, E.S. (1962), The Accumulation of Risky Capital: A Sequential Utility Analysis. *Econometrica* **30**, 729–43.

van der Ploeg, F. and de Zeeuw, A.J. (1992), International Aspects of Pollution Control. *Environmental and Resource Economics* **2**, 117–39.

Pigou, A.C. (1920), *The Economics of Welfare*. 4th edn. New York: Macmillan.

Polansky, S. (1992), Do Oil Producers Act as Oligopolists? *Journal of Environmental Economics and Management* **23**, 216–47.

Pontryagin, L.S., Boltyanskii, B., Gamkrelidze, R. and Mischenko, E. (1962), *Mathematical Theory of Optimal Processes*. New York: Wiley-Interscience.

Radner, R. (1967), Efficiency Prices for Infinite Horizon Production Programs. *Review of Economic Studies* **34**, 51–66.

Ramsey, F.P. (1928), A Mathematical Theory of Saving. *Economic Journal* **38**, 543–59.

Repetto, R., Magrath, W., Wells, M., Beer, C. and Rossini, F. (1989), *Wasting Assets: Natural Resources in the National Income* Accounts. Washington, DC: World Resources Institute.

Romer, P.M. (1986a), Increasing Returns and Long Run Growth. *Journal of Political Economy* **94**, 1002–37.

Romer, P.M. (1986b), Cake Eating, Chattering, and Jumps: Existence Results for Variational Problems. *Econometrica* **54**(4), 897–908.

Samuelson, P.A. (1961), The Evaluation of Social Income: Capital Formation and Wealth, in Lutz and Hague (eds), *The Theory of Capital*, Proceedings from the IEA Conference, New York: St Martin's Press.

Samuelson, P.A. (1965), Proof that Properly Anticipated Prices Fluctuate Randomly. *Industrial Management Review* **6**, 41–9.

Seierstad, A. (1982), Differentiability Properties of the Optimal Value Function in Control Theory. *Journal of Economic Dynamics and Control* **4**, 303–10.

Seierstad, A. and Sydsaeter, K. (1987), *Optimal Control Theory with Economic Applications*. Amsterdam: North Holland.

Sheng, F. (1995), *Real Value of Nature*, Gland, Switzerland: World Wildlife Fund International.

Solow, R.M. (1956), A Contribution to the Theory of Economic Growth. *Quarterly Journal of Economics* **70**, 65–94.

Spence, M. and Starrett, D. (1975), Most Rapid Paths in Accumulation Problems. *International Economic Review* **16**, 388–403.

Stiglitz, J.E. (1982), Self-Selection and Pareto Efficient Taxation. *Journal of Public Economics* **17**, 213–40.

Stratonovich, R.L. (1966), A New Representation for Stochastic Integrals and Equations. *Journal of SIAM Control and Optimization* **4**, 362–71.

Tahvonen, O. (1994), Carbon Dioxide Abatement as a Differential Game. *European Journal of Political Economy* **10**, 685–705.

Tahvonen, O. and Salo S. (1996), Non convexities in Optimal Pollution Accumulation. *Journal of Environmental Economics and Management* **31**, 160–77.

Vincent, J. and Hartwick, J. (1997), Forest Resources and the National Income Accounts: Concepts and Experience. Harvard University (mimeographed).

Warming, J. (1911), Om Grundrente af Fiskegrunde (On rent of Fishing Grounds). *Nationalekonomisk Tidsskrift* **49**, 499–505.

Weitzman, M.L. (1976), On the Welfare Significance of National Product in a Dynamic Economy. *The Quarterly Journal of Economics* **90**, 156–62.

Weitzman, M.L. (1997), Sustainability and Technical Progress. *The Scandinavian Journal of Economics* **99**, 1–13.

Weitzman, M.L. (1998), Comprehensive NDP and the Sustainability-Equivalent Principle. Harvard University.

Weitzman, M.L. (2000), The Linearized Hamiltonian as a Comprehensive NDP. *Environment and Development Economics* **5**, 55–68.

Weitzman, M.L. (2001), *A Contribution to the Theory of Welfare Accounting*. *Scandinavian Journal of Economics* **103**, 1–24.

Weitzman, M.L. (2002), Income, Capital, and the Maximum Principle. Book Manuscript, http://post.economics.harvard.edu/faculty/weitzman/new_book.html.

Weitzman, M.L. (2003), *Income, Wealth, and the Maximum Principle*. Harvard University Press.

Weitzman, M.L. and Löfgren, K.G. (1997), On the Welfare Significance of Green Accounting as Taught by Parable. *Journal of Environmental Economics and Management* **32**, 139–53.

Wishart, D.M.G. and Olsder, G.J. (1979) Discontinuous Stackelberg Solutions. *International Journal of System Sciences* **10**, 1359–68.

Index